COOKING
AS
COURTSHIP

COOKING
AS
COURTSHIP

SUSAN WIEGAND

DRAWINGS BY

KENT WILLIAMS

PENELOPE PRESS
Wichita • San Francisco

Cooking as Courtship

1997

ISBN 0-9657069-1-5

PENELOPE PRESS

The design and execution of this book owe much to the following gentlemen: David Pickell for his knowledge of type; Barry George for his extensive collection of technology and his generosity; and the fine artist, Marc Bosworth, for his kind collaboration in creating and producing the cover of the first, limited edition which so informed the final design. Kent Williams cannot be thanked enough for his contribution of both art and effort.

Chefs Sharon Redgrave and Tanya Tandoc are responsible for any real or valuable cooking information which may have slipped into the text. Thanks go out as well to the many others, especially Paul Edwards, whose comments and criticisms led to large and small improvements. All misinformation, error and plain lies are solely attributable to the author.

Appreciation and affection go to Independent Printing, The Wichita Bindery and all Kinko's stores.

Printed by Rand Graphics, Inc.
Wichita, Kansas.

For Cora and Sam

Contents

COOKING AS COURTSHIP

Introductory explanations and insistences to spur the faint of heart and calm the enthusiastic.

COOKING AS A MEANS of courtship. Courtship as a means of drawing others toward you and persuading them to remain of their own free will. It may be courtship of an intended love, though it might as soon be a parent or child or colleagues or friends or a very old and beloved love. Cooking as courtship because food will somehow be prepared and served, perhaps elaborately, but probably not. Perhaps by you, but not always.

Some squirm, uncomfortable with the idea of courting others, or confused by the thought that food might be for something besides maintaining one's weight. They imagine it dishonest to do anything sheerly for the pleasure of another, fearing it may even be a betrayal of oneself.

Others wonder why anyone would bother to mention, let alone discuss at length, the courting of others through food. "Naturally one courts others and of course that courtship takes place through the offering of food; metaphor for sustenance, for sex, gesture or token of love, of affection, care and concern, devotion," they remark dismissively. "In Hindu culture the gods themselves are courted with gorgeous, extravagant offerings of food, which the deities then generously share with their beloved devotees. What were you planning to say about it?"

Oh dear.

The author of this book should be far more successful than I at courtship. Yet such a one, having much sweeter things to do, might not have the inclination to write. Certainly the author should be a much better cook than I. But then a talented chef would never have been pressed to learn how to effect courtship at mealtime in the almost certain absence of an excellent entrée. Sublime food will seduce with little further effort, and chefs have only to remember not to be very very awful.

I TELL YOU NOW and you will know later: This is not a cookbook. In order to cook you will likely want to acquire a few real cookbooks written by real cooks. For reference and occasional inspiration, if not for clear instructions. It makes little difference which books you choose, as long as you choose wisely. In order to cook as a means of courtship you might as soon offer another a bite of apple as prepare and serve an awe-inspiring repast. It is a matter of something else entirely.

Try to believe this is not a book of rules and does not mean to proscribe a style of living nor being. Opinion and admonitions are just that. Sometimes it may seem the same thought is repeated over and over and that the whole book could be distilled into a single sentence, a phrase, a word, if only the right one had surfaced. Clearly it didn't.

The pages before you fall into two main parts: first a collection of essays meandering around various facets of cooking in the context of courtship; then a mess of what might be mistaken for recipes. A third, appended bit offers information mined casually from the heads of professional chefs. Anything that seems wrong to you probably is, for you. Commandments for one are crimes for another.

You will be fine. Anything made in love[1] and offered freely will warm and court.

_____

[1] That word. Good, I suppose, that it comes up so soon, since so many believe one only courts those with whom one hopes to share romantic love. This book is not so much about romantic love. It is about large love, the love that encompasses all things, even those things you don't particularly like. So to do anything in love does not at all mean to Be In Love. It means maybe to be within love, to be love, as opposed to hate and all its many avatars. It means to forsake the thieves of love, to banish greed and pride and desire and anger and jealousy and fear. It is harder than you might think to bring such strength to romantic love itself. Easier perhaps to love truly that which does not mean so much to you.

THE COMPLETE KITCHEN

In which the more likely kitchen tools are noted and their relative importance put forth.

A FRIEND RECENTLY OUTFITTED his kitchen with everything he thought he would need. "I want to cook at home more," he told me earnestly. Pots and pans, knives, bowls, appliances of all sorts, tools and utensils I'd heard of but never before seen, vinegars, oils, spices, herbs. He'd long since acquired dishes, glasses, tableware. Still, it was an expensive day.

I suppose there is no reason not to do it this way if you have a good deal of money and even more cupboard space. Or if you are for some personal reason committed to radically increasing the role of cooking in your life.

Even so, there is no imperative for such a monumental investment of money and space.

Maybe you acquire a big ceramic or porcelain or metal bowl, suitable for tossing salads or pastas, for mixing up cookies or cakes or muffins or bread. A saucepan large enough for cooking pasta and another, slightly smaller, for cooking sauce at the same time. Or just the bigger one. A sauté pan. Erring on the large size if you are only to have one. Some wooden spoons. A corkscrew bottle opener. A can opener. A chef's knife. A cutting board. A teapot. Some means to make coffee. Something that will contain the things that must go into the oven. Plates, bowls or rounded mugs, knives, spoons and forks. These things—and maybe even a few of these could be foregone—and you can cook.[1]

As you begin to cook a bit and perhaps a bit more and others begin to explore your kitchen for themselves, you will become aware of things that you would like to have. Maybe a colander for straining pasta and cleaning vegetables. Strawberries are mesmerizing when being rinsed in steel or copper. Maybe you need a hand mixer, or maybe just one of those squiggly tools designed to mash up vegetables. Maybe a platter for serving things too big to fit on a dinner plate, and bowls of various sizes. People start giving you gifts for your kitchen. Your mother hands on a few precious things she no longer needs. You notice bargains on well used kitchen things at garage sales in your neighborhood. You acquire measuring paraphernalia, cups and spoons. A wooden salad bowl and serving utensils in the shape of giraffes sent by friends from Nairobi. A toaster and a coffee grinder. Baking pans. A Dutch oven. Who knows what you will need until you need it? And how will you need it unless you are cooking and discover that you cannot live without it, at least not comfortably?

Naturally, there will always be the first go at a recipe when you become aware of all the things you do not have. But rather than anticipating and prepurchasing all of the possible conveniences and inconveniencing yourself terribly trying to use a zoo of tools you are unfamiliar with, you have the enviable opportunity to challenge your creativity in getting around the absence of all sorts of "indispensable items". Embrace that other freedom which springs from limitation. Surprise yourself by how little is needed. You will learn soon enough what is missing and might be acquired. Wait and watch and reign in desire until it becomes need, real and without emotion or urgency and you can see clearly what will fill

---

1 Or another can come to your house and cook something. Sitting smugly and thinking, "I really do plan to adhere exclusively to the restaurant delivery method of home dining, and am really just looking for the section on romantic candle placement," you may have forgotten that someone might come to your home and want to make dinner for you. Who knows why. Could be under almost any pretext. I often make dinner for a friend who plays the piano. He plays and I cook. Someone else might have a Wolf stove I envy. Or a fireplace. Or the bed I care to sleep in tonight. Or my roommate has his college football team in town for the Big Game and I don't want to be at home and I don't feel like going out, so I go to a friend's house and say, "I want to make dinner for us. Do you mind?" There are any number of reasons someone besides your mother might want to come over and cook in your kitchen. You would have to be a grumpy discontent to refuse this offer. A kitchen that has been cooked in and cleaned up is nice for days. The dust is gone. There are leftovers in the refrigerator. The sterile aspect of a non-cook house is mussed and a richer order that includes all aspects of life descends like sun and moonlight.

it. Do not go rushing out to assuage every whim and brief craving. I implore you. Such indulgence is destroying more than just us. If you keep your eyes open and hunt wisely and not greedily as you go about your day, you will find what you lack. Or perhaps someone will recognize your craving and find the right thing for you or lead you to it. It helps if you make known what it is you need and why you think you need it. Another may hear you who knows how to do without the item you consider necessary but which will take up an extraordinary amount of rare counter space and rarer cash. And they will share their knowledge.

Consider as well that the fewer luxury cooking tools and appliances you have in your kitchen, the more impressed people will be by the food you prepare. If your kitchen looks like the display window at Williams-Sonoma, people expect so much, pressure mounts, humor flies out the window, and with it many possibilities. Let your collection of kitchen toys and tools grow only as quickly as you do.

You can see that I remain baffled as to what needs absolutely to be in a kitchen. However, feel free to make use of the following list of things you might want to have in your kitchen and my opinion as to why. You will find that your Most Favored Recipes will require some few things that I could not have foreseen. Go get them. Listed below are the tools and trinkets which will make it possible for you and for others to cook in your kitchen with only adventurous inconvenience.[2]

INDISPENSABLE THINGS (can't possibly cook without them)

IMAGINATION

HUMOR

PATIENCE

---

[2] This list is offered with good intentions and all, but in truth almost any cookbook published this year has a better, more useful list of tools for you to consider. It seems to be the fashion. I think what we can take away from this is that we have lost the cultural knowledge of what tools are required for cooking, and so it is almost foolish to write a cookbook without giving a list of tools needed, as though we were a bunch of second graders who needed to be told to get out paper and pencils in order to do our math problems. French cookbooks from as recently as your mother's youth do not even list the ingredients for certain sauces used in a recipe, figuring that anyone in a kitchen knows full well how to make a Béarnaise. How far we are from there. I don't even know anyone who is completely sure how to boil an egg.

Back to the point at hand, as this isn't really a cookbook, this isn't really a list of what you need to cook. It is a list of stuff you might want to have in your kitchen for all sorts of reasons.

ADVISABLE TOOLS (can cook more easily with than without them)

BOARD

For chopping and other events. Any decent wood chopping board is a treasure. It might be a beautiful piece of wood, or a bunch of glued together bits of decent wood, or a plank of not particularly nice wood. It hardly matters. In addition to being a tool, it is a very nice way to serve cheese, or hot garlic breads, or anything that needs to be cut while serving. Big round fruit, for example. Ignoring aesthetics, which on occasion happens, a nylon cutting board works, and I have heard some particularly wary mothers say that nylon is hygienically superior to wood. Whatever. If you find a board you love, give similar boards freely to others as gifts. More than one board in a kitchen is just fine. I am thinking of acquiring a third. A really big one this time.

People who like to roast meats are well served by a carving board, which is very different from a chopping board. Carving boards are designed to drain the juices from the meat as it is being carved. They might be slanted to this purpose, or the board might have gutters carved into it. In either case there will be a receptacle toward which the juice drains. Some have spikes imbedded into them to keep the meat in place while it is being carved. All these are excellent qualities for a carving board, but horrible for a chopping board. For chopping you need the surface to be flat and continuous. Which in turn is terrible for carving as the juice from the meat runs quickly off the board, relentlessly seeking a lowest point which will eventually and unfortunately be the floor. Carve on a platter if you do not have a carving board, but be careful of the meat slipping out from under the knife.

BOWL

One largish bowl that is suitable for mixing and for serving would be very hard to live without. The bowl can be used for one-bowl pastas, for serving more complicated pastas and rices, for vegetable side dishes, for tossing and serving salads, for mixing brownies or cookies, and in the case of my own bowl, as a water dish for visiting rottweilers and mastiffs. Just one bowl. Big enough that visiting shi-tzus can't drink from it at all. Everything is complemented by any of the many white ceramics and porcelains and stonewares available from around the world and for sale in even the most remote spots. Once in a while you will find or another will give to you a bowl, perhaps plain, perhaps of many colors. A bowl made by someone with an eye and a hand and a mind for shape and depth and weight and color. You might not recognize it as the bowl right off, but it will make itself known as time passes and it is the bowl you prefer. The bowl you are constantly looking for and can't find because it is already in use. Today, I have two. Or three. All gifts. One large and white and slightly decorated in relief. An Italian ceramic thing that came complete with a chip on the edge and a blemish on the finish of the interior. So I don't worry about it. Another is small and pale blue and painted with strange flowers from some Asian imagination. Bigger than a very big cereal bowl. Strange thing and yet always in use. A third which almost doesn't count as a bowl. Still a gift, but this time with overtones of inheritance. Better described as a serving dish with a cover. Oval, footed, perfect in size, delightful in its restrained, almost intellectual romance. Not so confident of its beauty that it has forgotten to be useful.[3]

Find a bowl that suits you, and use it all the time. Acquiring others as it happens.

COLANDER

Which is to say, a bowl with holes in it. Sometimes a bowl formed of wire mesh. Use it for draining liquid from other things, or for keeping food from going down the drain while you are trying to wash it. Pasta, vegetables, shellfish, things out of jars or cans. Stainless steel is beautiful and my choice. I saw enamel colanders in many colors while shopping for a wedding gift last week. Mom has an awful aluminum one with bent feet, but it works fine. Plastic is available and will do. Sometimes you can get someone to give you a copper colander as gift. Colanders that are not eyesores are also good for serving just-washed fruit as the fruit that falls to the bottom doesn't get water logged Place it on the table and make sure everyone has access to knives and napkins.

Until you find yourself in possession of such a thing, vegetables and fruit can be washed and drained in plastic bags that you punch holes in or any loosely woven fabric sack, or in the salad spinner, or in whatever works for you. Pasta can be drained awkwardly using the cover of the pot it was cooked in.

CAN OPENER

There may be people in this country who never open cans of anything and so never need one. You will not be counted among them anytime soon. And I'll bet most of those people have a can opener in their kitchen anyway, just in case. Nothing more foolish than to not be able to get at your food. While it is likely that you will at some point inherit a can opener, it is also likely that it will be difficult to use in some way. Otherwise why would anyone get rid of it? One day when you feel flush and in a

---

[3] A soup tureen, as it turns out. Although I am not so sure, now that I think on it, as the cover does not have one of those nitches for the ladle to poke out.

temperament of generosity toward yourself, get a strong can opener with coated handles and a tight mechanism. Certainly they can be found at the grocery store, but you will be more assured of quality at a kitchen supply or hardware store. Estate sales are a good place to find them as well. A little the worse for wear, but if it was well made to begin with it will be good for a long while.

COOKIE SHEET

Sometimes you want to make cookies. They are what love is made of. If you are planning to buy a cookie sheet, get one that is weighted to hold the heat. It is a bit more expensive than the cheapest alternatives, but very worth it.

Still, even if you never make cookies, and even if you have only a traditional pan, inherited or found, you will be happier with a cookie sheet than without. Endlessly, it is the surface for holding things in the oven. It keeps foods from falling though the oven rack. It keeps your sanity intact. A cooking surface. Flat and stable. It cannot be knocked over. It can be recruited for tasks like some sort of marine infantry. A platter in a pinch. A cover to a large pot. And then again, you might need to make cookies.

CORKSCREW

You need to decide for yourself which kind you prefer, but you must have one. Even if you never drink wine. Someone might come over to your house with a tall green bottle and will not be thrilled a second time to have to open it by pushing the cork down the neck. Tiresome and messy, and not in a particularly provocative way. Your corkscrew should open bottles as well. As with all tools, you will be immeasurably happier if you have a well-made corkscrew. Corkscrews do some hard work and some healthy amount of torque might be exerted on them. Naturally you don't want the thing to break off in a cork, nor slice open someone's hand, and those are sufficient reason to acquire a good one. But further than that, the experience of opening a bottle of wine or beer or soda will be vastly improved by the quality of the device used. It should certainly be strong and capable, but it might also be antique or beautiful or exquisitely simple and solid and classic in design. One will get over a disappointing encounter with the tool. But to have had it be a good thing, a delightful thing, a thing unnoticed perhaps but absorbed and experienced nonetheless, is akin to having gorgeous fabrics drape your body, and for such stuff as pleases the senses and the imagination to be the last thing one touches before they touch skin.

DISHES

There is a whole section on dishes somewhere in this book. It is more important than you might think to set a decent table.[4]

FOOD

Have some in your kitchen. See Have on Hand.

GRATER

A simple thing, an ingenious tool that you can live without. But why? You can get graters that are like small towers with different sorts of grating textures on each side. Or you can find yourself with one of the planar graters, a flat thing that you lean against the counter while you crate against it. Even if you have a food processor for grating large quantities of things, you might still consider acquiring a hand grater. It is always nice to not use electricity if you don't have to. And often grating things requires a bit of muscle. It is very nice to feel your strength in this unchallenging task. Very nice in a completely unnoticed sort of way for some other you might politely ask to do some grating for you. Much sweeter a task than hauling out the processor and making a racket while exercising only the strength of an index finger, which interrupts conversation and makes for more dishes to do later. And it might very well be some golden rule of existence on this planet that if you can do it just as easily with your own power as with power stolen from the earth, you should.

Consider as well that if your grater has a variety of grating surfaces and one of them is very fine and non-directional, you can enjoy freshly grated nutmeg, which is the perfect complement to many pastas and soups. If you find you dearly love nutmeg, you can get a small grater made just for that. Ask for it at your favorite cooking or hardware store.

Then there is the cheese planer, which slices cheese thinly off the top of a hunk in a regular and graceful sort of way.[5]

Mind you, people do go years without any sort of cheese grater, arduously slicing and shaving cheeses. Parmesan and its siblings can even benefit from alternative methods of disintegration. And of course you can buy them grated. Other cheeses can be sliced

---

[4] In fact, the section on dishes lies in the chapter on setting the table. Not that you will necessarily set a table each time you use your dishes, but it seemed like a good time to flog that particular horse. You'll see what I mean.

[5] It is not as easy and safe as it seems. Be careful how you hold the cheese while you plane it, and don't exert lots of pressure. You are not, any more than I have been, exempt from planing off a bit of your hand.

and then julienned (chopped into slim strips) for use in omelets and the like. To not have a cheese grater also establishes you firmly as an amateur without drastically hindering your ability to cook. Liberated from expectations, confident that every edible morsel you produce will be appreciated, you will also probably use less cheese than other people, which is considerate and wise.

I must mention a completely unnecessary and medieval contraption involving a cylindrical grater and a long handle that grates long curls of parmesan or romano or the like which are an elegant complement to all kinds of steamed vegetables and the tops of pastas. Frivolous and perfect. It is the very best way to grate parmesan and other hard cheeses for tumbling over food about to be served. You surely don't need one, but should one come your way, accept it.

KNIVES

Spend your money on a good, 8-inch chef's knife. It will take you far. Pick up different knives and feel them before you choose which one to buy. The more truthful you are during the selection process, the happier you will be with your choice. A good knife store should have sales people who can talk to you about what to look for in a knife far better than I can. If they don't, go to a different store. Don't order knives off late night t.v.

There are other knives you might want to have. A bread knife, which is long, uniformly thin, and has a serrated (scalloped) edge. Such a serrated blade is also invaluable for slicing up tomatoes, although a very sharp chef's knife is even better. A small knife for everything the chef's knife is too big for. A paring knife, to those in the know, a darling, tiny thing that is practically just another finger. Sharper, of course. Maybe a 4-inch blade. A steak knife will just barely do if you are very dexterous and very short of cash.[6]

There is certainly no need to rush out and buy one of those nifty blocks with a bunch of knives stuck into it. Even if it is on sale. Takes up space and makes people think you know how to cook. Or it can label you as the domestic equivalent of a snow bunny. Better to be a novice.

Novice or not, learn how to sharpen knives, or find out which of your friends are good at the art and get them to do your knives now and again. They will do this in exchange for almost nothing. They like to pretend it is a great task; but in truth, people who know how to sharpen knives love to do it and need to find other knives to sharpen or

---

6 "No it won't!" Tony howls. Oh, but it did do for many years.

they risk sharpening their own knives down to nubs. You do need to have a knife sharpening tool, and it should be the tool of preference for the person who is going to do the sharpening.

LADLE

For soups and sauces. The only trick to buying a ladle, besides remembering to, is to look for one with a hook at the end of the handle which will keep it from slipping into the pot. Unfortunately, most ladles do not have this feature. Too many designers of kitchen tools think it is more important to hang your ladle decoratively on the wall than to keep it from falling into the soup. If you end up with one of these awful ladles, I recommend making a mess of your counter by setting the ladle down between uses rather than leaving it in the pot or bowl and allowing the handle to slip into the pot. Neither solution is particularly elegant, but the first is more palatable to others who may not like watching you root around in the soup. Also, you are less likely to accidentally utter distasteful expressions as your hand is scalded and your sleeve dips into the sauce. Less likely to shock and offend respected others with horrifying displays of temper. Something to consider as you are holding the ladle and weighing the costs of placing it sloppily on the counter or of sacrificing another dish to hold it.

Another quality of ladles is weight. Your ladle should feel substantial. Imagine the mechanics of a shallow vessel filled with fluid at the far end of a long, thin length of wood or metal: Would a heavy ladle be preferable to the light one? Less likely to be tipped indiscreetly and spill soup on the wrong lap?[7] It probably depends enormously on the design. Which suggests you might have to pay a little more than you thought.

OVEN

Whatever oven you have in your home is fine. If it is really not fine, or simply not there, consider purchasing a good quality and largish toaster oven. If you like baked and roasted foods and require the heat of an oven, consider instead or in addition to what you have, a freestanding convection oven. Convection means that the air in the oven is circulated, which allows foods to cook more evenly and a bit more quickly, but otherwise with all the wonderful qualities of roasting and baking and broiling. They are not so easy to find these days. It seems they were marketed on the quality of cooking more quickly, and never caught on because for speed one surely would choose a microwave.

---

[7] I would like to point out that I don't believe fluid mechanics are counted among the basic laws of physics.

On that note, microwave ovens are misnamed. They are better replacements for stoves than for the traditional, radiant oven.

OVEN MITTS

Get several that you like, and keep them next to the stove and oven at all times. You used to be able to get leather mitts at the Cheyenne Rodeo. Current aesthetic has brought all-cotton mitts into the stores, which is a great boon to anyone whose hands are not perfectly smooth at all times. So nasty are the synthetic interiors of most mitts, you might find yourself more willing to burn hands than try to slip them inside the mitts. Sturdy dish towels work well as an alternative, although you may find that you frequently burn the tops of hands on the racks and roofs of ovens since only the palms are protected. The white terry cloth towels sold in hardware and warehouse stores by the dozen are perfect.[7] Grab opposing corners, and the towel will just fit around most pasta pots and casseroles. Avoid cute, thematic pot holders and towels. Avoid cute, thematic anything.

PASTA OR STOCK POT

A big pot with two strong handles, one on each side near the top. Ideally, find yourself an 8-qt, stainless steel pot with a good cover. Try to avoid aluminum. It is important for the pot to be big enough that when a pound of pasta is placed in boiling water, the pasta is able to move around, roiling with the boiling motion of the water. Also, the more water in the pot, the less cooling effect the pasta will have on the water, and the sooner the water will return to boiling. A pasta pot is also an excellent vessel for making chili or risotto. You can survive with so small as a 3-quart pot, but it is like living in a too-small apartment. Whatever is cooking in the pot will be forever splattering on the stove and counters, bubbling over. Stirring becomes an exercise in dexterity and diplomacy. Your patience is brought to the fore. What's the point? Isn't the day difficult enough? Plus, while a 3-quart pot will take you as far as one pound of pasta, if you find yourself with more than four delicate diners at your table, you will be stumped by how to cook enough food for them. An extra pound of pasta and more sauce is no effort at all, unless you are restricted by your minimalist cookware.

Your pot should have a cover that fits nicely, for sometimes it will be needed. For example, when you want to cook rice. Or when you want to disguise the fact that you

---

[7] In fact they come in handy all over the house. Cheap and robust, they can be bleached back to white in all but the most extreme cases and are quite sexy in their disingenuousness. I won't name names, but I assure you they come highly recommended.

didn't wash it yet, or if you want to place it in the refrigerator, or if you need to keep insects or small animals from exploring the contents.

PEPPER MILL

The generally tall device used for grinding pepper. You don't need one. Ground pepper can be bought in any store.

But you would be a fool. Freshly ground pepper is sublime and worth the weight of the mill in gold. I especially like to grind pepper onto sandwiches, getting it all over the plate or counter. It is the best toy in a kitchen. Find one that feels good in your hand, is easy to use and feels as strong as you are. Not too large, maybe even quite small. Not tall at all. The grinding mechanism is what is important. The design can be anything. You will need to buy whole peppercorns for your mill and you might have your choice of black, red, or white peppercorns, or a combination of all three. All the colors are from the same tree, fruit in various stages of ripeness. White pepper on its own is considered irreplaceable in pale sauces by some cooks (and I confess that aesthetics have indeed restrained me from grinding black pepper into a few things, however they cried for the spice.) Other dishes look anemic without the traditional black and tan punctuation. You might consider two pepper grinders if you tend to more subtly colored recipes. Until you decide on such extravagance, you can buy ground white pepper.

In another scenario, you could find yourself with two pepper grinders because each is set to grind pepper to different coarseness. Coarse and crunchy for some more rustic things. Fine, powdery grind for silkier foods. Both filled with black peppercorns. Might as well put white peppercorns into the finer grinder. Or don't think about it all. Enjoy the indulgence of two pepper mills filled with the same peppercorns.[8]

REFRIGERATOR

I feel a little parochial mentioning this. After all, most of the world cooks much better food than I do without any access to refrigeration. But here in the western world, cooking often involves perishables, and while you would probably do fine without one if you didn't eat meat or dairy products, many people whom you wish to make comfortable in your home will look askance at the absence of refrigeration. They will get nervous about nothing and probably come down with some psychosomatic intestinal

---

[8] I am informed by professional chefs that one can adjust the grind of one's peppermill. I did know that, but I find that if the mill is adjusted by any besides a professional chef, and even then, there is a good chance the whole thing will come unscrewed and peppercorns will fly all over the place. Which is at once festive and annoying.

complaint tomorrow. And then you will certainly feel compelled to get a refrigerator. Might as well get one now. It needn't be very large, and if you have any consideration for energy usage it should be quite small. It is in every case the single largest electricity consumer in your home.

Excavate for failed experiments and forgotten leftovers every few months. Preferably on the day the trash is taken out. Look in the drawers for last season's fruits and vegetables. Keep an open box or small bowl of baking soda inside and change it occasionally. Sam's trick for people who don't use their refrigerator much and tend to leave things in it overly long is to keep the temperature lower than standard. He's right. Food still gets old and moldy in time but it doesn't rot so quickly.

Feeling rather prudish talking about this at all, I protest that you will spoil appetites (and you know which appetites I am talking about) with a mangy refrigerator. You may even destroy hope in the heart of someone dear, discourage their senses by an assault on nose and eyes. Pray they do not touch anything, or that they have a sudden moment of amnesia and draw no conclusions about your character from the state of affairs in your refrigerator.

When you do have to clean the thing, use warm soapy water and a sponge very carefully. If you don't clean your refrigerator, someone else will eventually feel compelled to tackle it for the sake of community health. Your laziness may cheer, but your reputation will suffer.

SAUCE PANS

Sauce pans have vertical sides, are deep enough to hold lots of liquid, and have a single, long handle. You should have maybe three. Small, Medium and Large. 1, 2 & 4 quart. To be extremely Spartan, have just one medium size sauce pan, suitable for boiling enough pasta for two. The large one is large enough to pose as a pasta or stock pot.

The having of several sauce pans is not only about variety, but about quantity. Cooking even a simple meal might involve the cooking of several things simultaneously or one after another, but in any case you need pans for each thing or you will be forever having to transfer stuff from a pan to some other vessel and then back again, let alone the washing out that will have to take place in between. Sauce pans are therefore great gifts, as are bowls. "Too many" would only mean there is no more room in the cupboard.

SAUTÉ PANS

Round and not very deep. The things you cook eggs in. They are also used to sauté vegetables, which is a French habit and a not bad one. If possible, have both a very small sauté pan—maybe 6 or 8 inches in diameter for sautéing mushrooms and the like[9]—as well as a larger sauté pan, 14 inches or so, for cooking real foods. Or something in between. Since I don't eat mushrooms, I have lived for some time with only a single, 10-inch sauté pan, a French, cast iron thing I acquired somehow, and which keeps following me around from house to house.[10] The pans might have curved sides and perhaps a solid non-stick surface.[11] Or the sides might rise at a right angle to the cooking surface, in which case it might be called a "sauterne" by cooks in the know. The pan should not be any deeper than two or three inches, so you can see what you are cooking. Deeper than that and you have a sauce pan on your hands. Which is absolutely fine, as long as you are not making an omelet.

Sauté pans should boast a heat-proof handle. They often need to be snatched quickly

---

[9] As if anything were like mushrooms.

[10] Every once in a while I will notice several people gathered around it as though it were some kind of alien landed. "This is a beautiful pan" they will breathe in awe. It is a nice pan, but sometimes I wonder if they are merely seduced by the bright, rich blue enamel exterior of the thing.

[11] Not Teflon, which is no longer manufactured but which you might inherit or ignorantly acquire in a second-hand, flea market fashion. Health hazards aside, it scrapes off the bottom of the pan with the lightest touch of metal. The pan is ruined, no one wants to eat what was being cooked, and courtship is soured when you fly across the kitchen screaming "NO!" as your darling, disposing of inhibition, stirs the mushrooms with the tip of a chef's knife.

from the stove after attention has wandered, too much time has passed, and one easily forgets to grab a protective cloth.[12]

SILVERWARE

There is a section about silverware tucked into the chapter on setting the table. I think the point was: You and your guests will eat with the forks and knives and spoons, so vanity should be forsaken in favor of functionality and sensuality. Would you buy a screwdriver with a witty or modern or beautifully sculpted, but barely functional handle?

SINK

With running water or without. A place to wash and prepare fruits and vegetables. A place to pour unwanted liquids. A place to place dishes at the end of the meal. Whatever your sink, keep it as empty as possible at all times. Clean it regularly with scouring stuff. You might even consider it the biggest and last thing to clean at the end of any cooking session. Just after the last pots have been carefully set on the counter to dry. If you have a counter. Long before the last wine and water glasses find their way back into the kitchen. Sink and counters and all surfaces and tools and dishes should always be ready for the next thing. Just like you.

SOME MEANS TO MAKE COFFEE

Entirely up to you. See Coffee & Tea.

SOME WAY TO BOIL WATER

A teapot is a good choice. A sauce pan will work. Electric kettles are divine.

SPATULA

For pancakes, and anything else that needs to be flipped or removed whole from a cooking surface. You might be able to live without one if you don't make pancakes and would never consider sautéing eggplant or making cookies, but it is one of those things people are extremely surprised to discover you do not have.[13]

---

[12] I cannot resist making the perverse observation that nursing another's injury can provoke very warm, friendly feelings from both men and women. Cutting off the tiniest tip of finger quite accidentally one evening in Paris led to a memorable if brief romance. On the other hand, some people sicken at the sight of blood.

[13] Perhaps I am projecting my own, still raw pain at the mocking I once received for not possessing a spatula. I should never have invited those actors over for barbecue. Try claiming that a neighbor borrowed it earlier in the week. Or launch into a sincere admission of how you never much liked the word "spatula" and have never been able to bring yourself to ask for one in the store. Or you could just look at them blankly, as I did, disbelieving that they should be so callous toward the feelings of the person making them dinner.

SPATULA, RUBBER

Similar to a regular spatula in that it is a flat thing attached to a handle, a rubber spatula is for scooping the last bits of anything out of a bowl. The best of them are heat resistant, have wooden handles and a rounded rectangular rubber end that is strong and flexible. Many are made all of plastic and are almost worthless as they cannot flex snugly to the sides of the bowl. You might as well use a spoon. A rubber spatula is certainly something you can live without. All it means is that you have dirtier dishes to wash. And you forego the sensual delight of caressing the sides of bowls and pans with a tool designed perfectly for the chore. The most frugal among us also love rubber spatulas because they give us the sensation of not wasting even a drop of anything. Children hate them because there is so little left to lick out of the bowl. Try using yours judiciously and appropriately to the situation at hand.

Keep it in the container with the wooden spoons. See Wooden Spoons.

SPOONS

A variety of spoons for stirring and serving. Again, see Wooden Spoons. Acquire a slotted spoon. It's for scooping things out of liquid without having to scoop up the liquid as well. It comes up more often than you might think, perhaps even especially for the occasional cook.

STOVE

Some sort of surface to cook on. Gas is preferred by people who like to cook. Electric is preferred by people who have bad memories of gas stoves from other times and places. You will probably be limited by what is in your home already. If you have no stove or no kitchen to speak of, you can purchase single or double electric burners which plug into a regular socket. I've used one to cook dinner for six or twelve on plenty of occasions. The only drawback is the same one for conventional electric stoves except worse: water takes forever to boil. Alternatively, you can get one of those nifty, double burner propane stoves (e.g., a Coleman camp stove) and have an excellent source of cooking heat which you can take camping with you if you should be so lucky as to go camping.[14] If you develop a passion for cooking with gas, you can always upgrade to a professional gas burner that runs on gas or propane. Water boils in the blink of a jaded eye.

---

[14] Do get a propane tank, or keep a few extra little bottles of propane on hand. I do not recommend running out of fuel halfway through cooking a meal, although I have done it and it turned out fine. Just luck that there had been plenty for all without that last pasta dish.

TOASTER OR TOASTER OVEN

Life as we know it and perhaps love itself is virtually impossible without the toaster. Toast, which is to say warm, delicious bread, slightly crisp where it wasn't to begin with, is more than anything the food of deep affection. Symbolic and simple. Unassuming, unpretentious, unbearably kind. The last thing one can eat before they cannot stand food at all. The first thing one considers when hunger returns. It requires almost no attention on the part of the person offering it, and is, for many people, the stuff life is made of. See Toast.

Toaster ovens are even better than traditional toasters, although never so charming as a rounded, chrome Sunbeam. Beyond toast, you can heat leftover pizza or kimma nan or roast two potatoes or make enough garlic bread for two without turning on the big oven. Can't do that in the Sunbeam.

TOWELS

Get yourself a stack of smallish, clean, cotton towels and be done with it. The kind sold in packs of twelve at stores everywhere work wonderfully. The kind described above for use as oven mitts. Clean, white, terry cloth towels. Some people set the table with them, using them as both placemats and as napkins. Adorable. Imaginative, casual, sensible. Provocative like clean skin. Or, if you are a speck more refined than that, you may prefer French dish towels. Again all cotton, often in a textured weave, white or pastel with a couple of wide stripes in a darker shade, sometimes with a pattern of fruit or some words woven through the stripe. Or you can walk a plain path, choosing those larger, thinner, very American, white squares of cotton. Flour sack towels. The sort women used to embroider the corners of with wisdom and pictures of teapots and farm animals. I would look for these at the hardware store in town.

Please do not fall prey to "designer" patterns. Typically not of the highest quality, they begin to disintegrate almost as soon as they are unwrapped, and you end up with towels that bring no pleasure for a lamentably long time. Having paid to indulge sentiment rather than respect for material or construction, from the first time you dry your hands these towels disappoint the senses. It is downhill from there.

On the other hand, there are sturdy cotton towels to be found in colors and patterns which are neither cute nor fashionable. You might feel a sort of camaraderie with them which can help you recognize them. Can't tell you where, but they can be found, and since so few people recognize and purchase for quality, they can often be found on sale. Stock up and give them as gifts.

Do not, under any circumstances, use bathroom towels in the kitchen. They are bad sizes, too thick and therefore awkward for drying dishes, and it makes your guests wonder what else you are too lazy to do correctly.[15]

WIRE WHISK

I've lived without one but I won't again. I am not even sure what I use them for but when they are not available I miss them. They also provide a sculptural complement to the wooden spoons and rubber spatula standing in a vessel near the stove. The best of them have a wood or metal or plastic handle, in any case something which is larger in diameter than the bundle of wires which form the whisk. Certainly they are wonderful for mixing sauces, for beating eggs, and for finishing whipped cream. (The stronger amongst us can make whipped cream from start to finish with a large wire whisk. Very impressive. Meringue is a little easier, but also impressive.) Have as many different sizes as you feel will be useful.

WOODEN SPOONS

Lots of wooden spoons. Buy them by the bag and put them in some container on or near the stove. Use them without discretion. Use them to taste whatever you are making, a unique sensual experience which has the added advantage of cutting way back on burnt tongues and lips. For that matter, eat your entire meal with one, right out of the pan it was cooked in. Give your companion their own spoon, or share.

A few notes concerning the use of wooden spoons. Artists will insist that the secret to a beautiful painting is the use of many brushes and the frequent cleaning of those brushes. Same thing applies to spoons. Don't use the same spoon in two different pans. And until you know your beloved very well, and perhaps even then, try not to put the spoon you just had in your mouth back into the pan. Or at least be understanding if they balk or object. Accept that people are raised with different versions of hygiene. Be patient and not angry, whichever side of this fence you fall on. They may not be disturbed for themselves, knowing well what deep kisses they plan to share with you before the day is out, but rather at the idea. At the thought that you might regard such earthiness as appropriate in general company.[16]

---

[15] Of course, they also might wonder where else the towels have been.

[16] This is an unavoidably tricky point, and I must confess I believe it is easier for the one with a more open approach to the sharing of cooties to adapt and be generous. I am such a one, so you needn't suppose I am making things easy for myself.

CONVENIENT THINGS (now and then useful, but honestly, who'd miss them?)

A BAKING DISH

Some stuff has to go in the oven and you need to put it on something. Garlic bread, for example, or roasted potatoes, or brownies, or lasagna. A cookie sheet or foil for the first, parchment for the second, or nothing for either in a pinch, but for the third and fourth?

A square or rectangular dish about two inches deep is broadly useful. You might also choose to own a loaf pan for making banana bread or pumpkin or zucchini or cranberry bread, or pound cake if you are that sort of person. A deep baking dish with a cover is prized by people who like roasted animals. I am particularly greedy concerning potatoes and carrots and onions that have been roasted along with the roast-whatever. Pyrex or Corningware is good, or some kind of enamel-coated cast-iron thing. Create makeshift foil covers when necessary. Some friends and family have found themselves with terra cotta or other clay, covered pots and swear by them. If a birthday falls on Valentine's Day, heart-shaped cake pans might be indispensable. Pie plates are as handy as they can possibly be, standing in as serving dishes on many occasions, holding a chicken for roasting, and being filled occasionally with a chocolate or pumpkin pie.

A REALLY BIG POT

For making large amounts of pasta, soup, chili or stew for large numbers of what are often large people.

A REALLY SMALL SAUCE PAN

For cooking small stuff quickly and gracefully and for reheating leftovers for your lunch.

HAND HELD MIXER

You cannot make whipped cream, nor meringue nor the chocolate pie in this book unless you have an electric mixer. Oh, maybe you are extraordinary and inherited your grandmother's forearms and are willing to take on the task of beating cream or egg whites to soft stiffness with a whisk. But maybe you aren't and you didn't. Of course, you can do almost anything you might have done with a hand mixer with a stationary, countertop, but nonetheless electric mixer, should you have the good fortune to have one of those. What you can't do is mash potatoes to velvet in the pot they were cooked in. That would be a shame.

COFFEE GRINDER

If you or anyone you like is a great fan of coffee, get one. I am not entirely sure that it makes a difference—surely not so large a difference as the quality of the coffee you buy or the frequency with which you restock your supply—but there are many people for whom it is ritual to grind coffee before making it into that seductive and poisonous nectar. And since ritual is the half of it, just go along with whatever they claim is important. Their happiness and comfort is the only thing you need to worry about.

You can use it to grind up spices if it turns out that you don't use it for coffee.

MORE SERVING BOWLS AND PLATTERS

Technically speaking, food can be served from pots and pans. Often dinner plates can stand in as serving platters.[17] But you will be happier having big dishes made for serving. Food loves to be in them. They feel good in hands as they are passed around. They are no extravagance as many things are made directly in them. They will wander toward you and you should welcome them, buying them when necessary, finding them and trapping them as they sneak past, accepting them and keeping them with dignity in your home. Wash them well and store them such that they are easy to get at and won't break while you are trying to extract one or another of them.

WOODEN SALAD BOWL

A standard sometimes forgotten, unnoticed but ever appreciated in the visual and tactile below-consciousness. Warm and comfortable. People like to hold them. Food looks nice in them. The more they are used the better they are. And you can drop them on the floor and they almost never break. Perhaps you would also like to invest in a set of salad servers, those oversized fork and spoon things that are so handy for serving not just greens but also lots of the other warm and cold things you might find on your table.

A wooden bowl does not make the A-list of kitchen tools because there are other sorts of bowls which can easily be used in its place. But they are not the same, especially not for salad. Also, putting it on the A-list might encourage you to run out and get one when it would be much wiser to wait until you find a wonderful wooden bowl which you are driven to acquire regardless of whether or not you need it.

---

17 If you have been discreet and tasteful in your choice of dishes. See the Dishes section in Setting Tables.

JUNK (those things that might be used if they're at hand)

BLENDER

If you are fond of making soup, any blender will be a treasure for you. If you do not lean in that direction, you might get by very nicely with a minipimer, which is a sort of handheld blender, or your hand mixer creatively manipulated. Neither is so powerful as a real blender and will not make so smooth a smoothie, but they will allow you to make mashed carrots in an instant and are easier to wash than a whole blender. Also use your blender, or the minipimer for that matter[18] to make fruity drinks, with or without alcohol. You might also use them to make faux steamed milk for coffee in the morning. A magic trick described somewhere else.

FOOD PROCESSOR

If you do have one, use it to make pesto, to make cookies quickly, to chop onions and slice potatoes and grate cheeses, whir up salad dressings in a moment. Do not use it as a blender. It cannot contain liquid like that. If you do not like chopping things but also shy away from owning so ominous a machine, consider one of the small versions, or one of the still smaller versions that hold barely a cup of anything. They are even preferable for chopping garlic.

GARLIC PRESS

If you must have one, get one and don't be cheap. The last thing you want is a flimsy garlic press. Better not to get one at all. In fact, don't get one at all. Marcella Hazan scorns the use of the garlic press, claiming that much of the power of the garlic is crushed into submission by the violent action of the press. She recommends chopping or slicing or some other knife-based approach to the cloves.[19]

---

[18] Haven't tried the hand mixer for this. That the two whisks don't fit nicely in a glass is probably the reason. But I think there are more fundamental reasons in addition to the circumstantial ones. But you give it a try if you think it will work. The minipimer, by the way, is more generically referred to as an immersion blender. It is exactly what you would expect a one-whisk hand mixer to look like, knowing as you must, that it was designed by a team of male designers. Yes, phallic, but please do not take this cruel and whiny little appliance out of the kitchen.

[19] I know cooking technique is not my area of expertise, but allow me to offer you a tip for getting garlic cloves out of their jammies. Cut off the end that was attached to the base of the bulb. Place a chef's knife with a broad blade on top of the clove, which is lying on a chopping board. Hold the handle of the knife with one hand; then press down on the blade with the palm of the other hand. The clove will be smashed and the stiff covering sufficiently damaged for it to be removed easily. If you were planning to neatly slice the garlic for something special, don't do this. Otherwise, do a few or many and then chop them all at the same time.

MICROWAVE OVEN

I wouldn't have one, but I do use them when I am in other kitchens. They make me question my own ethics, which is probably good except that I am not wild about the answers. If you do have one and do use it, be careful about the noise they make for it is far from delightful. Do not in any case over-use the microwave. They were invented for Cooking as Anything But Courtship. And of course for reheating previously cooked meals into reincarnations of themselves, which done thoughtfully and respectfully might very well be the stuff courtship is made of.[20] You can reheat whole vessels of things, or you can assemble a meal on a plate, minus anything that should remain cool, cover it if you like, and then microwave that whole plate.

Metal cannot be used in a microwave. Ceramic, glass and plastic only. Pyrex containers are a marvelous choice. For potatoes, the microwave is a loud but swift way to cook them. Mash them, or serve as though they had been baked.

MUFFIN TINS

I confess I am afraid to own them. I have a thing for muffins and would happily spend every weekend morning for the rest of my life baking some slight variation on my favorite muffin recipe, which seems unwise. You do what you think is right, but if you cannot behave responsibly, sell your muffin tin for a dime at the next garage sale.

PIZZA BOARD

A girlfriend has one and uses it to make what might be sublime pizzas except that they always seem to be covered with mushrooms of one sort or another. I don't believe the board has anything to do with that, but I still decline to possess one. For another person, a pizza board might be just the tool, the thing which makes making food simple and seductive to the chef and delightful to all others.

SALAD SPINNER

At once useful and annoying because they do the job better than anything else, but take up so much space in the cupboard. In its absence, put the greens in the center of a towel, gather up the edges and whir it about over your head. This is better done outdoors, especially if you are at someone else's house. There is an interim device, a

---

[20] Don't forget that reheating leftovers was done for centuries without the advantage of microwaves. Slowly on the stove, no more than medium heat, with a bit of added liquid. Slowly in the oven, or in the toaster oven or small convection oven. You might change containers, as twice baked-on food is very difficult to clean. Not impossible, so you needn't throw the pan away, but difficult.

wire basket, which expands to accommodate the greens, with handles so it can be whirred about (again, outdoors), but which can only be acquired through inheritance or diligent attendance at garage and estate sales. It folds into a more compact thing for storage, and is so lovely, this web of wires, that it may remain on the counter indefinitely without ever offending.

FORBIDDEN ITEMS

DIET COOKBOOKS

YES, BUT WHAT do you really need to cook? Something that will work as a stove, a vessel for cooking, a pan of some sort, a bowl, a knife, a spoon. A flat surface of some sort that can be made clean enough for your tastes where you can prepare food. Access to water. Potable water is best. It need not be near the heat source. A refrigerator. Maria thinks you should have a refrigerator. People live and cook without them. And if it is perennially summer, you can probably forego the stove. Now we are down to a knife, a bowl, a spoon, a flat place, and a source of water. That's all you really need in order to go to the grocery, buy some stuff and bring it home and feed someone.[21]

Everything else is fluff, and you are living large in the soft lap of luxury.

---

[21] If you shop correctly, you don't even need that much. But you will not appear to be cooking.

USING COOKBOOKS

*In which the art of using cookbooks and the
recipes within them is explored.*

PEOPLE WHO HAVE a genuine
affection for food and enjoy experimenting with it often use cookbooks. They seek out and
delight in discovering new ideas concerning food. Some people are not particularly imaginative but appreciate the imaginations of others. Others use ideas found in cookbooks as
springboards for their own raucous experimentation in the kitchen or elsewhere. Full of
ideas and information, history and science and culture, there is no way to ignore the value
of cookbooks. And yet they often sit dusty on the shelf. Only one amongst them dog-eared
and splattered.

Anyone who ever ventures into the kitchen might use a cookbook. Old tricks are nice
and warm and comfortable, but new tricks can be refreshing and lend new aspect to the old

29

ones. Go on and try new things. You might like them. Consider how new knowledge and understanding might improve old standards and habits. Surprise yourself by conquering a new thing, acquiring facility with a new herb or technique. Surprise others. Play with your food. Challenge yourself, and then remember to come up laughing. No one wants to hear about how miserable you are that an attempted recipe failed any more than they want to hear you complain sex was no good last night. They will look at you like you are nuts, wondering why on earth you think that's a topic for conversation.[1]

Go ahead and use them.[2] Everyone does once in awhile, or should.

UNFORTUNATELY FOR YOU, using cookbooks is not so easy as opening up the most attractive book and having a go. All cookbooks are not created equal, and you still cannot judge a book by its cover. Good recipes often come from the strangest places. Individual cookbooks are relatively homogeneous in their approach to food. Which is to say, if there are a several recipes you like from one book, chances are many of the other recipes in the book will also be to your taste. Conversely, if you haven't much liked a number of things from a particular book, your chances of liking any recipe in that book, no matter how good it sounds, are slim. This is even somewhat true of the compiled cookbooks, where the recipes come from a wide variety of sources. The editors' taste will out. Only the books in which there is no editor per se, where it is simply a compilation of recipes from whomever had the time and inclination to send one in remain mysterious no matter how many recipes you have tried. No way to know what sort of thing is being offered up in the next recipe. No way of knowing who thought it delicious enough to share. Very scary. Very adventurous. All the other books, including this one, have a single kitchen and a single person or two with their singular tastes deciding yay or nay on each recipe and each ingredient within it. And you can tell, and you can use it to your advantage.

Which is all in saying, if you insist on being experimental[3] and using recipes from a variety of cookbooks, or if you cook so often that you need to adopt more than one new recipe each year, be discreet and sensible in your choice of books and of the recipes selected from them. And then be very honest about whether a recipe is worth repeating. If you are a rare cook, stick to experimenting with books of recipes which better cooks than yourself have recommended and from which you have enjoyed many meals cooked by others. Do not be

---

[1] Not that they wouldn't have been delighted to discuss what went wrong in either arena had you maintained your humor. But in the face of complaint, they will think, "Shut up and get over yourself," and will say as much if they are one of those blunt and frank-speaking friends so hard to find these days.

[2] Cookbooks. Not your friends.

[3] That is, experimenting in a conventional way with new things rather than experimenting in new ways with old things.

ambitious and wild until you have finished Ms. Child's masterpiece, *The Way to Cook*. Cover to cover.[4] Then you can have all the fun you want with any cookbook in the world.

Is it possible that you are among those people who are more comfortable with some guidelines, some instructions? It can be so comforting to have a cookbook on hand which you trust and which you feel confident will produce food that is wonderful to eat. It is as good as having a real cook for a neighbor who is always willing to spend an afternoon helping you come up with ideas for dinner. Maybe you like to use cookbooks, enjoy trying a new recipe, reveling slightly in the comfort of knowing someone somewhere, if only in a test kitchen, figured out that these particular amounts of these particular things work together. And indeed they do. Strangest things, cookbooks. You can walk into a house where you have never been and see sitting on the counter a meticulously prepared something which looks just exactly like something someone else once prepared for you.

WHICH BRINGS US to a very important courtship point for those of you who are using cookbooks: The person you are courting may very well have seen and smelled and tasted and enjoyed or not enjoyed this very same food at another place, another time, and with another person; and you might be inadvertently summoning up memories which will only in some circumstances be to your courtship advantage. More frequently they will be distracting, and at worst they may be damned destructive.

Some traditional and comforting foods have been elsewhere cited for the danger of serving them at all. Many cookies as well as hot chocolate fall firmly into this category, as does conventional spaghetti with meat sauce, roast turkey with stuffing, waffles, and a million other things we don't need to mention because we don't even eat them anymore so laden are they with baggage from our youth. Who can count the number of times they have sipped hot chocolate? How many memories involving maple syrup vie for position in their heart and mind, leaving your love with a jumble of what you hope will be good will? Specific nostalgia. As lethal and as beneficial as, and should be treated with the same respect reserved for, nitroglycerine. At once poisonous and life-giving. Dangerous and powerful foods, we could spend a whole chapter on them. [5]

---

[4] Hyperbole. What I actually think is you should open the book, look around in it for a half-hour or so, read one or two things carefully, and thereby gain respect for the huge amount you do not know about food and how to cook it. That humility will go almost as far as actual knowledge when you are in the kitchen trying to cook.

[5] We don't.

While less certain to provoke a nostalgic response than a more ubiquitous item,[6] food made by following recipes from fashionable cookbooks are the very scariest and potentially explosive because the recollection attached to it is so much more specific and individual. There cannot be more than a handful of times, perhaps only one very vivid image of that other evening on which they were served that unmistakable pasta tossed with brie, tomatoes, basil and garlic, or that particular spinach salad with warm mustard dressing. And whether the event was generally positive or positively negative doesn't even matter because their attention is now split between you and the last person who offered or shared this very, sensuous experience with them. Thin ice, as they say. You might easily find yourself suddenly home alone with a lot of cooled leftovers.

Be careful.

And do not forget that cookbooks, even unfashionable ones no one could have possibly experienced previously, are not at all appropriate when spontaneity is important. When your attention should lie elsewhere. When it should appear you know what you are doing, are confident of your own instincts and don't need a manual to tell you what to do step by step. Don't worry that you might not offer a plate to challenge the presentation of the finest chef, however much your guest might merit the finest of all things.[7] The more important thing is for the meal to be executed with the sole and sincere intent to delight and flatter and primarily to feed the beloved, making them aware that they are deeply cared for, and accomplished partly by not caring at all about how the offering holds to more universal standards of aesthetic or artistic or other value.

SOMETHING ELSE TO DO WITH BOOKS

Browse through them now and again, in your own home, or in a bookstore, or maybe while visiting with someone in their home, lingering at their kitchen table, wandering in and out of chaotic conversation. Browsing is a fine art which is too seldom honed to good use. You should try it, here and in many other places. You'd be surprised how much you can learn and about what. Little things that can transform your view of the world. Transform your

---

[6] Peanut butter cookies, for example. Which to the dismay of my mother I make oversized, both to make them unlike the actual cookies served to children and so not childish, and to make the experience even more akin to that of childhood, when cookies were almost as large as our hands. Always served with adult drinks, and not milk. To evoke childhood, especially its nicer parts, is very different from recreating it, in which case you will get more than just the nice parts. Yikes. Stand back unless you are a trained professional.

[7] As Rosalind so wisely points out to Orlando, one cannot trust the suitor who offers excellent love poetry. It shows that their attention lies with their own accomplishment and therefore in their own vanity rather than with the object of their attraction. And that object cannot help but notice. There is a great area of possibility where everything is good enough to please, but not so good as to provoke questions about priority.

world. Open up a new line of thought that would have remained ever closed, but which now opened so slightly encourages new thoughts and ideas and theories and observations to pour in from all sides. That, among all things, is most appealing to a would-be amour.

In this particular case you would be learning about food. More than that, and especially if you are browsing aloud in the company of a precious other, you will be learning about that other and what they think about food and possibly glean knowledge from their experience which is so much easier and less messy and time-consuming than learning it on your own.

Mostly you absorb slowly and in the most painless of fashions an understanding of what sorts of foods are placed with what other sorts when people who are very good with food are doing the placing. You read a few recipes for fettuccini alfredo and eventually you get the general idea. You peruse several descriptions of what to do with fennel and you begin to understand. Notice which herbs appear where and in combination with what else. Look up ingredients and recipes that interest you in the index. Look through cookbooks describing cuisines very different from your own. See how familiar ingredients are used in unfamiliar combination. Other notions may begin to wander into your head, ideas which do not hail from nowhere but which have some substance of knowledge or the beginnings of wisdom informing them. Open minds with open books before them, explosive and fertile. Look at anything which catches your eye. Browse through the table of contents and the index to see what sort of recipes are in the book. Flip through the pages to see if any particular list of ingredients catches your eye. Lemon grass, which almost no one knows what to do with, might show up. Read on. A recipe for something which has always been a mystery to you might appear one day. And then you will understand more than you did before.

Let worlds of ideas and thought-out thoughts wash over you, the one you are ready for, the one which will catapult you to the next idea of your own always the one that catches your eye. Thousands of well-paid and well-meaning researchers try daily to figure out why and how our brains are so good at this sort of sifting and sorting even when we make virtually no effort, and maybe even more so when we make no effort. But they can't figure it out. Your eyes sweep the page and inform inward, but no one knows what other parts of the body are consulted before the eyes are caught and slowed and the hand involuntarily moves to touch the words on the page and the lips silently move. "What is the process," they ponder, "by which one thing rather than another is selected as interesting and pertinent? How does it happen, and why, and how can we emulate it electronically, mechanically, or chemically?"

Which ponderance is of virtually no interest to you and me. You probably won't ever want to enlist any sort of robotic thing to take your place at any table with a glass of wine or cup of some other sultry poison on a Saturday afternoon in the chatty company of friends or family while paging through beautiful books about foods and all the wonderful things that can be done with them. And then doing them or not doing them but in any case having done something. The success not only in the capture but also in the pursuit, for what is captured in the course of the pursuit will be of great value.[8]

Browse[9] without ever bothering to on this and other subjects and you will advance all your courtship skills immensely. If only because you might come across things you want to try or explore and there you are, making others smile and glow without even trying. Which is the way they like it.

---

[8] Maybe not today, maybe not tomorrow, but soon and for the rest of your life.

[9] Do you know how to browse? Has this reverie been enough to illustrate? It is a technique of experiencing books, or anything else, in an intermediate manner and depth. You do not read nor absorb nor possess the whole thing, but you see enough and experience enough to know whether you need more, and in any case you come away knowing a little more than you did before. Open books and look at them. Read a paragraph, at least, maybe a page or two to get an impression of the voice of the author. Look at the table of contents to see what subjects appear to be addressed. The way the chapters are titled will also give you insight into the flavor of the book. They might be elegant, flippant, scholarly, direct, anything. Read the back cover and any other criticism of the book that comes packaged with it. It is all propaganda and you must read through the lines, but there is understanding to be had there as well. Practice browsing. There is no law that says you must read a whole book in order to be at all familiar with it. Just as you know some people only because you had a brief conversation with them once at a party or on a street corner, you can also know books casually, perhaps later deciding to get to know them better. They will wait for you.

FINDING RECIPES

In which you find or invent some several things worth making and which you can make very well.

IF YOU ARE GOING to cook, you need to cook something, and the set of instructions for cooking that thing, even if they exist only in your head, is a recipe. It might merely be your technique for slicing a pear and putting in a bowl which is somehow right, softly coaxing others to eat a pear which they would have otherwise passed by, thereby allowing them to delight in pear-deliciousness and your company at the same time and perhaps make an association of happiness and the source of it between the two. It might rather be a complicated series of ingredients and procedures for making a spiced tea which are written carefully on a piece of paper which you keep in a particular part of a particular drawer so you will be able to refer to it when you make the tea and not be forced to guess and remember and possibly fail to make the drink you desire. It might be a loose combination of ingredients and no particular procedure, but which when followed however inexactly leads to an irresistible and comfortable pasta or salad or soup or roasted thing or whatever. It might be a book full of things, all of which you enjoy cooking, the whole book being for you a recipe for cooking in general.

As you can imagine, these recipes do not descend from on high at the moment of your birth and attach themselves to you, even though you may eventually inherit one or several from your parents. No, you must discover and develop and otherwise hunt down and domesticate them to your own purposes. You must nurture them and care for them and keep them healthy so they will last many years and grow, perhaps fitfully, along with you. Many will enter your life for awhile and then wander off, the two of you having grown irreconcilably in separate directions.[1] You might on occasion look closely and critically at your stable of preferred recipes and check to see that none are unhappy with you, that none are undermining your hopes and dreams for yourself by frightening away your friends, showing up and appearing to be a perfectly fine thing for dinner, but underneath the warm exterior poisoning people against you.

You need to root out and make your own those few recipes for things you like well enough to revisit again and again, and which are not so fussy and precise that you actually need skills or concentration to make them.[2] They need to be on good terms with your friends and family, and should not betray preferences nor restrictions nor provoke allergic reactions. Naturally, your kitchen and tools should be able to accommodate these recipes, although you might very well have favorites which you only enjoy making when you have access to the garden or professional stove or company of some certain friend. They should be less rather than more labor intensive; you should neither notice nor care about the effort.[3] Your chosen recipes should not destroy your health, but since you are hardly going to be cooking everyday and subsisting on your own chefery, neither do they have to be relentlessly healthy and correct for daily bread.[4] Also, if you are going to have only a small

---

[1] For example, very few people are the experts at making macaroni and cheese from a box they were in their early twenties.

[2] Of course you may have extraordinary culinary skills and excellent concentration, but there are moments when you do not care to call on them for cooking, or when it might be inappropriate and undermining of higher goals to do so. I have seen more than one amour be more put off than seduced by a great display of effort and skill, for a variety of reasons. See footnote 8.

[3] Naturally this is different for everyone. I blanche at the thought of roasting and peeling the same Anaheim pepper which continents of people roast and peel without thinking the first thing. Funny, but I can't think of a single chore I happily do but millions of others think is too much effort. Cooking at all, maybe. Documenting my every tiny opinion, certainly. Sweet of you to read along.

[4] Which conveniently explains and excuses most of the recipes found in this book. Mind you, you might find it easier to eat well by feeding yourself than by any other means. Which explains the rest of the recipes in this book.

number of recipes at your immediate disposal, it is very nice for them to be recipes which are amenable to variation. Chocolate soufflé, for example, would not come under the heading "Amenable to Variation". Salads, pastas, soups, sandwiches, marinades, muffins, enchiladas and risottos do.

How do you find your recipes? According to me, there are several ways and all of them incorporate a small amount of trial and error. Willingness to fail, and humility and humor because you will, are invaluable in the hunt for your house specialties.

ONE

Notice when you are served something you really like, and then at a convenient moment ask politely and sincerely for the recipe. Friends and other hosts are usually generous, willing at least to point toward the cookbook in which the original recipe is located. Be forewarned, however, that they often withhold, as they have every right to do, spontaneous or premeditated alterations on the original instructions.[5]

A variation on this way of acquiring recipes is to watch carefully while someone who knows how to cook is making something you like very much and to ask questions about what they are doing. Eventually you will come to understand the underlying structure of the dish and be able to recreate it in your own fashion with only the barest inkling of ingredients and method—which is all a recipe ever is anyway, however fanatically you may choose to follow it. Watch and copy. Notice what is being combined with what else and in what general amounts. Ask questions. Over time this course of observation will give you a foundation of knowledge which will enable you to behave sensibly around other groups of ingredients as well.[6] If you seem in over your head, if your attempt to remember the temperature of the oven seems to be displacing information about how or how much oil was used earlier in the process, you can always retreat and ask for the recipe in writing.

Again, most people will be flattered by the request and will be happy to hand over the recipe in some scant or elaborate form. But there are people who will be flustered by

---

[5] One friend, who has remained a good friend in spite of this, insists to this day her recipe for muffins comes from the side of the 100% Bran box. "Maybe I use more butter than they suggest," she offers when I call to tell her that once again my attempt to make muffins from this recipe has failed. Abroad and far from any bran at all, I tried other muffin recipes until I found one in *The Joy of Cooking* that I could play with without ruining. To each their own muffin. Mine never involve bran. Why should they? I can always go to her house or to the bakery for that sort of thing.

[6] When very young I made tapioca pudding, assiduously following the recipe on the back of the box. Unfortunately I misread the box and put in a quarter cup of salt instead of sugar. So now I know that a quarter cup of salt is inappropriate for something that is to serve six people. I always recommend learning from other people's mistakes.

the request, who will respond in a less than generous way. Let them be. They might not really know the recipe, are flying by the seat of their pants, and fear horribly they will be revealed in their charade. Or they might have been sworn to secrecy by the great-grandmother who passed this family recipe into their care moments before passing away. Or they might be among those people who lie spontaneously when asked even such unthreatening questions as where they purchased an article of clothing, considering their knowledge to be part of their wealth and believing that if shared its value is diminished. Alternatively, your friend may be literally unable to respond to a request for something because they are in the process of entertaining a bunch of people. Have some sense of timing.

Have some sense of discretion as well. If you beg, borrow or steal a recipe from someone, make it your own. You might alter the amounts of some ingredients, add or subtract mushrooms or some other expendable item, choose some very different form of presentation, anything which makes it yours and not theirs. If the recipe is directly from a cookbook, then you needn't worry. Hundreds of people in hundreds of kitchens are creating the exact same delicacy down to the garnish and the author is raking in royalties. On the other hand, if you recreate a friend's signature dish and then serve it at every opportunity, you should not be surprised if you seem not to see much of that friend any more.

TWO

Look through cookbooks for recipes which list ingredients you like, or seek out recipes for things you remember enjoying, and then try those recipes on for size. This method of hunting up recipes requires a substantial amount of patience. You often have to try a recipe a couple of times before you get it to work, and then another time or two to make it suit your tastes. Even then it may not work out for circumstantial reasons: your oven isn't sufficiently dependable, the grocery stops stocking some of the ingredients, the mess from preparation is too horrible, things like that. But if you keep your eyes open and are willing to eat toast for dinner now and again, it works. Later on you don't have to credit anyone for your virtuosity, nor risk becoming bitter because a friend of yours effortlessly serves up a particular something you have failed to conquer.

The trickiest part about learning from books is the touchy-feely part. Many recipes depend upon some cooking knowledge, and some familiarity with the nature of food. They are not simply a set of instructions that anyone who can read can follow, as many people claim. Recipes are riddled with directions like "beaten eggs", but there is no way for you to know you must beat the eggs with a fork or a whisk until they turn lemon yellow and drizzle off the utensil in a smooth ribbon or the cake won't really do what a cake is supposed to do. There is no one in your kitchen saying "THIS is what the dough should feel like before you roll it out." No. You have to figure it out for yourself, and there is pretty much no chance you will get it right the first time. For that matter, you don't want to get it right the first time. Then you will have learned nothing about the process. Best to get it terribly wrong, then call one of your cook friends and tell them the whole pathetic story. They will be happy to point out the several ways in which you may have erred. Needless to say, their comments could help you learn about things that didn't actually go wrong but might have at a later date if they hadn't drawn your attention to their importance. You learn in double time and still, with all this help, can claim the recipes as your own.

Getting a good grasp on a recipe which depends upon your knowing what the food should be like at various points in the process will take several attempts within a very small number of days so you can remember from one try to the next what you did and what you changed and how that affected the final product. Once you have mastered a basic recipe, and know where you must be careful and where you can relax, you might with confidence vary it for effect or to accommodate seasonal and regional foods and the contents of your refrigerator.

Browse cookbooks without motive and reject anything requiring special tools or appliances or having more than about ten ingredients until you are a very comfortable cook. Do not be ambitious. Even if by some miracle you successfully execute a delicate and complicated dish, you will probably not have had much fun, will be ragged from the strain of unfamiliar concentration, and won't be inclined to play in the kitchen again anytime soon. Push yourself but gently and without large leaps which might leave you suddenly lost in the middle of nowhere. Consider this process akin to pursuing a self-designed and directed work-out regimen. The important things are to keep showing up at the gym or on the field or wherever and to not succumb to enthusiasm which could lead to injury or even to extreme and debilitating soreness which would preclude the continued pursuit of strength and flexibility. Same here. Moderation. Persistence. Modesty and humility. The ability to admire others who are further along than you are in their development as an athlete or as a cook. To ask for advice and to accept counsel that was unasked for but appropriate anyway. To politely screen inappropriate counsel.

If you are impatient, seek out and commission a trainer.

THREE

Keep your eye out for likely recipes in restaurants. A difficult path because you get even less designation of amounts than I am willing to give in this book. Clever because chefs in restaurants are endlessly imaginative and there is next to no chance that anyone else will make such a thing in a private home and so you do not risk serving an inferior or at best matching version of something already wrought with previous intimate associations.

How can you get such recipes? Sometimes you can beg the chef for it. Sometimes you can convince a cooking magazine to wrangle the recipe from the restaurant and publish it several months down the road when the ingredients are no longer freshly available. Or you can hone your genius for ingredient identification and try to recreate the dish at home with skills you barely possess and a vague idea of what might be in the recipe. I tried that once. A better approach is to describe the dish to a friend who knows how to cook really well, and ask them what they think is in it. Or take them to the restaurant and let them figure it out in person. Or call the next day and ask what was in the dish under the pretext of trying to discover what might have been responsible for an allergic reaction you suffered after leaving the restaurant. Chefs always fall for that one. You don't get precise amounts, but you can get precise ingredients and general amounts. Then you can combine this knowledge of ingredients with knowledge about how to make things which you have gleaned from cookbooks and from cooking friends, and weave together something resembling what you so enjoyed at the restaurant. Your best direction from here is to improve it to your own tastes and using your own imagination rather than trying ever harder to mimic exactly what the professional chef created with ingredients and tools which are oft times not even available to you, and being necessarily and so foolishly disappointed.

GO

However you do it, find something you like to make and which people like to eat[7] and which is not too elaborate.[8] Maybe three or four things. Know them so intimately that you

---

[7] For example, there is probably no need to get really good at making okra tortas.

[8] Sure you can have extremely elaborate dishes which you enjoy making, and can make at a moment's notice. But overly elaborate meals, like too-expensive gifts, make people nervous. And I ask you, Who is going to clean up the mess after the execution of an extravagant concoction? Some people are virtually incapable of becoming all quivery and romantic if there are dishes in the sink. I don't need to tell you how precious momentum can be lost during even 10 minutes of clean-up time. It's as bad as the drive back from a restaurant. On the other hand, if you can make doing the dishes as provocative as slow-dancing by firelight, bravo.

could make them in your sleep. You may have to. Learn them so well that even if you do not have any of the ingredients on hand, you can create a reasonable facsimile of the dish. Spontaneity. Flexibility. Creativity. Competence. Humor. Excellent qualities in a cook,[9] and especially important when you fail miserably and are dialing for take-out. Temper or any evidence of a bruised ego is extremely inappropriate. Impress your companion with your humor, your sanity, and your good taste in delivery food.

ABOUT THE RECIPES in this book: they are homogeneous and dull. Interesting only because everyone is so surprised to find me cooking anything at all. Delicious only because everyone is drunk or famished or otherwise distracted by the time they sit down to the table. Documented here solely because they are the only things I know how to make, and so all that is available for me to demonstrate how you might go about feeding your friends and would-be loved ones without all the trouble of actually becoming an excellent cook. I wouldn't bother trying to emulate any of these recipes, were I you. The tastes you crave, the flavors you favor cannot be the same as mine because you were not raised in my mother's house. You did not discover garlic in Massachusetts, far from any fresh vegetables. Your roommate was not from India. You did not linger for years in Sharon's kitchen and garden. You did not have two plum trees in your yard when you were small. Your best love did not teach you how to make peanut butter cookies. You did not work at the Flea Street Cafe. You didn't get to spend weeks being fed by Jennifer. You did not live in France and England and Spain and learn about those peculiar approaches to food. You are not so finicky about what you eat in the first place. Maybe you like mushrooms and olives.

You will find your own recipes, will find your own flavors you like to use. The important thing is to choose foods others like as well. No point in cooking things no one else wants to eat. That will not charm a soul. Be comfortable with some few recipes so you can make them without attending to a recipe book. It is extremely difficult to pay attention to a guest if your nose is in a book and you are concerned you will miss a step and ruin a dinner which is supposed to seduce. They might wander off, finally eating and enjoying the delicious meal you labored over in the midst of a flirtation with someone else entirely.

If your cooking style requires your complete attention, you should do it by yourself before anyone arrives. Much better to know recipes you can make while chatting with others, or at least while listening to them and enjoying the conversation. That way no one feels as though you have slaved away for them and that they now owe you something in return for your great effort, if only the courtesy of feigning enjoyment. You want them to

---

[9] Or a colleague or a friend or a parent or a child or a lover or a spouse or just about anybody.

feel as though it were absolutely no trouble for you to offer them this delicious meal, all trouble and travail rendered enjoyable, or at least untroubling, because it was done with them in mind. And if they don't like summer squash, for heaven's sake you didn't know and are terribly sorry and they shouldn't trouble themselves about it. If you feel your face fall as a guest politely explains that they can't stand the watermelon you drove ten miles in horrible heat to pick up, you are being vile. The only thought you should have when someone doesn't want something you have offered is, "What else do I have in the house which might be a nice dessert for them since they won't enjoy the watermelon?" Any other response will make them feel terrible for being themselves. If they end up in your arms after such a display on your part, you had best wonder what they want from you to have so quickly forgiven or forgotten such dreadful proof of character.

Whatever you choose to cook and serve is what others will be eating. Find recipes that will make everyone happy, tossing your delight to the side first. It's your kitchen. You can always find something to eat. The others, they are at your mercy.

HAVE ON HAND

In which the contents of cupboards and refrigerators are examined and suggestions are made.

WHAT SHOULD BE in the refrigerator? In the cupboard? In the freezer? What should you have all the time within reach and what should be bought only when it is required for something you plan to prepare today? What should you buy at the grocery store, at the vegetable market, at the specialty foods stores, and when?

When one does not cook frequently, when one is out of the habit, it is almost impossible to imagine what one should have for food in the house. The cupboard might be full, but for the life of you there is nothing to eat. Who bought this stuff? you inquire of yourself, and the answers fall like hail. An ex-mate or roommate, your mother, a sibling or some other good soul who thought your cupboard was bare. Perhaps you are yourself the culprit,

43

living long months and even years with the carnage of an ill-fated trip to one of those warehouse stores. The best intentions go awry in those caverns of gross consumption. Or perhaps your shelves are truly bare, the light in the refrigerator reflecting eerily and too brightly off the unobstructed white interior walls. The cupboards like Christmas morning in Whoville. Steeling yourself to the task of making dinner, desiring to take control of your meals, you start in bravely. You imagine yourself competent and wise concerning things edible. You chop and stir. How bad can it be? Of course you know how to cook. You used to cook. Your mother knows how to cook. You worked in a restaurant once and it didn't look that hard. And at the end of two hours you have an ugly lump of stuff that doesn't taste good at all and you go to bed hungry.

I'm so sorry. It happens all the time. It certainly happens to me. You shouldn't feel bad about it. You need to start from the beginning all over again. Forget everything you once thought you knew and reinvent sustenance for yourself.

How?

First, you better go to the store.

Oh, no. You wander aimless through the supermarket for an hour, perusing the aisles for something you might want to eat. Nothing looks right, nothing looks good. Without a list of specific ingredients needed for a recipe you are planning to attempt later that same day nothing even makes much sense. Eventually you find yourself at the check out with a jar of salsa, some crackers and maybe a pint of ice cream. If you had any spine you would walk out empty-handed, and you probably should since you already have salsa, crackers and ice cream you still haven't eaten from the last time you tried to go to the grocery store without a plan. It's tough. And frankly, the grocery stores and their suppliers are partly to blame. They are not in the business of helping you cook well and for the purpose of courting your friends and family. They are in the business of selling you high-margin, prepared products whose main value does not rest in the quality of the ingredients nor their interesting combination but rather in how much easier you think it will make your life. How much less time you believe you will spend dealing with food and eating it. How little of your precious attention you will be required to pay to your food.

It's a way of looking at the world. But one might as soon think one's life would be easier if one or two or ten people came over for three hours or six or nine, spending a meal and all that surrounds it laughing and eating and talking about dangerous topics.[1] Easier because when others are happy it is easy to be happy and it is easier to live one's life when one is

---

[1] Life might also be easier if you refrain from poisoning yourself and your friends with things you cannot pronounce and some things you can pronounce just fine but which probably don't count as food but which are listed on most labels of most things in the supermarket. Think of all the time you might not have to spend in the hospital later. I also imagine everyone's life would be easier, particularly those lives currently in childhood,

happy. Life might also be easier if one only cooks anything at all maybe once a week; the rest of the time snacking on leftovers, ordering pizza or Indian take-out and eating with friends at their homes or in the delicious restaurants we have the privilege to live amongst. Even if circumstances, finances or children dictate that one cooks at home with regularity, frequent evenings in which cooking is more courtship than culinary chore are not a bad idea. And if these evenings are designed to furnish leftovers for days to come, cooking as a chore might become as infrequent as replacing the shelf paper. Wouldn't that be wild and nice?

But how to get from here to there. How to get into the grocery store and out of it again with a bag of good foods in your arms and with your humor intact. How to find yourself with a cupboard which is not so much full as frank with suggestion of things you could make for dinner tonight. How to get from feeding yourself in as quick and easy a fashion as possible according to the outline offered by ten thousand commercials which you hear and see daily and arrive at cooking Zen. How to leave the world in which food is a horrible burden, a chore, a whirling and mysterious black hole where time and energy and money are sucked away at an alarming rate and must be tamed like those ancient wild rivers by pre-prepared stuffs whisked to readiness in ever speedier heating technologies. How to find the wherewithal to wander wide-eyed into the sultry universe where Marcella and Julia and their spiritual siblings thrust strong hands into warm bowls of pasta and have to ask a friendly observer to hold the glass of wine or water to their lips. A path grown thick with brambles.

You're so lucky you found this book. And so lucky you found this chapter which might eventually get around to giving you some idea of what should be in your cupboard and how it might have gotten there so you have a half a chance of ever being able to make anything at all in your kitchen without that frantic trip to the grocery store at 8 PM. Of course, you might accept that the best way to stock your kitchen is to make a few of the things you suspect you will like, suffer those mid-recipe visits to the grocery (or have someone suffer them for you), and eventually have all those things which should live at your house. Then you can get to know them and how they work. Just a few things, mind you. Not a world of foods. No Krishna you. You do not have to be lover to twenty thousand. Just one or two. Just one for the moment. Keep track of as little as possible. Do as little as possible. Be confident and comfortable with everything in your kitchen, everything in your house for that matter, even if that means you have nearly nothing.[2]

---

if we stop eating things that arrive at the house in a package or several layers of packages, all of which must be somehow disposed of. And millions of lives will be made first more difficult and then perhaps less so if a lot of the energy and resource-intensive manufacturing of food ground to a slow halt. It's just an idea. One I ponder as I drink toxin-riddled coffee with hormone-heavy cream. It doesn't ever stop, does it?

[2] One memorable dinner served by one to another was fresh gnocchi tossed with salt and butter and grated

Meanwhile, as you slowly move toward having a kitchen in which food can be made without thought and without getting dressed to go to the store, remember this: Do not teach yourself to make anything that will not be delicious. Do not spend a moment of time nor a fraction of a dollar on anything you do not want to make, want to eat, or want to offer to others. There is no reason to. Kids will eat what you give them,[3] and adults can find their own food if it comes to that.

Now, to find out what might be delicious to you and then to furnish your kitchen so you can create it without too much effort.

THE RARE AND RELUCTANT cook who has lost the trail can be helped along enormously by a trip to an elegant and well-stocked neighborhood market. The food in such stores is more appetizing than in regular supermarkets, partially because it is presented with more care in order to sell it at higher prices to a lazy and affluent clientele but also because the stuff is simply better. Good food that does not flash to appeal to the childish eye. Fewer bizarre pink cupcakes in cellophane, more pastries from local bakeries. Fewer frozen vegetables, more organic produce. Fewer colorful, sugary breakfast cereals, more pastas and sauces. Less Budweiser, more small vineyards and independent breweries. Less sliced bread, more round, crusty bread. And of course there is less of everything just generally which can help dismantle the cloak of confusion that often settles onto the novice shopper in supermarkets.[4]

But perhaps that is just me.

---

parmesan, eaten while lounging on a very old kilim covering the sloping floor of a small living room just up the hill from the Abbesses metro. A salad of no complexity. Darkness banished with a candle. You see, you barely need a kitchen at all.

[3] Having no children of my own, I am stripped of credibility on the topic. I was a child, though, and hung with children and still do. And I have noticed that if you give them cucumber sandwiches and tomato soup, they will live and very well. If you want to serve them pancakes for dinner, go ahead. If you are making something fabulous and strange, let them eat that, or be happy with some bland element of the meal. That they like hot dogs is no reason to feed them such things. Plenty of children grow to strong gorgeous adulthood without eating any of the stuffs recommended by the food councils. Consider that tribes in Africa which have no access to milk or meat have the lowest incidence of osteoporosis in the world and they keep their very white teeth until they die. Consider that millions of children in this country are so far below the poverty level they never eat anything we would consider a meal in their whole lives, and yet they manage nonetheless to arrive at adulthood with sufficiently large and healthy bodies to bear children of their own. You can plow through this very large can of worms yourself. Meanwhile, try to be compassionate to their young tastes without pandering.

[4] It is only when I have been abroad or in Manhattan for any length of time that I miss these temples of food. I walk into them with awe and relief, and leave with things I am glad to have found. On other occasions, it is too often an exercise in remembering how far my whole culture has strayed from respecting food for what it is and from feeding people what they need to eat rather than what is convenient and profitable for the food industry to sell. And I can't find what I want.

If you are in the mood to share and enjoy food or wish you were but can't seem to remember what is so nifty about it and none of it seems to be in your home, trundle down to your local farmers market in the early morning and browse for an hour or two. Don't buy anything. Keep your hands free and your shoulders weightless. Look at all the vegetables and fruit. Touch them and smell them if it seems no one will mind too much. Definitely smell the herbs. Romantic, perhaps, but who cares. You won't run into anyone there who will think less of you for enjoying a farmers market. Ask the vendors about things you don't recognize and then ask what one might do with them. Find the honey table and taste some. Watch what other people are buying and how much and what else. Accept samples. Drink some coffee or tea or juice or water and let the whole idea of colorful, fresh food going directly from the hands of those who grew it into the hands of those whom it is to sustain wash over you. Still, don't buy anything. Wait awhile. Let the suspense build. Then choose and buy a piece of fruit and eat it. You can splurge on bunches of vegetables and dozens of fruits on another occasion when you have some idea of what to do with them.[5]

Mind you, the farmers market is not the place to find things to keep handy in the kitchen. This is where you find all the things you need immediately, whenever that might be. But not now. Perishables, you can call them. In regarding them you have an opportunity to think about what sorts of things you do like and would like to be able to make, and can be more wise when you are shopping for the surrounding items. The staples and condiments. Those things you must go to a store of some sort to acquire. For those things I suggest you try one of the afore mentioned exquisite markets which can be found in most cities. I realize these stores are fiendishly expensive, but once you know what is available in the world, you will be able to take much better advantage of the discount stores which currently abound. If you don't know what is in the real stores, if you are not in constant conversation with things of excellent quality, you will forget what excellence is and what it feels like to be near and the discount stores, let alone capitalism itself, will have you at their mercy, will sell you scandalously inferior stuffs and you won't even notice.

So go. Wander around one of these places just to get an idea of the possibilities. Lingering near the deli counter might give you ideas for things you could make yourself. Know what sorts of things can be found in these havens so later you can use them as cupboards. Get used to being around excellent things. Grow accustomed to places where food is appreciated and enjoyed and take part in the festivities.[6]

---

[5] If you do give into the temptation to buy a week's worth of stuff on your first trip out, you will be unhappy two weeks later when you find it all rotting in the crisper.

[6] Besides, when such stores have promotions it is likely to be a sampling of goose liver pate or sundried tomato puree on an herbed crostini, and not some new version of cheez wiz on a trisquit.

BUT WHAT SHOULD be in your kitchen? I reluctantly return to the difficult and mundane problem of what should be in the kitchen all the time and as a welcoming committee for more perishable and exotic delicacies. I should think the list would be brief. For example:

POTS AND PANS

And bowls and knives and spoons. See The Complete Kitchen.

STUFF TO EAT WITH

See Dishes.

SALT AND PEPPER

And perhaps garlic and crushed red pepper.

OIL

Some kind of oil. Olive oil, maybe. Or just vegetable oil. Or a nut oil.

BREAD

Loaves of it in the freezer.

DRY PASTA

Or rice or potatoes or cornmeal or some kind of basic, barely perishable food.

Beyond that you are in an arena of personal taste.[7]

For example, when younger, immortal and shopping for a house of six mostly male twenty-somethings our grocery list was this: Minute Maid frozen orange juice, whipped butter, milk, light cream, French roast coffee beans, boneless skinless breast of chicken, Bonne Maman preserves, Thomas' English muffins, Adam's peanut butter, Philadelphia

---

[7] Will suggestions even help? Will it be of assistance to know what is in the kitchens of people who do cook? Or will it simply destroy what small confidence you have built up to know how many little things are going to clutter your kitchen if you succumb to the idea of cooking in such a way that people want to eat? Would you believe me if I assured you that there is no absolute need for distracting and irritating clutter? Are you already halfway back to the frozen food section of the supermarket? Are you only offering me polite attention, all the time thinking to yourself that anyone who lists oil among the critical items to have in a kitchen is not going to espouse a sufficiently low-fat form of cooking to suit your sick little obsession with what you consider health? Please be patient. If you cook well and in a distracting fashion, you will be able to afford a few extra calories.

whipped cream cheese, sharpest cheddar cheese, plain yogurt, carrots, onions, green onions, lettuce and garlic, eggs, Raisin Bran, Ramen noodles, fresh pasta, frozen peas and other vegetables, Beck's beer, parmesan cheese, graham crackers. Lots of all of it. Rice, mustard, soy sauce, olive oil, rice or other vinegars, herbs and spices favoring parsley and basil and oregano, Bisquick, flour, sugar, and unsweetened chocolate as needed. We ate very well and only visited the whole foods store around the corner for fresh vegetables and ginger, exotic cheeses and very cheap French wines.

But now, that grocery list is wrong for me. Too much meat and milk. Too much food.[8]

For sustenance, a store of dry or frozen pasta along with a small selection of bottled pasta sauces. Or rice. Mom loves potatoes. Cornmeal for polenta is a warm change of pace. Bread. A loaf or two in the freezer is wise, and they help keep the cold steady if your freezer is not otherwise well-stocked. Toast is always an excellent thing to eat, and a wonderful thing to offer. Butter and preserves for toast purposes. Breakfast cereal, for house guests if not for you. Some crackers you like, but not so much so you gobble them up the minute they get into the house. Animal crackers if you know children who visit. Juice, for both the children and the house guests. Graham crackers if you are a friend of mine. Whatever anyone might need for coffee or tea.

In the cupboard, in bottles and jars and cans: Tomato sauce and other sorts of canned tomatoes. Olive and other oils. Sugar and honey. Vinegars. Marsala wine. Vermouth. Soy sauce. Bottled herbs and spices. Peanut butter. There are people whose cupboard might as well be empty if there are no tins of sardines or jars of herring in sauce. Popcorn that is less than a year old. An extra can or two of things you find you actually use. Beans or vegetables or canned crab. Tuna. Sugar and brown sugar, flour, baking soda. Vanilla extract. Walnuts or pecans, or some kind of nut that can be nibbled or thrown into a salad or sauce or sautéed with butter and brown sugar. Caviar. Chopped chilis. Raisins or other dried fruit. Sundried tomatoes. Bittersweet chocolate. Who could know what you might like to have around?

For spices and herbs[9] you might want to have parsley, rosemary, thyme, oregano, basil, maybe cilantro, maybe sage, marjoram, cinnamon, cloves, cumin, dry mustard, crushed red pepper, maybe nutmeg, maybe coriander, maybe even the very extravagant cardamom if

---

8 Unless, of course, I happen to be shopping for a warehouse full of mostly male twenty-something-close-to thir-ties, in which case nothing is too much. Still, it doesn't seem right any longer to subsist on meat. The odd barbecue, but other than that an easy vegetarian existence and no one seems to mind or notice. Mind you, I throw a lot of cookies into this equation.

9 Say, do you know the difference between spices and herbs? Spices are the berries or bark of an aromatic plant. Herbs are the stems and leaves. Ginger and garlic are neither. The first is a rhizome and the second a bulb.

you cook in an exotic fashion and like to serve Indian spice tea or coffee.[10] Rifle through cookbooks at the bookstore for sections describing the uses of various herbs and spices. Ask people whose cooking you admire what flavors they use and for what. They will enjoy telling you and you might learn something.

In the refrigerator, a good mustard or two, ketchup if you are that sort of person, and mayonnaise if you like that. Capers, if you are me. Salsa. Parmesan cheese. Worcestershire Sauce, maybe fish sauce, certainly Tabasco sauce, lemon juice in a bottle in addition to lemons. Depends what you have decided to cook when you cook.[11] You don't have to be able to cook very many things, and they don't have to be wildly different in character, so your kitchen needn't look like the condiment aisle at the market.[12]

In the freezer, coffee and ice creams. Ice. The loaves of bread. Extra butter. A bag of bagels. Cranberries. Leftover soups and sauces.

PLEASE BE CAREFUL when you go to the store. Most of the stuff you find in the supermarket you won't ever have occasion to use. It might seem like a good idea, the label claims it will be endlessly nourishing and delicious and convenient, but rarely rarely is it. Wait until you want something for more than a day, or wait until you find yourself in need of it, and then go get it. You don't need much and probably shouldn't have too much food in your kitchen. It makes people nervous if it looks like you're set up for the possibility of siege warfare.[13] Or they might expect that you will be an excellent cook since your kitchen is so well-stocked and then won't be impressed by anything you do.

Still, I haven't answered the question, have not fulfilled the promise of the chapter: What absolutely must be in the kitchen so you can prepare a meal for another?

Nothing, really. Nothing at all. Just you and someone you want to feed.

---

[10] Who, you? But if you want to try: Regular tea or coffee, milk, sugar and ground cardamom simmered together. A friend throws in a small amount of ground black pepper. Maybe some other stuff as well. I think he picked up that trick in Nepal. A good and not too shocking alternative to hot chocolate, which familiar drink can provoke the wrong sort of childlike mood in many people. You do what seems best. Risking rejection, or risking regression. Hmm ... Perhaps just some regular old spiked coffee and to bed.

[11] There is an appendix of shopping lists for different styles of cooking. For reference. In case you are concerned about their usefulness, I assure you they were compiled by real cooks and not by me.

[12] All the recipes in this book, for example, can be attempted and with some success with barely a fifth of the things I've just mentioned as important.

[13] On the other hand, you will be very popular in the event of an earthquake or whatever regional disaster might keep you from the market for a few days.

ABOUT
AMOUNTS[1]

*In which you are admonished to pay some,
but not too much attention.*

WHEN YOU BEGIN cooking,
should you begin cooking, you might think it is best, even imperative, to adhere to amounts
dictated by recipes. One cup sugar. A half cup olive oil. A quarter teaspoon thyme. Two

---

[1] There was early criticism of the near absence of exact amounts in the recipes in this book. In response I
discreetly shrieked that these are my recipes, recipes for foods I actually cook for family and for friends and for
loves and it hardly seems wise to let others know exactly how I make them. Where would that leave me? With
a repertoire of recipes my intimates can find at the table of any literate person with sufficient sense to buy this
book. You're lucky I include complete lists of ingredients. The recipes in this book are offered only to illustrate
a manner of cooking, a philosophy for feeding others in which it is unlikely that the exact same amounts would
ever be used twice to create the same recipe. This approach has plenty of historical precedence. Besides, truth
be told I don't know the exact amounts.

eggs. Like that. Alternatively you may be too-quickly enlightened, having watched Julia Child at too early an age, and think too carelessly that any amount of anything will be just fine.

Truth, as usual, appears to linger somewhere in between, with occasional visits to each extreme. Some knowledge, some good portion of awareness and evolving wisdom will guide you well. It is not too hard to notice that eggs come in many sizes, that herbs and spices are inconsistently intense, and that sweetness is a matter of taste. Even if you do stick strictly to dictated amounts, the variation in the final product can be significant. How large a step is it then to take some control over the variations? To know what more or less thyme will do to a dish and decide for yourself if it needs more or less or none or something else entirely. To know whether you prefer the effect of more egg or less egg, and determine on your own, given the size of eggs on hand, how many to use. The recipe is a good place to start. More or less two eggs. Two medium eggs. Maybe two small eggs, if you prefer less egg, or just one large egg. Or three small eggs, or even three medium or two large eggs, if you want the cakiness of more egg. You, you you you, decide. You are the cook.

You see, cooking is no more precise than any other endeavor in the material world. Olive and other oils have great variety of flavor, and if the oil is being used for flavor the quality and intensity might be considered. If the oil is being used as a medium, one's preference for oiliness is of interest.[2] The right degree of sweetness of a sauce or a cookie is very much a matter of taste. American cookbooks tend to make both desserts and savory dishes sweeter than necessary for deliciousness. Sugar, fat and salt are the most direct way to stimulate the sense of taste and are overused for that reason.[3]

If you could see me, you would see a woman shaking her head and rolling her eyes, frustrated as can be at the wide-spread practice of obsessive measuring and adherence to recipes. Food is so variable it seems silly to suggest let alone dictate amounts for anything besides baked stuff or candies. Even then, recipes can usually be adjusted to taste without harm. More frequently, one has only obscure or untrustworthy directions to begin with, bare clues about where to start and with what. The recipe for bruschetta pilfered from the menu of a local trattoria lets on that roma tomatoes, garlic, basil and olive oil are present. How much? Who knows. If the recipe came from a book, you might be equally adrift. You are captive to how strong your garlic is and how much you feel like peeling and chopping up. You must decide how much green basil you want to see amongst the red, even if the recipe was specific about how many leaves to use. How can you not notice that leaves come

---

[2] One excellent cook, in addition to many friends, simply halves the oil and doubles the garlic suggested in any recipe. That's a good rule, if you love garlic and have not been trained to need great amounts of fat to feel something is delicious. A middle ground between the excesses of regular recipes and the excesses of fat-free cooking.

[3] Kind of like using a vibrator all of the time.

in many sizes? You may want to start the whole process by looking to see how many tomatoes you bought and how big they are. Maybe there should be a bit of salt and pepper and sugar in the mixture since there almost always is, and adding them certainly works, but sometimes you forget the salt or the pepper or the sugar and it is fine as well. You would never forget the garlic, of course, but if you did, or if the garlic used was not pungent enough, you would know soon enough because it wouldn't be wonderful.[4] You wouldn't want to eat any. Your guests would still be talking instead of eating and laughing at their efforts to keep the bits of tomato on the toasts. You would turn around and it would still be there. Would a recipe have helped? Wouldn't it be better to have instructions to look at to insure that nothing important is forgotten? Yes, but no. Because the garlic might still be weak, the tomatoes not sweet enough, or the recipe itself flawed in the context of your own tastes and the habits of your friends. The bruschetta would be all wrong and the only solace you would have is to blame the failure on someone else. "The book said to do it that way. It's not my fault it didn't work." Yes, well. Forgive everyone for not caring too much, and go about making it better.

Of course "making it better" will require you to be able to determine what is wrong with it. Can you decide if it needs salt or garlic or sugar or more basil or more oil? Do you know a little bit about what each ingredient contributes so you can resolve that common lament: It needs something. How very important it is to have some idea of what various foods do in conjunction with other foods so when you use more or use less you have some good idea what will happen. Important both so that you do not make some horrible mistake and render inedible perfectly good food, but also so that you can experiment and explore and create ever more delicious somethings with confidence. No good at all being cavalier about amounts before your time. Things can turn ugly in the blink of an eye, and you might end up forever afraid of making anything that has not been previously tested in a professional kitchen and given the stamp of approval by a NYC cookbook publisher.

Be wary as you become wise. Wisdom in some areas means you must be humble and know there are other and myriad areas where it would not be right to improvise just yet. Perhaps you have a good grasp on garlic and an array of herbs popular in Italy. Play as you like with them. But when you decide one day to try making a southeast Asian vegetable dish, even if it happens to include basil which it might, use a recipe and use it carefully. You cannot leap wildly and exuberantly about until you have checked that you have ground to

---

4 Unless of course the basil and tomatoes were of such luscious ripeness that their mingling in aromatic oil from the olive were sufficient all by itself. A hint or no garlic at all being very very fine in this case. You see, you see? The possibilities are endless. You cannot go wrong unless you don't care, don't notice when what you offer is not good, neglect to acquire good ingredients, refuse to learn to taste and appreciate texture and flavor, forget to notice if your guests are enjoying themselves. Bad qualities all around, I'd say, steering well clear of your bed.

stand on and leap from and that dangerous precipices are a little ways off. It's no good bouncing about hoping you will by chance land on some solid ground. Neither physics nor cooking nor courtship work that way. Who knows how they work, but they don't work like that. You always need something to leap from.[5]

That is why you need to have a rudimentary grasp of amounts. Now, how.

SOMEHOW YOU WILL acquire knowledge about amounts of ingredients and you will be able to raise your eyebrows with the finest chefs when a recipe calls for an unorthodox amount of some ingredient or another.[6] Mind you, such heresy is exactly the sort of stuff famous chefs are made of. But their successful rejection of traditional rules for cooking rises from their understanding of them. The more intimately they understand the existing dogma, the more profound and revelatory will be their refutation. For you, a beginning of understanding will allow you to begin inventing and straying on your own. Increasing understanding will increase your inventiveness and expand the radius of your wanderings. To start, know that a cup of salt is never right, unless you are cooking for more than 300, or if the salt is being used in some process and then discarded or rinsed off well before serving whatever it is. A cup of sugar is often right, but not if the recipe is to be served prior to dessert. Later you may learn that a cup of capers is almost never right, parmesan goes in at the last moment, and lemon should not be combined with milk, but that with care it can be mingled with cream. Still further along, discover that ginger can be used in extremely small amounts or in prodigious amounts, and that both effects are glorious and lead to soft sighs and purrs that begin below the belly.[7]

Begin to gather this sort of knowledge by browsing through cookbooks. Notice the amounts associated with different ingredients and what role the various ingredients seem to have in the recipe. Note whether a particular ingredient is a large part of the recipe, or a grace note. Notice when it is used and how it is prepared before being combined with the other ingredients. Read instructions for preparation. Read anything having to do with

---

[5] By the way, you aren't going to find it in this book. This is only about leaping form. Try *The Way to Cook, The Silver Palate Cookbook, The Greens Cookbook, The Joy of Cooking, Fannie Farmer*, Escoffier, books by Pepin. Or ask a smart, kind, sympathetic, non-snooty friend who cooks to recommend a book from which you might leap. Or take a cooking class. Or work for a few months in a restaurant. Or get deeply involved with someone who loves to cook and knows how.

[6] I do not mean in judgment or disdain. Eyebrows can go up in simple recognition that something is not as it usually is. A gesture that suggests no condemnation, but rather increased interest and heightened attentiveness as the predictable has been forsaken.

[7] Why don't you add your own footnote here.

cooking and food. You will absorb more than you notice. Even lists of ingredients on prepared foods will give you knowledge.[8]

Then when you are feeling adventurous, or particularly safe and secure, follow a few recipes—recipes from real cookbooks. Any recipes will do. As long as you are at it, you may as well find recipes which involve some of the special things you particularly want to know about. The less stuff in a recipe, the easier it will be to see how one single ingredient affects it. Too few things, though, and you will not be able to see how different elements affect each other. Seven to twelve ingredients, perhaps. Make brownies with less egg and then with more egg. Make a pasta sauce with less garlic and then with more. Put in double the amount of an herb or spice than is called for. Leave it out entirely, adding it at the last moment if it turns out to be indispensable. Exchange one ingredient for another you think will be an interesting alternative. Decide if you like what happens. Banish your ego and be willing to accept that an experiment failed. Find recipes that combine ingredients in ways you have not before tried. Discover that garlic and ginger go beautifully together. Notice how mustard can be used as an ingredient rather than a condiment. Find nutmeg in all sorts of sauces and soups. Grated on top when not mixed into the dish itself. Figure out how to cook with beans. With chili peppers. Indeed, knowledge and understanding of amounts is inextricable from knowledge and understanding of the ingredients themselves. Know about beans and about chili peppers, what they are like, their flavor and texture, and then you will know better how much of them you want to add to the risotto or soup or salad or pasta you are making.

Or find a recipe for something you are already familiar with, and which you like quite a bit since you will be having it on several occasions. A dressing for a salad. Soup. A casserole, a frittata, an omelet, a torte. Not a soufflé nor a mousse. Not flaming anything. Nothing which seems like it must be done Just So. You might not want to use a favorite recipe from a friend if you tend to have high expectations of yourself. You will surely not make it as well on your first try as they do any day of the week, and you risk becoming quickly frustrated and bricking off the kitchen in a fit of pique. No sense at all in giving yourself opportunity to compare your developing skills to those of other, more experienced cooks and possibly lose heart. For that matter, no sense in learning how to make something you can just as easily get someone else to make for you. Sure you are using the recipe

---

[8] I confess I once elucidated most of a recipe for Caesar dressing from the backs of several bottles at the gourmet grocery. It was a busy day leading up to the festivities of the Book Burning and Exchange; friends appearing out of nowhere and others disappearing as mysteriously. All day with eyes open, but still no recipe presented itself. We all knew there was something special about Caesar dressing, but couldn't remember what it was. No vinegar, it turns out. Lemon juice and olive oil; plus garlic, egg, anchovy, and parmesan, of course. Ground pepper to finish. And large, rustic croutons. A little fresh thyme, if you like. Make it properly and people will eat it right out of the bowl with their hands and not even notice.

primarily to learn about amounts—as well as to become acquainted with ingredients and have the opportunity to practice cooking technique—but the hard truth is whatever you experiment with at this time will become the cornerstone of your repertoire of things you know how to make. If you have borrowed a favorite recipe from a friend, and then proceed to make some version of it for every dinner party for the next decade, you stand a good chance of offending and an even better chance of being considered unimaginative and thoughtless.

However you do it, as long as you do it politely and legally, find a recipe or several for things you would like to make. Before you begin to play with your food, make whatever it is you have chosen exactly according to the recipe you have found. Or as exactly as you can in your particular kitchen. If there are difficult to find ingredients you are missing or tools required which you do not possess and are in no hurry to add to your collection, pause. Call someone who knows how to cook and ask them if artichoke hearts are really all that important in this particular soup recipe. I cannot think of a single ingredient that might not be indispensable in one recipe, while frivolous and perhaps even better left out of another. Even salt has moments when it is not needed.[9] Consider amounts with the intent to arrive at a spot where not having measuring spoons and cups in the kitchen won't bother you. As you make the chosen recipe, notice how much of the different ingredients you are using. When you taste the final product, think about what went into it and how it might be different if you had used more or less of something, or left it out altogether. Taste the stuff at different stages, before some ingredients have been added to learn more on that count. Taste your ingredients. Imagine how the addition of another herb, or some nuts or raisins, or a different vegetable or some cream might effect the dish. Ask others what they think and be the beneficiary of much hard experience. You will hear tales of woe and of triumph; there will be much laughter and storytelling, confessions and contradictions.[10] You will eventually find yourself not caring very deeply what any recipe has to say about how much garlic and crushed red pepper you should use. You will know yourself to be the final judge of that. If the recipe is by a cook whom you trust and admire, you may want to give weight to their thoughts on the matter. In all cases you decide what you want to do, and then you do it. Even if it is following a recipe to the letter.

---

9 Cordelia would never have believed it, but then I do not believe pre-historic Gaul had many sources of parmesan cheese or anchovy paste, or even many lemons for that matter, or garlic. Lear, though, he knew. A man before his time. "Loves me like salt, does she? I see through her little ruse. Tomorrow she will favor orange zest and then where will my kingdom be?"

10 IF it is a crowd who cooks, be it casually or professionally; a crowd not bent on appearing impressive; friends who do not fear foolishness in themselves nor deride it in others.

Whatever you choose to do, remember that when you approach cooking as courtship it doesn't matter what others have done before you or might choose to do after you. All that matters is that what you do at any moment be sincere, pure in its intent, and without expectation for return. Your beloved, or whomever is fortunate enough to find themselves at your table, will have no grounds for comparing you to anyone or anything else in the whole world, thoughtlessly happy as they are with whatever is in front of them.

PERHAPS YOU ARE RELUCTANT to learn. You shake your head and say, "Cooking as courtship I can see. I accept the idea that feeding someone well might make them feel a little or a lot more warmly toward me personally. But this stuff about using recipes as mere suggestion is going too far. People more clever than myself have thought this all out, determined the amounts, and I am not going to waste my time learning how to be flexible in the kitchen. I am sure I will feed my darlings much better if I just follow the recipes in the books. That way I can serve them a wider variety of impressive things, without having to think too much about it, and that must be good. Variety. Right?"

Oh, yes. Right. Variety is very good. In fact, your darling might begin to consider a wider variety of entertainments if you take this approach to feeding them. Consider A: Your guest informs you as you are beginning to cook up a delicious something they are allergic to or can't stand or otherwise prefer not to ingest a certain element of the thing you are about to make.[11] Consider B: Neither of you is exactly dressed to go to the store, but a particular sort of something is desired by the other. Something which you would be happy to make if only you had ... But you don't. Consider C: Another good friend borrowed your cookbook yesterday. Consider, although it is difficult and sad to do so, how many times one body walks away from another simply because life was too dull, too regimented, too predictable. They find a love who is inspired by them, who inspires in them creativity and boldness, with whom they can play and reveal themselves. Not that the first love couldn't have thrown aside ideas and preconceptions and allegiance to lifestyle and come out to play themselves, but if they don't, they haven't.

---

11 Mind you, you needn't listen too carefully to any of their ideas about what should be in the meal unless they are prefaced with medical authority of some sort, e.g. "Goat cheese makes me sick," or the authority of an on-off switch, e.g. "If it is very spicy-hot, I won't be able to eat it." And you should listen very carefully to polite displays of deep revulsion, e.g. "Are you going to cook this eggplant?" It is self-assured, controlling comments like "Go easy on the ginger. I'm not wild about it," which you can ignore utterly, simply nodding in their direction as though you heard them. That is a food prejudice, and indeed if you have any evidence they have unknowingly eaten things with lots of ginger in it, you can ignore them without feeling the smallest bit evil. Besides, like it's even possible to have too much ginger.

You had better know how to make something and how to make it with more or less or none or a slightly different version of any particular ingredient. That's what I think. "Where's the respect for the art of the author of the cookbook?" you ask. Oh, for heaven's sake, someone is hungry, perhaps for something, and the more quickly and deliciously and humorously you feed them, and all the better with something which is exactly what they wanted except better and surprising and scrumptious on its own, the more quickly they will retire back to the chaise or the lounge or wherever it is you would have them. Don't undermine yourself with purist ideas about the merit of any particular recipe. Don't be fussing and trying to measure out amounts primly and precisely when you might be exhibiting spontaneity, dexterity and sureness of movement and intention. A relaxed nature. Even should goofiness or ineptitude be your persona of choice—an act which works extremely well for a small percentage of people—you still need to get better than edible food in front of another with some haste and with little apparent effort. Otherwise they will not understand why you are not just ordering delivery, will regret you were not clever enough to have leftovers in the fridge. Trying too hard. People are extremely sensitive to it, don't like it, draw away from it, wish you wouldn't, so don't. Or at least don't appear to. Even more important perhaps is that you do not ever allow yourself to feel you are trying too hard. If you do, or if you sense that you are losing the allegiance of your audience as they instinctively desert someone doomed to failure or check out before they are forced into feeling grateful, stop immediately and say, "This is too complicated to pay attention to with you over there. How about some toast?"

Then, of course, it must be added: Use the measuring instruments if you wish, follow instructions exactly, but follow them as friends instead of jailers and relax. In general it just doesn't matter. Cooking for the most part is a far less precise science than most cookbooks would suggest. Relative amounts are what is most important, if anything is, therefore it is fine to use whatever cup you have on hand as long as you use the same sort of cup for all the ingredients. Insistence that you must use one-fourth of a teaspoon rather than a whole teaspoon of marjoram is in violent opposition to the whole idea of cooking as courtship. Certainly that 3/4 teaspoon will change the way the dish tastes and for people who are picky and precise and full of ideas about how things should taste that might be a very big deal indeed. But perhaps the author chose an exact amount only so that the reader would feel secure. In most cases, changing the amount of an ingredient will simply change the way something tastes, not necessarily for the better nor for the worse. Which is all to say, please let your use of cookbooks be referential rather than reverential.

Having said that, chemistry instructions should not be toyed with unless you become quite an advanced cook and need to spend more effort disguising your proficiency than creating fabulous foods. Chemistry instructions are pretty easy to notice because they involve all the things that are essentially flavorless. Oils, water, flour, salt, eggs, baking soda and baking powder. Some things have both flavor and chemistry value. Vinegar and lemon and alcohols, for example. Instructions on the order of mixing things together and the amount of time and sort of heat for cooking should also be heeded.

As it happens, there is lots of room for flexibility even in these chemistry experiments—obviously since plenty of people cook beautifully with nearly no resources—but it does take a bit of experimentation under the watchful gaze of a mentor, present or in print, before you can move freely about inside the restrictions of the physical world. Bake obediently until you can disregard instructions intelligently.[12]

FOLLOW RECIPES TO the letter if you like, but consider that you might eventually, sooner rather than later, adjust them to your taste and to the ingredients available. Altering them if only to be certain that your culinary expression of affection is not word for word that of another. Or because you notice that regardless of how safe it may make you feel and certain of success, if you persist in following instructions your nose will have been very unfortunately in a book and you won't have heard a word of conversation for possibly hours. Which sadly means you will be an hour behind in both subject and momentum when you do finally get dinner on the table and address yourself to the minds and souls at hand. Good strategy, if you like to sleep alone. Better, I should think, to depend upon recipes you are comfortable with, have already transcended in terms of exact amounts and participating ingredients,[13] and which you know people like, or at least have good reason

---

[12] Another Susan takes all my thoughts about amounts and casts them out with a single chocolate chip cookie. Single? I should rather say many several, they were so delicious I lost count. Asking for the recipe, she tells me a long story about trying the recipe in the Stars cookbook and finding that the cookies were not at all like the those served in the restaurant. (Mind you this is a woman who can tell when a favorite bakery has changed flour suppliers.) Addressing her dismay to the restaurant, the baker finally confesses she had converted the amounts from weight to volume measurements to accommodate home cooks who rarely have scales. Hmmm. It's true though. Ingredients change volume with humidity and other variables. So Susan and the baker work together and figure out what the weight measurements are for a small batch. Some specific number of grams of this, some specific number of grams of that. Perfect. Susan orders chocolate pieces from a cafe in Seattle to make the cookies still more wonderful.

[13] We haven't discussed this yet, and perhaps for good reason. There are two sorts of stabilities, mathematically speaking. One is the equivalent of pin balanced on its point on top of the point of another pin. The other is illustrated by a marble at the bottom of a bowl. Both are stable, but the first cannot stand even the slightest push from the stable point while the second can be pushed around quite dramatically and even violently before the marble finally slips over the edge of the bowl. Some recipes are like the first: They work just fine if conditions are perfect and you do everything exactly right. Other recipes, all the recipes in this book, for example, are stable in the second manner: You can fool with them almost endlessly, as long as you don't do anything foolish like turn the bowl over. The first sort cannot be transcended. The second sort may be best that way. Having said that, it's interesting to look at an original recipe years later to see how far you've wandered, and to consider different routes from center.

to think they will. Know what you are doing. Do what you want. Hold within yourself knowledge of what has gone before and acceptance that you do not know what will come next. A constant balance between the two, neither resting solidly on former successes, neither flailing about with no substance within grasp.

A final suggestion: Do your experimenting on your own time or with people who already love you so much that no amount of praiseworthy food would increase their affection, and no amount of delivered pizza will hurt it.[14]

---

[14] That will take too much time, you complain? Well. Did you make love beautifully the first time? Even within several years of picking up the sport? Of course not, but a healthy amount of good humor and an honest desire to learn, an enthusiasm and willingness even, pleaded your cause and probably everyone waited patiently for you to become tolerable and then even longer for you to become competent. Try try and try again, they say, although I don't think this is what they were talking about. And it is remarkable how many rustic meals, honestly prepared, people will gladly accept if the conversation and wine are good and the food isn't getting worse. Remarkable how few previously frozen, recently microwaved meals you can serve before people begin to decline invitations to dine at all. Unless, of course, company and conversation are of legendary proportions.

INVITING THEM

In which we put forth sneaky ways of seeding and growing friendship and acquaintance, if not love.

EASY ENOUGH TO select your guest of honor.[1] To take aim and fuel your own desires with healthy fantasy. But how do you get that figment of your imagination into your home and begin the irksome and possibly impossible task of turning sweet dream into radiant flesh and laughter and warmth of all sorts? Hells of a thousand varieties lie between those states of grace. Admiring from afar is fine for a time, even forever, but if courtship insists itself upon you, if conjuring a relationship of

---

[1] Easy enough, anyway, to make a poor selection. To choose unwisely. All the more reason to get them to your home, to cook for them, to start learning more about them in the revealing arena of an offered and shared meal, to become wise concerning them, and then get on with it. Of course, now they know where you live and if your selection is very very poor, you may have a problem. See footnote 3.

some sort becomes a matter of importance to you, you will need correspondence. They must get near enough to touch. Words need to be exchanged and experiences shared. Coffees and tea and dinners and movies and walks in parks and along rivers and through museums and down alleyways will heighten your desire to bring them back to your home, to feed them and love them and keep them full and happy. Whoever they are that you would draw into your life. Whatever they will be when they get there. Courtship of any sort will lead to food. Even business dealings, social climbing and politickings of the finest quality take place in the dining rooms of private homes. And though the guidelines may become more formal, the process of invitation and seducing towards acceptance your desired companion or companions remains the same.

For now, and to avoid such subjects more likely to prove nauseating than entertaining, let us suppose you have only the most humble and honest of courtship aims. Friendship. Love. Camaraderie, casual or commercial. How will you invite that other to your home? Under what pretext and with what level of formality do you invite them? How far in advance and by what means? How do you arrive at the point where an invitation to dinner is not presumptuous? What series of events, of previous invitations leading to one of significance, must take place? A difficult enough puzzle of tasks even before considering the many instances when to convince the guest of importance to come at all you might have to round up a slightly larger party. How do you invite these people, in what attitude, when, and for what? And once they are assembled, what path do you take to midnight, the object of your interest in your home and well fed, your very discreet and well-mannered friends having made their excuses and vanished into the night? There you are, alone together, and there is no further counsel to be had here.[2]

Nuts and bolts sorts of stuff, mind you, and hard to focus upon when you are only thinking about larger desires. Whom did you invite, and how? To what and for what apparent "why"? How did you get the desirable one to agree to attend this little event? None of this is easy, even for the accomplished professional. Many are the morsels whose defining characteristic at first appears to be "Elusive." Many are the friends who cannot be trusted in the company of someone you are trying to impress. Few are the evenings or mornings or afternoons when everything comes together and the next day you wander through your responsibilities basking in the warmth of having gotten it right the day before. It might be as close as we come to divinity: all-giving and full of grace.[3]

---

[2] Other chapters of this book will escort you as far as that wild shore. Note especially Graciousness and The Technical Production.

[3] Monstrous sorts who do not understand generosity without agenda will ruin your mood. It makes them nervous and suspicious. There is no good solution. Offer them nothing. Make them ask for it. Then say no about two-thirds the time. The rest of the time say yes, but act as though it is a great effort for you. Later, if

THERE ARE SEVERAL approaches to inviting people to your home for a meal. Some are more dependable than others. Some are almost always more off-putting than inviting. None of them work flawlessly on every occasion. Before exploring the ins and outs of a longer guest list, let's look at how you will get yourself and your would-be beloved[4] into a private home, any private home, with the purpose of sharing a meal.

Often a pretext is useful. The way into another's heart is never through portals that open broadly onto the street. A maze to be negotiated, griffins at the gate, dogs to be distracted with loaves of bread, locks and traps to be unwound and undone. Perhaps they have a painting you would like to see, an art collection of some reputation. Maybe in conversation they mention a newly built porch you could admire or flowers recently planted. You meet at their house before going to a movie or a play or a club. In many cases it is easier to get yourself invited to someone else's home than to get them into your own. Once you have made that first brief visit, which should be very brief and encompass no more than a cup of coffee or a single drink, you are in an excellent position to later invite them to your own home for a more lengthy visit. Dinner perhaps. Reversed, this is a method of getting yourself invited to someone else's house. Invite them into your own home for some silliness of purpose. They will naturally admire your taste in abodes and insist you must come see their home sometime. "I'd love to," you reply. Is it possible that neither of you have homes worth visiting? Or that one of you has a home pleasant to be in and the other an ill-kept or otherwise uncomfortable and uninviting place of residence? If the latter is you, fix it or accept that you can be found wanting for such oversight and insensibility. If the latter is the other, wonder and consider why that might be and whether or not it bothers you.

When conversation allows it, mention that you occasionally cook for friends. Don't mention that you do it well. Just that you do. How easy then to include them in the next dinner party. Not threatening. The sort of thing a potential mate might regard as very attractive in the possible other. The ability to entertain casually. The having of friends. That's a good sign. Better still, the sharing of friends. In some circles, perhaps all circles, an expression of highest regard.[5]

---

they become comfortable enough to accept normal gestures of goodwill from you, they will regard your generosity as something they have won and which is special to them. Then terrible trouble because they might well notice that you treat a number of friends similarly. A fight ensues. You try to explain. They think you are sleeping with the neighbor because you lent them some olive oil. As I said. There is nothing much to do with these people. Maybe it is best after all to just treat them well and watch them squirm. Maybe they will get used to it.

[4] If it is already your beloved, you should have no problem getting them to the table. In fact, you may damage the affair beyond repair if you neglect to invite them to a private dinner.

[5] Don't underestimate this, nor the separating force of refusing to share friends.

Of course, there is no reason you cannot invite someone straight-away to your home for dinner or ask them to accompany you to dinner at the home of another.[6] However you do it—and there are a thousand thousand ways and means—make them feel comfortable and want to say Yes. Present the occasion as an existing thing and offer them a sincere and unassuming invitation to join in. Set them at ease and dissolve any concern they might have that you are asking too much of them too quickly. While you are bracing yourself for rejection and rehearsing in your head your casual acceptance of a cruel "No", try to remember that there is a second being with all their quirks of character involved and listen carefully for clues which will improve your chances of a sweet "Yes" on the next occasion. For example, some people are enormously nervous in groups of more than four or five, and would never attend a party that was to be larger than that. Others won't go anywhere so dangerous as another's house unless they are sure there will be a huge crowd and that they will know two or three amongst them. You might not be able to know this beforehand, and you might offer the wrong thing. Don't alter the form to try to suit them.[7] Say something like, "Oh, sorry. Another time then." Don't forget to add, "Please feel free to change your mind. I know you would enjoy the others who will be there." On another not terribly distant occasion spontaneously invite them to something else which is equally written in stone. You never know what people will decide to do, what change of heart you might inspire by your kindness and lack of judgment.

If even so unassuming an invitation seems still too familiar, consider accumulating smaller moments, something like building blocks toward real courtship.

For example, as an alternative to the too too brusque technique of sidling up beside the one whose laugh captivates you and inviting them away for a passion-filled weekend in Rome, you stop by their desk, or office, or home or you call first, but in any case you say, "I'm on my way to the cafe X for a latté. Want to join me?" Or perhaps one Tuesday in the early evening you call them up and say, "I'm going to go see the new Almodovar film at 7:05 at the Kabuki. Would you like to join me?" The specific request gives them something to say Yes or No to. Maybe they already saw it, but inquire "Would you consider seeing the new Stallone film at 7:20 instead?" Maybe you would, maybe you wouldn't.[8] Maybe they are busy—most people have plans for tonight—but they have the occasion to say, "No, I can't. My mother is helping me build a cabinet tonight. But I'd love to another time. Call

---

6 No, you won't be the impressively casual cook, but who cares? A well-fed person is a well-fed person. As long as the host doesn't have any extracurricular interest in your companion, you should be fine.

7 It probably doesn't even exist anyway. You made it up as a pretext for inviting them to your home. If you change your story mid-stream you will be busted. On the other hand, honesty is always good.

8 I find such a negotiation is itself worth several dates worth of getting-to-know-you.

me again."[9] The goal is to accumulate a countless number of such incidents.[10] A few such casual afternoon minutes over coffee or barrels of popcorn in the dark, and you are well on your way to long evenings at home, not alone.

THE LARGER PARTY

Now, whom else should you invite? This is a very hard part. One handy rule of thumb is: Whoever calls that week gets invited. Right up until the first round of cocktails is served. Past that, be curt and say, "I have twenty people here. I'll call you later." Maybe dig up a friend or two that you don't see enough of and invite them. Sometimes such haphazard casting is disastrous but more often it is magic. There is a moment an hour before or the day before when you roll through your mind who will be coming for dinner, and you will think to yourself, "Oh no, what have I done?" Those are the best nights. And if such a dinner or party is combined with the more sweet presence of someone you actually adore and plan to flirt with, all the better if the party is not composed of your inner circle who might feel called upon to tease you, to bring up historical topics best left untouched for a few more days, or forget in their loud and ancient intimacy that there is a stranger among you.

A motley and less than usual collection of dinner companions can be a warmer climate. They won't notice that you are paying more attention to this guest than you have to others, or that your attention is of a slightly different quality. Give them enough to eat and drink, introduce them thoroughly to each other, and they won't notice anything at all. Your most precious guest will have plenty of time to acclimate themselves to the surroundings during the chaos of preparing and enjoying dinner in sparkling company. You can pay discreet attention to them, allowing yourself to be occupied with dinner or with others if they seem to need a little time to observe. You can enjoy opportunities to anticipate their needs and fill them, or you can practice not being overly attentive. You can watch the other in a social group, and that other can watch you, and you both can learn lots. No one feels awkward for having nothing to say, even for hours.[11]

---

[9] You should be a sufficiently skilled interpreter of the human voice to tell if it was a sincere if small disappointment that they can't join you, or if they just made up that bit about their mother having time for woodworking to put off saying, "No way, not with you, never with you." Err in your own favor once or twice and then catch the hint.

[10] Countless because you are not keeping count, not because there are so many you can't count them. Of course you can count them. The trick is not to.

[11] This does depend on the clamor and jabbering of a relaxed, opinionated and non-judgmental crowd. How to encourage such a melee instead of the too-frequent and excruciating dullness of people reluctant to offer their intimate selves and most honest thoughts, for whatever reason, is currently a mystery to me. Sometimes I think it has to do with the projection of the host, whether or not that person is conversant and interested in

You can do this in the company of your very closest friends as well, but it might be a trial by fire for all involved. Friends will watch you closely, observing your prey, comparing qualities to those of a former love. Very dangerous ground to walk so early. On the other hand, if your friends are kind and trustworthy, and lucky you if they are, they can be the perfect solution to dilute the concentrated stuff between you and another, dissolving what could be poisonous to something fairly therapeutic. Also, if you have chosen your friends well over the years and cared for them properly, they are extremely valuable eyes through which to observe a new love. One sometimes useful ploy is to invite them all over, plus your preferred one and another stranger or two. Don't tell everyone about the hoped-for romance. Enjoy the evening and see what your friends think of your new companion.[12] Imply, if you like, that you are without designs so your friends won't be tempted to be nice. See if they think you should maybe have some designs. See if your would-be-amour likes your friends. See how they all behave themselves.

Still unsure about how the invitation should take place? Think some more. Be creative at the same time as you are thoughtful and compassionate. Considerate of their position, current or dissolving attachments, fears and feelings. No need to worry or sculpt your behavior to these elements, but consideration and compassion are always appropriate. They build patience and tolerance which are invaluable during courtship. Invaluable at all times. If there is already a friendship or a textured acquaintance[13] between you and the one you wish to spend more time with, it can be easy enough to simply invite them over for dinner. Alone even. For no reason and with frankness of purpose: "Come over for dinner tonight." If tonight is bad, ask them to pick a night. How hard is that? Too hard. Too direct. Too without reason. Not spontaneous, you whine. Oh, for heaven's sakes. Be indirect then. It works almost as well. Perhaps after a long afternoon of hunting down a particular piece of scuba equipment or the perfect gift for someone's mom, or at the end of a strenuous hike

thoughts and views beyond their own. Whether guests are thoughtlessly confident that they will not be deemed idiots or jerks for any opinion or question they might care to offer, or whether they sense that a party line must be towed and so close up their interesting selves for the night and talk only about investments and golf and previous episodes of revelry. Sometimes I think it has all to do with lighting. Obviously, a room filled with sparkling eyes and an ocean of mingling voices and laughter does depend on having a nice supply of thinking, loving people, and a great dirth of attention-starved pedants.

12 And see what you think of your current circle in the context of this new, possibly wonderful thing you have attracted. It is not unheard of for a smitten soul to suddenly decide all their pals are monstrous and dull in contrast and to drop them wholesale. In one legendary case, a lover threw out an address book altogether. Too bad later when she left him. But would she have stayed for even those few lovely moments if she had known the truth about the company he had been keeping? And is he not better off for having to find new friends at a higher standard? Hard to say.

13 What does THAT mean? Tony asks all the hard questions. I mean you are not friends, but recognize each other as interesting and somewhat kindred souls. That you would not choose their shoulder to cry on, but you might later tell them about what upset you. A potential friend in the right series of circumstances. Someone who falls between your best friend and your best friend's sister's business partner in the hierarchy of your heart.

up and down a nearby mountain, or a cultural expedition through a city's galleries and museums, you return to your house and because you are not stupid, you spontaneously and effortlessly suggest they stay and have a bite to eat. Make it be the easiest thing in the world. Pull garlic bread from your freezer. Make a delicious pasta from whatever you have in your refrigerator. Heat up a myriad of leftovers from an Indian feast the night before. Make an omelet. Order a pizza. If they are game, send them to the store for some fresh ingredient you couldn't possibly have had on hand, or for a bottle of wine. Or go yourself, leaving them with something to nibble, something to drink and the leisure to explore your house unobserved. Make it seem effortless. Make it be effortless. Continue talking and listening while you prepare whatever it is. Spill something all over yourself so that you have to go take a quick shower and change into something more comfortable. If they are filthy from a long day of exercise and adventure, invite them to take advantage of your bathroom. Which is clean, of course.[14] Give them comfy clothes to borrow, preferably things you can spare as they may never be returned. Feed them something appropriate and delicious and not intimidating. This is not the time to try a tricky new recipe. Not the time to impress them with your famous scampi flambé.

DID YOU NOTICE that all of the above techniques rest rather solidly on the assumption that you have some sort of correspondence in the first place? It is difficult to invite someone to your home for dinner, to find yourself in the enviable position of feeding their divine selves with earthly foods when you do not have occasion to speak with them. Hard to ask someone you just met in a bar to your home. I really can't offer any tips for that scenario. On the other hand, the desired one might be someone you don't know but someone you know knows. In which case, your friend can easily invite that person to your house as their guest. A few hints usually work, or the very direct, "Come for dinner and

---

14 Oh, here is a book all by itself: How to Keep Your Bathroom from Ruining Your Chance at Romance. Learn how to clean a bathroom, and then do it regularly. Or hire someone, and have them clean the rest of your house as well. A disgusting bathroom has kept more women from spending the evening in increasing states of undress at the home of another than perhaps anything besides bad personal hygiene. Of course, if you smelled bad and looked slimy, they probably wouldn't have spent the day with you, wouldn't have agreed to let you make them dinner, and wouldn't have found their way into your bathroom in the first place. Don't mess up your momentum. The sink, the counters and all the paraphernalia on them, the tub, the toilet, the floors, walls and ceiling, and the towels are all things that must be cleaned often. Sorry. And knowing you will snap at me for sexism, I will say I have met men who care, but women care more often. Way more often. Maybe because they are arranged in such a way that they are more vulnerable to disease. Maybe because many of them never get as filthy as men do to begin with. I couldn't say. But women don't respond well to a scary bathroom, unless, of course it's their own. This would be further discussed in yet another book: The Effects of 400 Years of Peculiar Sexism on Daily Behavior and Perception.

bring that friend of yours." You might also generously support the courtships of others by extending such invitations.

BEYOND ROMANCE

Inviting people and not inviting people to any event is always an exercise in wisdom, wit, and usually incompetence as well. Modern folk seem to seldom possess the manners and independence which would make them both easy to invite and to not invite. They don't respond when they do receive an invitation, complain if they don't receive an invitation early enough, show up late, and all too often arrive so frantic from a busy day you rather wish they had had the good sense to stop at a spa or a bar on their way over.

And that's when they are on the invitation list.

Friends who discover they weren't included might sulk, fish for an invitation, or even show up unannounced.[15] Their bad behavior can in turn be credited back to you in part if you have been at all elusive or dishonest about throwing a party in order to avoid confronting those who weren't included. Get over it. Like they invite you to every party they throw. Be honest. Call them up for recipes. Tell them whom you are inviting and gossip about who's doing what these days. Before you finish the conversation say, "I'll let you know how the evening goes." Coyness and evasion will be interpreted badly, here as anywhere. Don't be tempted. As long as there is some reason why the guest list is limited, they should be able to accept not making the cut.[16] And you need to live with the truth that when you exclude people, no matter how real your reasons, feelings can be hurt.

We are still left with the question, Whom to Invite, and of course, How to Invite Them. I am alone in this practice, but I find that never inviting anyone you don't like works well. If they happen to call that week, don't mention the party. I don't care how old an acquaintance they are. I don't care if they have invited you to their home on several occasions.[17] You are never, as far as I am concerned, required to invite unpleasant people to dinner. Never never never required to cook for them if they do happen to show up at your home. Claim you have dinner reservations and offer them a quick drink of tap water. Leave your house yourself if they won't.

---

[15] I now avoid the whole thing by never having a list and inviting everyone I speak to between the time I decide to have a party and the actual start of that party. The toughest thing about this approach is remembering that everyone doesn't do it this way.

[16] If you seem to be inviting everyone but them, you should maybe ask yourself why.

[17] If they are truly terrible, you should also decline invitation. Then you will not feel the need to reciprocate. If you do accept invitations from people you dislike, it might be time for a little heart to heart with yourself.

Whom you should invite is anyone you enjoy, whose company is nourishment to your soul. You are feeding them. They can feed you. You should invite anyone who is simply nice to have around. Sweet people make a wonderful side dish at a spicy party. No one you will have to protect, though. Invite people who talk and people who listen, especially if they happen to be the same people. If possible, and palatable, invite relatives for non-family parties. It confuses them and makes you their favorite relation. Invite people who have invited you to their home and whom you like enough to see again. If you never return an invitation, you won't get a lot more from that source. Which might be just fine. Invite people you barely know at the lightest opportunity. If you are not courting anyone in particular, court the world in general. Which is not to say issue an APB about your dinner or garden party, but relax a little about exactly how many people are going to be at the table. Encourage friends to bring friends. Never say no, unless you have a most excellent and urgent reason.[18] Who knows what they might bring by.

Now, how are you going to invite these select few? In person or via missile of some sort? Is there a reason for the gathering? How far in advance are you letting out the word? What atmosphere are you hoping to attain? Are you clever? Formal? Do you have a fax modem? E-mail?

If it is very spontaneous, as is likely if you are planning to cook, phone calls and messages, email and passing comments will do. If there is an occasion involved as well, the fax or email is wonderful as you can include a great deal of information, more than you would be comfortable leaving on voice mail or with the distracted ten-year-old who is taking your message, and they get it as quickly as possible. Assuming their fax or computer is in their home or in their office. Don't send difficult-to-get faxes for social reasons. Electronic mail if it works for everyone works very well. Whatever message sending ability you have, use it.[19] Invite everyone and make sure they all know how to get to your home. Send very good directions. Evenings are ruined by an hour spent lost because of bad directions.

If you have anything over a week of notice, feel free to mail a real, physical invitation.[20] Your options are endless. From the silliest postcard to the most abstruse poetic parlance. Paper, fabric, wood, metal, small packages of trinkets or herbs; I've seen so much and have

---

[18] For example, the suggested guest is another, more important guest's loathed ex-spouse. "No," you might say, "I don't really think they would enjoy the party much. Maybe another time."

[19] Whatever you use, don't assume it works perfectly. It is little solace the day after a party to learn that a message was lost.

[20] You can send out invitations even later than that, but you do risk getting calls from disgruntled invitees who suffered the vagaries of the mail service and received the invitation after the event. To diminish the risk of social repudiation, call everyone to let them know that an invitation is on its way and to please come whether they receive it in time or not.

much more to see. You can make your point and impress your friends and their colleagues with your style, if not with your foresight. In any case, if there is information beyond, "Come by for dinner around eight on Saturday." a written message of some sort is probably not only in good taste but in good sense as well. If it is someone's birthday or other celebration, a theme, or if there is some other activity to be pursued, they will want to be prepared, want to have some clue how to dress, want know if children are welcome, what sorts of moods will be acceptable, and like that.

Also take note: An interesting, intriguing invitation can sometimes rile difficult-to-get guests out of their homebound languor. An invitation can set the atmosphere of the party and prepare your guests such that they arrive molten, having spent the days since receiving the invitation sinking into your notion of celebration.

However you do it, get them there. Then make them glad they came.

GRACIOUSNESS

In which you are asked to give reign to some best self.

WHAT COULD BE MEANT by that?
Surely you are not being admonished to follow some arbitrary set of rules for social comportment. Surely no one is suggesting you do anything at all for form's sake. No no no. Graciousness here does not at all mean, "Impress others with how beautifully you do things." No one should ever spend good moments at your house and leave thinking, "I could never compete with that." Making people feel as though you are better at something than they are is not gracious at all.

Of course maybe you are an extremely good host, and people do come to your house hoping for and expecting a certain high level of beauty and grace. In which case, you shouldn't be reading this book. Or rather if you are, you should be reading it for the purpose of toning down your style so that it might be unobtrusive on those occasions when you do not want to impress others with your entertaining skills but rather want them to fall madly in love with you. Accidentally exposed fallibility, and good humor while you humbly reveal your weaknesses and allow that others have strengths you can admire and which complement your own: A different sort of approach to social interaction from the one typically expounded upon in magazines devoted to selling you trinkets and devices which make it ever easier for you to be formally gracious according to the fashions of the day. But it is that other thing, that aspect which does not necessarily benefit from taller candelabras and more exotic flowers which has the best chance of furthering a courtship of any sort.[1]

So perhaps we might say we are talking about how to be gracious without appearing to be especially so. Only the most jaded eye should be able to observe your machinations and remark with admiration, "You are extraordinarily gracious, aren't you? How did you get to be that way?" At which point you demure and do something just slightly goofy and clearly not graceful in an impromptu gesture to pull your disguise of gracelessness back over your extremely gracious self. Everyone else will be drawn to you because in your presence they feel fabulous, treated as such by one who is clearly fabulous themselves. The one who sniffed you out still more impressed by this display of highly evolved grace. And each will sense they are worthy of respect and admiration and honor because they are respected and admired and honored.[2] And feeling that way, will without effort go on to behave toward others in a similar fashion.

The burden is upon you. It is all in your hands. You get to do the very best you can, including choosing your guests and friends wisely. You get to bring them into your home or enter theirs as one czarina might visit the respected dominion of an admired other. And you get to do a million chores,[3] indirect, unstudied, and without agenda or interest which will slowly and softly but unambiguously reveal your regard for them, for their well-being and comfort. And see if they take to that sort of thing.[4] You get to feed them and sustain

---

[1] Except the kind of courtship in which you are applying for the position of Gracious Host. Even then it is trickier than that, and the applicant who exhibits disarming and guileless, almost accidental grace often wins out.

[2] Careful. Gracious people are sometimes accused of being shamelessly flirtatious by naive and priggish types who have not yet digested the complexity of human interaction. Of course they are flirts, indiscriminately so. All "flirting" means is to favor another with your full attention: Intellectual, romantic, sensual, sexual, whatever.

[3] Tony wants to know what I mean by chores. Get them a drink. Set the table. Put their wet jacket in a place where it will dry during the course of their visit. At their home, you might read to the children, arrange some flowers, set the table. Like that. Chores, sweet and endless. Do them.

[4] Some people don't, you know, considering themselves unworthy regardless of your actions. Doubly lamentable because they will also think less of you for being good to them. Others take to it all too well, having been seeking just that sort of thing and they try to entrap you into a contract in which you must treat them with honor and they treat you with disdain. Stay so far from those people. Treat them with extraordinary kindness

them and create warmth where there had been none. Gifts one might more readily ask or expect of a deity than another human—unexpected and therefore disarming. Courtship continues and thrives in such thoughtless generosity, a favorite and fertile soil.

POINT

Even so, and with all that heavy wax on the subject, when you do finally cook something for another it is extremely and unspeakably important that you do not make that person feel as though you are doing them some great favor.

First of all, you're not. Food is easy to come by, everyone has a favorite dish and chances are you are not making it.[5] Whatever you feed someone is a gift, and gifts must be given freely and without expectation of appreciation or return. Really and truly. Even though it might seem possible to disguise and hide your motives, possible to believe you can play another as easily as a recorder, you can't. When you give it must be without anticipation for a particular result. Without thought or concern for your own interests or desires.[6] Have you ever tried to force a child to play with a new toy? Have you ever criticized a friend for not having said "thank you"? Quickly enough? Sincerely enough? Have you ever told a lover how lucky they are you do what you do? Of course not.

Not that it is easy to go to great lengths of effort and creativity and not expect appreciative acknowledgment. You might notice such thoughts as, "I may as well have ordered a pizza for all they care," meandering across your mind as you chop up ginger and onions or stir a sauce slowly as it thickens. The key is this: The moment you feel underappreciated, stop whatever you are doing. Not because others aren't paying sufficient homage and don't deserve your efforts, but because you do not possess sufficient lightness of heart to do it well. In the case of cooking, set everything aside[7] and call for that pizza.[8] Or, if you want to disguise your humor, turn off all the lights and announce that everything has burned[9] and that you think it would be a good idea to head straight for a restaurant.

---

for they are unhappy. It is not entirely their fault they act in such poisonous ways. But keep the same distance you would from a rattlesnake or a grizzly. No need to kill them or wrestle power from them or get very close at all. You can't and shouldn't avoid these people, but neither should you court and mate with them. That's what I think. Others disagree.

[5] If you do make someone's favorite dish, especially if it's something you are not particularly fond of, and they do not notice or seem to much care, don't make it again.

[6] At least in the most important cases. Who cares if you easily seduce someone of no importance.

[7] Wrapping up what you can for later use. A nasty disposition is no reason to waste good food.

[8] See PIZZA.

[9] Let something inessential burn for inspiration and dramatic effect if you are not a very good liar.

Under no circumstances should you cook the meal and then sulk throughout the evening and into the next day.

Enough of this. Cook when you want to cook. Feed those you want to feed. Give until you are tired of giving. Then stop without remark.[10] The secret is no one cares.

COUNTERPOINT

The other secret is they care deeply. I am not the only one who finds little charm in a badly prepared cup of coffee and burnt toast. Mine is not the only heart which leaps at the promise of a good meal not cooked by me. I cannot be the only woman who, having eaten well, desires but to curl up on the bed of the cook and live out her days their love slave.

A charged thing, food, and while it may be served effortlessly and mindlessly, it cannot, must not, be done badly. Nor should it ever be received as a meaningless gesture. To take being fed for granted, as a chore or service that has been bought and paid for and therefore may be expected is to forget and so betray the generosity of spirit and self which typically, and perhaps without exception, accompany the serving of food one wants to eat. Just as one can buy sexual favors, one can buy food. Good food, too. It is the emotional and artistic element which elevates both above bare sustenance and entertainment and which is beyond negotiation. Either it is freely offered or it isn't.

And all too often it isn't. Hence the burnt and tasteless meatloaf. The wilted iceberg salad. The grayish stringy beans. All evidence of a cook who is not feeling particularly giving, not particularly loved nor loving. Perhaps feeling even a bit abused. Probably a cook who is hoping never to be asked to cook again.

Too bad. To feed someone well is to love them gently and deeply. To get way deep inside of them, caressing them where fingers and feet cannot go. Feed your lovers with disingenuous abundance and with food which provokes their senses and you will probably be happy. Feed them with studied and measured delicacy or in a fashion which reeks of penury, and you might find their affections match your table. Do not feed them at all, and they will be unfed.[11] That lean and hungry look which foretold Julius Caesar's fate is one you probably don't want to see in your intimate chambers.

---

[10] In truth, sometimes a remark can be very useful. A great aunt of ours recently stopped right in the middle of cooking three different things and announced "I am sick of this meal." My sister and I recovered quickly from our surprise, shuttled her out of the kitchen, and finished the cooking. The meal was delicious and we were all in good spirits, although it did take my aunt a moment to recover hers. As usual, frankness worked like a charm to diffuse a simmering situation. Good thing, too, as excellent pizza is hard to find in Holmes Beach.

[11] Which is a perverse courtship technique all its own. See Not Cooking as Courtship.

Go ahead and think of cooking as a hobby, as a method of stress management, an outlet for artistic creativity, a money saving device, whatever. Regardless of the reason, in the end you are feeding people. Deadly[12] cooks forget this and then go on to forget that feeding people is not such a big deal. Rapt in pride for their accomplishments,[13] they expect praise and admiration for the simple feat of feeding others. Not unlike lovers who ask about their performance, needing to be assured it was brilliant; who make love not as an expression of affection for the beloved, but rather as an opportunity to expose their talents and to attract compliments. The thing caressed and adored never the other person but rather the self-same ego.[14]

Back at the table, the person who unwittingly ate the meal feels empty, realizing to late they have not been fed at all.

CONFUSED? WONDERING whether it is the host or the guest who is being instructed to be gracious? Twisting about, trying to see where to place the blame when a meal is soured by bad humor and a loud absence of generosity and grace? Surprise. You are responsible at all times. You are also responsible for deciding when the behavior of another is intolerable and then further responsible for disentangling yourself from contact with the insufferable being.[15]

If you are cooking and are not happy about it, Stop. If another is unhappy in the kitchen, check with yourself silently to see if it is because you have either taken their efforts for granted or otherwise neglected or offended them. Correct the situation, or otherwise extend yourself to make it possible for them to refind a place of comfort, even if it means taking their place at the stove.[16] If they are cooking in a mean or pompous or otherwise

---

[12] I steal the idea and the term shamelessly from Peter Brooks' *The Empty Space*. He uses it it to describe and refer to the sort of theater in which all is performed exactly as you would expect, according to convention, suffocating under its own cultural weight. The sort of theater once seen convinces the viewer they hate theater.

[13] In the highly unnoticeable film, Mr. Frost, a latter-day incarnation of Satan, when not busy murdering people, chopping them up and burying them in the backyard, spends his time cooking elaborate dishes, taking Polaroids of them and then throwing the food out. What kind of monster would cook food only for the aesthetic exercise of culinary virtuosity? Too many, it seems to me, although they usually serve the food as an additional crime, caring only about gathering praise.

[14] I read about this somewhere.

[15] Shall I mention that forgiveness is the greatest form of grace? Insufferable tonight is not the same as insufferable. You have to be Solomon. Please don't make big mistakes that cannot be corrected and then say I told you to do it. First of all, I didn't, and second of all no one would care if I had.

[16] "You sit down and let me chop/stir/wash for awhile," would be one way to extract someone from something in which they are mired, but which they would never admit hating. Taking a stance of savior or remarking that their humor has soured is deeply impolite and fabulously ineffective. I have never found anyone to accept an offer which is contingent upon their admitting they have lost grace.

disturbing attitude, forgetting it is all a continuous communication and communion with their guests and not an exhibit for a panel of judges, protect yourself and do not fall into their trap. Play your role politely rather than to the hilt. Be a good, healthy person, and good, healthy people will fall into your sphere of gravity.[17] You will find that you dine well and often in the company of excellent friends and loves. Mindless, habitual, guileless and frank consideration and kindness will do it.

Without grace, however awkward or strangely manifested, there is no courtship.

---

17 Conversely, do not accept abuse and abusive people will drop from sight. Such a neat trick. I'm always surprised more people do not employ it.

SETTING TABLES

*In which the objects and objectives surrounding the serving of
food are put forth incompletely and with ambivalence.*

WHEN YOU SERVE food at a table or on some
such flat thing, you may very well want to pay some attention to the surface and its surroundings or ask someone else to. Of course you do not need to have a table at all. Laps
work very nicely—bare skin and fine garments protected from warm plates and sticky
sauces by a tray or a second large napkin. And if you do set a table, it need not be a dining
table. It might be a coffee table or a picnic bench or the floor. I heard tell of one romantic
meal served on the corner of a bed.[1] For everyone else who is not playing such powerful

---

[1] I don't imagine it would work more than once or twice, and should certainly be attempted only in the absence
of a table and exclusively in the confines of a studio apartment, but if the story is true it can be very effective
in that moment.

and direct games of courtship, tables should be large enough for comfort and sturdy enough for peace of mind, well-placed and compassionately lit, set somehow with ceramic and metal and glass and wood and wax and cloth.[2] Flowers, if you like, and if the view across the table will not be obstructed.

There are many ways to set any table on any occasion. De rigeur are plates or bowls or both, forks and knives and spoons, vessels for drinking and napkins. Even if you are planning to eat on the front stoop, these things still must be pulled from cupboards and drawers or wherever they live and placed on a counter near where the food is to be served up, which might very well be by the stove, but could be on a buffet in the living room or on the picnic table outside or on the front stoop. It hardly matters. You have only to get the dishes and utensils out to the place where they will be needed. Their charm will reside in themselves and not their placement so much, although it is always possible to make your casual jumble of stuff more rather than less attractive to the eye and spirit. Go ahead and try.

But perhaps you have a table and you want to set it for a meal. You want to make it appealing. When your guests are asked to sit down to the meal and their attention turns from whatever was holding it and they focus on the table, you want them to sigh softly in joy and relief that for the next few hours they have nothing to do but to eat and drink and enjoy themselves and the company around them. A set for dining, light bouncing on and off glass and metal and glaze and fabric (even if it is only the corner of a counter set with china and silver on placemats fashioned from napkins or towels), they will know that the evening is theirs. Conversation continues, stronger now in the secure knowledge that they were expected for dinner. If the table is a jumble and does not promise anything, they will continue as before, although probably with a pall of confusion, wondering whether they were really invited for dinner, or if they misunderstood, have arrived inconveniently, and you are just being polite.[3]

---

[2] This is going to be a problem for some of you. What about plastic, you cry, or whatever other material you have chosen and I have not listed. Look. I don't really care what you use as replacement for the traditional materials, and I am not going to attempt to prophesize materials to come. I feel rather generous not mentioning linen, cotton and hemp specifically, trusting that you will discover for yourself that those are the only fibers you should use. I don't care if your plates are bronze, your cups ceramic, and your forks made of glass. I don't care if every last thing on the table is made of plastic. As long as everything performs its function well and does not insult your guests with distracting ugliness of shape, color, texture or taste, no one cares. Most people, however, will use ceramic for plates, as it holds rather than transfers heat, metal for flatware because it can be sharp and rarely breaks and glass for vessels because they can see what is in them. People also use these materials because they are traditional and therefore readily available. Be clever and creative if you like, but please stop short of making the meal and the conversation of others difficult to enjoy.

Unless, come to think of it, you are not cooking as courtship but rather as statement. Serving food that cannot actually be eaten with the tools at hand. Plates that discolor or spill whatever is placed on them. Forks that crumble into shards. Vessels that dissolve in liquid. It could be a very provocative event. Thought provoking, anyway. I leave you to it.

[3] Barely, I might add. Mind you, even when such misunderstandings do happen, if you are happy about the error

A very small amount of concrete information on setting a table is offered here because you have to decide for yourself how you want to set a table. Some people set a table with fine linen and silver and china and chargers[4] and candelabra and crystal vases full of roses. Those would be people who have large weddings or long lineage. Others throw a curtain from the thrift store over a work table and go about setting places with flea market silver-plate, Salvation Army china, napkins ripped from muslin, estate sale candles held in empty bottles, and a little vase filled with dandelions. Couldn't say that one approach is any better than the other. Both might be wonderful, either might fail miserably. The only requirement is that you care about your guests. That you do not insult them with ugliness or cleverness or inconvenient extravagance. Tables and dishes and silverware and napkins are all discussed later in this chapter. Putting them together is a task of creativity and kindness.

SETTING A TABLE

Having said all that, here is how to set a table. First, choose your table. Make sure it is large enough for all your guests and that you have enough chairs. If you need to make the table larger, do that, or decide to allow people to eat anywhere they like. If you need more chairs, buy or borrow them. Check lighting to make sure you have something besides an overhead lamp.[5] Clean off the table and the chairs if needed. Put down a table cloth or placemats of some sort. Find your napkins. Make sure they are clean. Get out all the silverware you will need. Place the napkins and the silverware in some configuration around the table so as to suggest seating places. Chairs will also help to suggest places. Whereas napkins and silver can be placed almost anywhere within the place setting, glasses for water and wine want to be in the top right corner of the place setting. You can put them anywhere you want, but that is where people will look for them and you will have discussion of whose glass is whose if you get very far from tradition. Which is fine. Do have a water and a wine glass for each person if your store of glassware will allow.[6] Place the plates on the table if the

---

set the table as though you had planned the whole thing and looked forward to it all week. If they come to comprehend the situation, they will be thrilled and amazed that you so fabulously and effortlessly fed and entertained them. But all you had to do was set the table or ask someone else to do it while you threw more pasta in a pot. You see, it is not so hard to make others happy and to sponsor an evening of conversation and laughter. Which is exactly what courtship is made of. You can even order out and lose no effect if the table is set.

[4] Those are the large plates that are at your place when you arrive in a very fine restaurant and which are summarily removed when plates of food arrive. I am not sure of their purpose, and know nothing of their history, but that is what they are.

[5] A chandelier is different because its light comes from many small sources and typically it can be dimmed. See Technical Production for more discussion of lighting. The importance of light cannot be overemphasized.

[6] Although it is contrary to the American tradition of large glasses of ice water at the table, it is preferable in many cases to use small water glasses and to refill them from a carafe of cool or room temperature water. It is

food is to be served at the table. Leave them in the kitchen if plates are to be served up there. Place candles. Put flowers on the table only if they do not block views between guests. If someone brings you tall flowers, place them somewhere honorable but not on the table. Small sculpture or other interesting things can be an alternative to flowers and other purely decorative centerpieces. Mind you, they need not be in the center. You might want to set your guests around one end of the table, or only along the sides, freeing up both ends for flowers and candles and other things of visual interest or for platters and bowls of food. Unless you are serving a formal, course by course meal, you might place a salad in a bowl on the table at the beginning of the meal and thereby allow people who prefer to start with salad, those who prefer to end with it, and those who like to have salad with their meal to all do as they please. What difference can it make to you? And it might make a great difference to them. Fill a pitcher or carafe with water for the table. If you don't have one, use an empty, clear-glass wine bottle with the label removed, or buy some water in glass bottles for the occasion. Salt and pepper, because someone will want them. The corkscrew and whatever serving utensils you will need might all be placed in the center of the table, or on some nearby surface. Light candles or small lamps. Turn off any overhead fixture and leave it off. Lighting should entice your guests to the table, now a stage for what will certainly be a most excellent meal filled with shimmering conversation.

If you are serving the meal as a buffet, which is to say you are setting a surface from which people will take plates of food and utensils and go elsewhere to sit down, you can still arrange the buffet so it attracts your guests and sets the mood for the meal. Whatever that might be. You may also set a table where they will take their plates, be seated and dine.

---

not very healthy to drink ice water in the first place, and it is very hard to drink, as your throat must warm it to a decent temperature before allowing it to pass to the rest of you, which it can only do in very small amounts. In the USA people believe they need ice water, but it is a habit, and rarely rarely will it get drunk with the meal. If someone asks for ice water, give it to them. Otherwise they are no worse off than if they were dining at a three star restaurant in Paris.

The large glass of ice water is more about what was once the extraordinary luxury of ice, and for that reason if you are trying to impress a very traditional American crowd you might want to serve those tremendous goblets of ice water that condense over by the end of the meal so if you did try to pick it up it would slip out of your hand just before you suffered frostbite. An excellent design, when you look at it like that. Toddlers also love to play with ice, so you might want to serve it for that reason.

THE TABLE AND ACCOMPANYING CHAIRS

The table is a foundation for the meal. It will support everything from flowers and candles to plates and glasses and elbows and the attached heads and thoughts, let alone whatever books and other clutter which may be brought in to test or illustrate points in discussion. It will separate one body from another. Or connect them. A surface to rest held hands, or something to hide them below. Chairs hold whole bodies, for hours sometimes, each minute deliciously and without fanfare following upon the last. Backsides are at once forgiving and finicky. Yet there is not much to say about chairs since at the end of the day, if what is on and around the table captivates, almost anything will suffice for seating. Take care, as people will fashion chairs out of almost anything, judgment obscured by any number of things.[7]

If there is to be a table it is good for it to be nice in at least one or two ways. Perhaps it is a lovely table of fine wood or metal or concrete. Perhaps it is large and well-placed under an ancient tree. Perhaps it is in a warm sunny corner or there is a little lamp on it capable of making any old Tuesday dinner seem like Saturday night in Berlin. The table and its surroundings should not be unpleasant in any noticeable way. Legs and edges should not wack and stab at shins and knees and thighs. Forearms should not gather splinters. Light should not glare angrily from above or from any other direction. The table should not rock about threatening to capsize glasses and temperaments. Certainly it should be clean of all remnants of previous meals. Perhaps it is laid with a tablecloth or placemats. It should be large enough for the number of people who plan to crowd around it, sturdy enough to allow for passions, wide enough to encourage generosity of spirit, and it should be flat.

Both tables and chairs can be many things, many of which are, technically speaking, neither tables nor chairs. A beautiful table is a beautiful thing. Comfortable chairs that can be used around a table are to some a sort of holy grail. Spending lots of money is often a good way to acquire table and chairs, but it is hardly a fool-proof strategy.[8] If you are to have a table and chairs, acquire them wisely and ruthlessly. Get rid of things that don't work or are uncomfortable. If your table and chairs do not make you happy, find out why and fix it. Put a piece of plywood on a wrong table and cover it with a large piece of cloth if you must. Get some comfortable folding chairs to tide you over. They can be later used as extras for suddenly larger parties. However you do it, get content.

---

[7] My task has now and again been the rescue of sacred or deceptively fragile, chair-like items from a heavy fate. You can avoid asking for such trouble by habitually collecting orphaned chairs and leaving them handily about.

[8] I've noticed it often attracts fools and makes them still more foolish.

NOT THAT IT IS so easy to get content. It is not easy to know what is wrong and still more difficult perhaps to know what should be done. To understand why the table you have might be undermining your best efforts to feed others in your home, to discover what is wrong with it and determine what can be done to improve things, is an architectural, sculptural, decorative, functional and troublesome problem. And yet, so many things work just fine. You must find it, but there is a good chance that an excruciatingly simple solution will make it all right. So good a possibility, you might well be suspicious of any arduous, expensive, or otherwise complicated solutions offered by others.

Test your table. Sit down with something to read and something to drink. Are you happy, comfortable? If you got up to answer the door, would you bring your visitor back to the table with you, or would you lead them to some other seating place? You might even try this when you are expecting someone. See how they respond to sitting at the table when they don't have to. Notice whether guests in your home ever spontaneously sit down at your dining table. Notice whether you ever sit down at the table. This is only a first step. If you are comfortable and happy and others seem to be as well, you have only to press the test an inch further, asking close friends whose homes you admire and know to be comfortable what they think of your set-up, the furniture, the space, the lighting, the art or decorations. Ask if there is anything they particularly like or don't like and if there are any changes they would make if it were up to them. If they decline to offer suggestions and assure you that it is fine, you might have polite friends rather than a perfect room. Ask about particular things. Pester them until they are so annoyed with you, they will be delighted to tell you all the negative things about your dining area that have been ir- ritating them for years. Or alternatively, ask them to consider what might be improved and to let you know if they think of anything.[9]

Your table might be of poor proportions, the height or the position of the legs in- convenient, its sturdiness erratic, the chairs unwelcoming.[10] Lighting might be poor or cruel, the position of the table in the room awkward, you might have neglected to clean up

[9] More likely though, they will have a few things to say. And then it is for you to listen and not defend your- self, and to later consider their thoughts and decide for yourself if you want to take any to heart. When you ask someone's opinion you are not required to execute their ideas, but you are required to listen respectfully to what they have to say. Even and especially if you don't like it.

[10] Mind you, all this consideration does not take place in a vacuum and you must accept that your penniless artist cousin will be forgiven all kinds of crimes that someone who vacations in the Seychelles will be condemned for. Too bad for you. If your guests know that you take extravagant care of yourself but are content to let them eat from chipped ceramic on a folding table, it will never occur to them that you are interested in their well-being and that you are hoping they will choose to spend more time with you. Of course, if you are the penniless artist, you must still make your best effort and not take excessive advantage of your guests' understand- ing natures. Care for others at least as well as you care for yourself, and remember to care for yourself.

after some long forgotten meal, or there could be some lingering thing you no longer notice but which is vile. An old arrangement of flowers or a dead plant, piles of books or papers, a tablecloth, the cat's food dish. All sorts of things might take up residence on an unused table and make something perfectly fine horrid. Clean off your table if it is cluttered, then wash it thoroughly and the chairs and the floor around it.[11] Perhaps now it is a terrific table and very comfortable to sit at. Perhaps you discover you have a glorious piece of furniture you have forgotten to enjoy. Perhaps that is not the case at all and the table itself follows the dead flora out to the garbage pile. All the better to have a good go at cleaning the floor and rethinking what you should have in that part of your home.

But perhaps your truth lies somewhere in between. It is not a wonderful table, but neither is it crying for disposal. Make it work for you. Paint it, strip it, find some good table-cloths. Make it bigger with plywood and fabric when you need to. But don't worry too much about it. When it is time for a meal, you clean and set with care and imagination, and it will be ten thousand times greater a table than that of most kings.

If you must acquire a table, by all means get one that is large and strong (or small and strong if your space is limited) and which feels good under your hands and head. You will almost certainly have it forever so you might as well get something in some way excellent. It needn't be anything in particular. A solid surface at about table height. Don't concern yourself so much about what it looks like. Until you commit yourself to an elegant home, well furnished and filled with art, there is almost no table so ugly that it is not fine when

---

[11] Why not clean the whole room while you're at it?

clean and well set with linen and dishes and all the other paraphernalia. Better really to have an ugly table that is sturdy and comfortable than a beautiful table that is rickety and careless of knees.

Now, if you can buy or cleverly acquire a table that is large, sturdy and beautiful all at once, that would be the way to go. Wherever you go, wherever you put it, it will make the room magnificent and functional as nothing else can. In the dining room, the kitchen, in a library or an office, wherever. You can always use a good table.[12]

DISHES AND OTHER ACCESSORIES

Dishes you address once and then live with for a very long time. Not so strange, really. Many things are this way. If you do it well, you will never think of them again except occasionally to tell yourself, "I am so glad I bought these dishes." Your peace will not be disturbed by reminders of ancient bouts with bad taste. Only the infrequent, very observant guest will ever remark upon your dishes, and then only to say how very nice they are. Everyone else will be caught in your invisible web of excellent taste. If you do it badly, you will find no pleasure in setting your own table for guests and will find yourself frequently browsing porcelain displays and wondering if you are extravagant enough to throw out perfectly good dishes and start anew. Meanwhile your guests will silently wonder why you have such awful dishes.

Important considerations for dishes are 1) How food will look on them, 2) How likely they are to break (or, How easy they are to replace), and 3) What they will be like in all the possible contexts, of which there are probably only two or three. If you have any more interest in thinking about them, try to imagine how you might feel about them ten years from now.

Unfortunately, we as a nation are starting out on the wrong foot. No small thanks to a certain Japanese plate manufacturer which managed during the late seventies and throughout the eighties to make full sets of dishes so cheap and so seemingly practical (from freezer to nuclear reactor), nearly every house in the country seems to have been

---

12 I am not being very helpful on styles or where to find a table, am I? Me, I would go to garage sales and junk stores, perhaps to an auction or estate sale if I had a pocket half-full of money. Or I would build a table from steel or wood and concrete or granite. Or I would commission one of the crafts people or artists I know to make me a wonderful table. But I know people who have found lovely tables in retail stores. Still other friends with pockets full of money have bought tables from antique dealers and from design studios. Keep your eyes open and your heart. My sister waited for nine years to find her dining table. One night, tipped off by the empty front room, the police stopped by her house to enquire as to whether there had been a robbery and if everyone was OK. Undaunted, if slightly embarrassed, she held her ground and eventually came to own a most beautiful square table that seats two on each side and opens out to seat five thousand, or something like that.

poisoned by silly floral and even sillier earth-toned plates and bowls.[13] An especially lamentable situation since most people find it extremely difficult to replace sets of dishes until they are mostly broken. Which these particular dishes never are. Further lamentable because it is almost impossible to set a visually and sensually satisfying table with these dishes as raw material.

Dining tables then are yet another casualty of our cultural infatuation with the economics of the mass-produced and apparently practical. Like the Victorians before us, the romantics before them, and who knows who before that, the ability of machines to cheaply reproduce what might have once looked like something artful and which could be profitably sold as something useful or decorative proved too seductive to resist. Overly decorated or self-consciously spare and designed to appeal to the most sentimental veins and modern conceits of the impulse shopper, plates and bowls and cups and saucers and their kin have lost contact with principles of substance and aesthetic.[14]

Regardless of what you think, people are aware of the weight and texture of a plate, or of anything at all for that matter. They might not be able to articulate in every case what bothers them about a particular thing, what is wrong with a room or a suit of clothes or a table setting, but it will be unambiguously if indefinably wrong. And too bad for you who selected for the swift and fleeting appeal of surface rather than for the slower force of substance. Their eyes will have been drawn, but attention will not be held.

Think of them as t-shirts. In the largest number of cases, plates should be white, and occasionally, if you have a great deal of style, gravitate toward the modern or primitive and tend to serve pale food, black. In the realm of color, you should probably choose only those pigments which have been in use for hundreds of years. Anything made up to appeal by its newness alone will be overshadowed by next season's contender which will by definition be more new and therefore more appealing. Maybe, if you must, a bit of decoration, something conventional or unlikely that doesn't come anywhere near the food. Maybe a traditional, or utterly not traditional trim. Though there are glorious plates cluttered with odd and many-colored flowers, and many sweet plates in strange colors and designs from other times and other places. There is no good advice beyond Choose wisely, where wise

---

[13] Earth tone and floral are not silly in and of themselves. It's just that you must have an aesthetic which you trust as you trust your own dentist in order to select a plausible plate in either of these themes. A good rule of thumb, if you are not a world-famous art-collector, is to choose only designs that have been popular in the country of their manufacture for over 100 years.

[14] Not that everyone should have the same aesthetic. I mean to draw your attention to the clear if inexpressible difference between the person you would be delighted to spend the evening with and the person you want to spend your life with, even if the occasional evening ends up being a little dull. Likewise with your place setting. Try fresh cut flowers, or perhaps something in fabric, tablecloth or napkins, or garb on yourself or your other to re-inspire.

means with your whole self intact, free, creative, and with awareness of a greater world. Don't spend money or even devote shelf space to dishes that do not delight and support you.[15]

So you find yourself hunting for dishes. How does one think about how food will look on a plate? Not an easy a task when you are in the dish store admiring the colors and patterns as though you might be hanging the plate on the wall. For example, beige food on a beige plate is unappetizing. Unless it is a magnificent red, few will appreciate it and the rest will wonder what you were thinking. Blue does little for any food, except maybe vanilla ice cream, and then again only if it is a very nice blue. Claude Monet might be the last person who used yellow to good effect at the table. Try to recall the last time you were served food on anything besides a white plate in a good restaurant. Dishes are not art. For the most part they will be covered up, and then they will be dirty. That is why one might recommend to the reluctant chef, especially one who has no aesthetic point to make or ax to grind, a plain white plate of Italian, French, English, Japanese, Czechoslovakian, Icelandic or American design.[16] Aplico if you can, anything "made in Italy" if you can't,[17] Buffalo China if you can find it. Sasaki if you are that sort of person. Avoid fashionable or flashy things here as everywhere.[18] On the other hand, if you see a dish design you truly love—and you must look deep into your heart to be sure you do indeed love the design—buy it all. Ignore my or anyone's opinions about what you should look for in a plate. Who

---

[15] As though I had not already said enough... While the proud owner of some of the most magnificent white plates ever made, I admit I also possess a veritable zoo of plates and bowls found at garage sales and white sales and strange stores that carry old things. I especially like to serve black bean quesadillas on some slightly small-ish, pale pink or blue or yellow plates for a sort of mild mariachi effect. Then there are those shallow bowls I got for dimes at a garage sale in Wichita that seem to be creamy white, but when you finish your soup or pudding, you find a silly flower and two leaves painted on the bottom. (Blue leaf, yellow leaf and pink flower, come to think of it, so they may want to hang with the mariachi plates sometime.) I just love them, and love that they are also oven proof. These are all fun, and like light friends, delightful to spend the odd evening or morning with. My white plates of substance and weight like the best spouse or dearest friend; perhaps not thrilling or amusing, but solid and strong, something to be proud of and happy to be with in all circumstances, never inappropriate, always supportive, at once unobtrusive and richly present, not needing to call attention to the self. I paid for them dearly with that stuff, money, as I pay for profound love and deep friendship with that stuff ego, both of which seem so valuable but aren't; pay not thoughtlessly, not without trepidation, and never regretting it. Good thing about plates, though: if you don't break them, you only pay once.

[16] Don't grimace at me like I'm dictating some kind of rigid minimalist aesthetic in every kitchen. White plates can be many things; traditional, modernist, romantic. For that matter, white can be many things. And if you would just keep reading, you would see that I am perfectly supportive of any forays you might want to take into more creative dish management. And consider that if it is boredom you fear (as if your dishes could save you), it is a lot cheaper to buy new table linens now and again and easier to store a variety of them. Once again we are stuck with plain dishes to go with the largest number of colors and prints. Blah blah blah. As if anyone cares. Get by without offense.

[17] Keep in mind that most of the Italian ceramics chip easily. Fortunately they are very affordable and painlessly replaced. And who really cares if plates are chipped?

[18] Which is to say, for the most part. Fashionable and flashy certainly have their place.

cares? They're just dishes. Just make very sure you love the design for all the right reasons, or that you have the budget to replace the whole lot in about three years. Or the humility to apologize for the dishes every time you serve dinner.[19] Indulge freely your desires for bright or fantastic expressions in ceramic or porcelain with the odd serving platter or teapot, vase or mugs. If your dishes are well-chosen and neutral,[20] almost anything you put on the table will complement and be complemented by them.

Now think honestly about how upset you will be if a particular plate gets broken and must be replaced. Lighter weight dishes generally break more easily than heavier ones, but that is not a rule. Cheaper ceramics chip easily. Do you care? A greater investment in the first place can mean fewer broken dishes in the long run but not necessarily. Spending a great deal of money on a very delicate and beautiful set of dishes will cause nothing but heartbreak and bankruptcy if you keep trying to replace them as one by one they shatter. You need to know deep in your heart that dishes and glasses break, and factor that, along with your own frugality and sentimentality, into your decision about what to acquire.[21]

The last thing not to forget when you are opening yourself up to the seduction of a thousand dish designs created solely to entice you is this: They will be present in a variety of places. Perhaps you have already settled on the home you plan to stay in until you are very old or dead, but it is more likely you will change homes a few times, that the plates will appear on an assortment of tables, and that the fabric elements, the napkins and tablecloths, not to mention the upholstery, the curtains, and your own clothing will wear out and be replaced with refreshing and perhaps newly fashionable things, or at least things in a different color. It would be a shame if a change in table linens rendered your dishes hideous.

Consider as well that you might be using the same dishes in both very formal and very informal environments, and that you might even want to use them in an outdoor space. This is not a restrictive consideration, as anything can be used anywhere. But it is something to ponder briefly in case you are personally opposed for aesthetic or practical reasons to the use of fragile, hand-painted porcelain in combination with redwood decking or stone patio. You don't want to be restricted from eating food from real plates just because

[19] Shameless disregard for aesthetics will work, but it is always a gamble that shameless disregard in one arena will wander into another, and you will be on your way to divorce court before dessert.

[20] Neutral. By which I mean any color that does not insult other colors. Any color if it is deeply and richly itself can be a neutral. Fashion colors, on the other hand, are never neutral. They are created specifically to exclude combination with other colors so that you are required to replace everything next year with the new colors which clash horribly with last year's colors. If you choose higher quality and non-fashion colors, usually made directly from pigments found in the earth, they always go together just fine and maybe extremely well, just like they do when they are part of the actual earth. Of course, many whites and the actual color of clay and metal and wood are also neutral.

[21] You might also factor in the general level of physical coordination amongst your friends, but it won't help when someone's clumsy cousin tags along and drops a stack of plates on the flagstone patio.

your guest wanted to dine by moonlight. Choose your dishes so that you will be happy using them anywhere in your home, or get a second set of dishes which can go places the first set can't.

Be true to yourself.[22] Do not succumb to the pulls on your sentimentality orchestrated by the armies of marketing wizards and dish designers who want you to spend money on dishes this year and next year as well. Even if you serve dinner all the time and not with lamentable rarity, you are still more likely to tire of a design than you are to wear out the plates. Deny yourself the fleet-footed pleasure of buying the first thing that catches your eye and your fickle heart.

And now, in the specific...

PLATES

It is possible that the dishes you choose will only have one size plate which will work for meals. But in some cases there will be both a dinner plate and a luncheon plate. Mainly this occurs in the higher quality and more expensive sorts of dishes. You can get some of both, or think for a moment about how you eat and how you like to feed others and decide if the big plate is what you need, or if the smaller plate, still larger than a salad plate, is appropriate. I have lived with only one and only the other, and both work just fine. Guests are encouraged to take their courses one at a time and tend to take seconds when they are using the smaller plates. If you like to serve a number of different things on a plate at one time, e.g. an entree, a vegetable, a side dish, etc., then you might prefer a bigger plate so that everything doesn't get crowded together.[23]

Another thing to notice is how deep the bowl, or indentation, of the plate is. Some are quite deep, and you can easily imagine quite a bit of sauce or syrup gathering on the plate. Other designs have barely any depth to them at all, and if you carry them any distance with any sauce on them, you are likely to find yourself mopping up the floor before you sit down to eat. It is entirely up to you. Think about the kinds of things you

---

[22] A self-righteous platitude, perhaps. But think how much easier it will be to be true to yourself in the process of buying dishes than it is in almost any other context. Perhaps being ruthlessly true here, you will learn secrets of how to be true in other, far more important arenas. Surely the exercise can't hurt. And at the end of the day, when you return from the wrong career to an ill-fitting home, at least your dishes will not taunt you. Turn down the lights and pretend for the moment your life is otherwise. Then begin plotting how to make it so.

[23] But if you are so brave as to be cooking many things at once and so dexterous as to have them all ready at the same time, what are you doing looking at this book? Why would you be browsing my advice at all? You should be over here, giving me tips on how to do more than one thing at a time. How to cook excellently for the people I adore, mirroring my complex and varied affection for them in the variety of foods I offer them. All at once. How do you do that?

like to eat and might consider cooking, and then think about what that would be like on the plate you are admiring.

Feel the heaviness of the plate, the texture of the design and the finish, the sharpness of its edges, and decide if it pleases you. Try to clear your mind of any theories or ideas you might have about what is right. Release yourself from any rules which may have accumulated in your head. Decide as you hold the plate in your hands whether it is the plate you want to hold and offer and wash and dry a thousand times.

Choose a good plate. You are going to have it for a long time.

BOWLS

Bowls are more difficult than plates. You might even want to rethink your plate decision if the bowl you choose does not work, either practically or aesthetically, with the plates you like. Obviously they do not have to match or anything like that. Although they may.

Look at bowls to see if there are any shapes that draw your eye. They are all different. Deep bowls, flat bowls, bowls on little pedestals, rice bowls. Hold them with both hands because you might want to use them for cafe au lait in the morning. Look at them carefully, imagining soup, cereal, sauces, berries inside. Keep in mind, if money or space is tight, it is possible to choose your coffee cups in such a way that you do not need bowls at all. A large, bowl-shaped cup and saucer will get you through almost anything, from soup to coffee and including ice cream.

Unfortunately there is nothing I can say to help you decide what sort of bowl is right for you. It is as individual a choice as mugs. The same things that were important for plates are important for bowls. Color, weight, texture, sharpness of edges, depth. Plus, a bowl is more sculpturally present on your table than a plate. Look at the bowl as you would a three dimensional work of art and decide whether it is the sort of thing you want to look at for ever.[24] Look at bowls on other tables and notice what you like and don't like about particular examples. Try not to develop involved theories. Then buy what is good for you and what you think will be good for your guests, and don't think about bowls ever again.[25]

---

[24] Or can stand to look at for a long time. Again, you are not buying art.

[25] Now that is not entirely true. You very well might, at some point in the future, decide to buy a different sort of bowl. Something might speak to your soul. And you should do it. Different bowls are good. Vessels in the abstract are powerful things. Need, or rather the lack of it, is no reason to refuse beauty.

Oh dear. I know you. You are thinking, "I am too busy to worry about bowls. I don't care what kind of bowl I serve stuff in. I'm not a cook. If the bowls turn out to be no good, I'll just ask someone who knows more than I do to go shopping with me and let them pick out bowls. I don't have time to learn about bowls."

And you are right. That can be an excellent technique for disarming someone, to defer to their taste, to ask assistance. And you are also right that in the end it doesn't matter what bowls you use as long as you are you and filled with good humor.

MUGS

Or cups or whatever it is you plan to serve coffee, tea, and hot chocolate in. I suppose it is because they are tied in with the drug ritual of coffee and tea, but it does seem people are particular about their mugs. They are not so particular about your mugs perhaps, but they are still affected. It's one more place where you do not so much need to please as to not annoy, although there is no reason to abstain from an opportunity to please.

There are so many things about mugs that can grate. Their shape, their color, their texture, and whatever design or distracting lettering or illustration some imbecile printed upon them. You can hardly spend a day in America without acquiring yet another mug with a corporate message scrawled across it. Leave them at the office, as you should all work-related things. Keeping in mind almost no joke survives being told to the same person more than once, ban cartoon joke mugs from your house as well. And refrain from buying them for others. You just encourage the industry. Mugs are easy to manufacture and cheap and have become the favorite arena in our culture for marketing mavens to convince you to buy yet another thing you don't need and won't or shouldn't use. How many times, after all, have you broken a mug? It's a constant struggle against a relentless ocean of mugs which you will only take from the shelf, and reluctantly at that, when every other vessel in the house is in use or in the sink. Better to wash some dishes.

Find cups you like for coffee and tea and other warm things and acquire a number of them. Generous or discreet, they needn't even match. Four is perhaps the smallest number you should have. Twelve of any one sort is probably as many as you want. Even then, you might want to divide their number between two or three colors or versions of your favored design. You don't want people to suspect you entertain so many people regularly. It destroys your credibility as a novice. Another approach is to collect two or three or four each of designs you particularly like, eventually having quite a nice supply that does not appear impressive nor intimidating.

In mug buying, notice and consider the many qualities of a ceramic vessel. For example, the proportion of height to diameter. I favor mugs which are just slightly taller than they are wide. Something more and less than four and a half inches for each dimension. Popular these days are mugs which are dramatically tall or dramatically wide. Some people prefer small, neat cups appropriate for strong coffee. Consider how much the bowl will hold and what is right for you and the most important others who will be using them. You may need several kinds of mugs and cups. An eclectic selection. You may not.

Notice whether you can hold the cup in one hand without using the handle. Notice the shape, the texture and thickness of the material and how it feels in your hand, the handle and whether it works. See if it feels right or if it is uncomfortable or seems unbalanced.[26] The color or colors. Remember, it will be in your kitchen and all over your house and it will have brown stuff in it. Which is not to say your mugs should match your furniture nor that they should be brown. No more than art should match the walls. Try to transcend the dictates of interior design magazines and home decorating catalogues. Try to find colors and patterns, if any, which appeal to you and which you can imagine still looking at ten years from now. Not that you will still be looking at them ten years from now, but you might be. In any case it is a very good touchstone for determining whether you will be able to enjoy your new mugs past

---

[26] What you are unused to almost always feels wrong to start with. Prisoners whose chains have been removed feel as though something were out of place. Try to get beyond your habits and prejudices when you are deciding about mugs, or mates, or anything at all. You'll be happier and we'll be happier.

next week.[27] Consider them and return to the store at a later date, or buy impulsively the mugs which capture your heart on a day when it is healthy. Your choice will be the first thing that you, or whoever is drinking their morning brew from it, will be able to focus upon. It will be the first sensual experience of the day, that cup, and perhaps the last thing they touch in the evening before they reach for you. No sense at all in choosing a mug because it looks good with your other dishes. It will hardly ever be anywhere near your other dishes. Of course, if you are pure at heart and clean of eye, things you choose because they appeal to you will almost invariably complement each other. In a serene or eclectic way, but nonetheless. You only risk a jarring and unpleasant effect if you allow ugly things you don't like to litter your home.

GLASSWARE

Will anyone object if we throw all glassware into this one category? After all, one is hardly going to have a different glass for every possible beverage and still be able to honestly lay claim to the advantages and allowances tendered reluctant and courtship-oriented cooks.

Officially, of course, there are a myriad of types of glasses: Stemware for the fermented drinks (red wine white wine and bubbly wine), water glasses, beer glasses, highballs and lowballs, teeny tiny cordial and aperitif glasses, giant cognac snifters, juice glasses, tumblers... For heaven's sake. Someone must be making quite a bit of money off all this glassware. Feel free to thwart them.

On the other hand, you do need to serve people drinks at your home whether you are planning to cook for them or not. Mugs won't do for merlot, unless you are trying to impress upon someone how utterly unable you are to manage your own life, which is a very different sort of courtship technique. And while no one is going to condemn you for serving wine in cafe glasses, they may be distressed by it being poured into a tall tumbler. In which case it is not propriety that is being forsaken but rather discretion, which is perilous.

Perhaps the best way to choose glassware is by selecting the least expensive glasses which appeal you. Glasses break. You do not want to spend much money on any one glass nor be too attached to it. Perhaps you can arrange for your tastes to be so proletariat that your favorite wine glass is the very glass used to hold Chianti in every

---

[27] As a rule you shouldn't let anything into your house for more than a week that you wouldn't be happy to have stay there forever. Which does imply that you should choose your dishes more carefully than you choose your weekend house guests.

second-rate Italian restaurant in the greater Americas. Purchase them in boxes of four at hardware stores or for change at almost any thrift store or garage sale.

Water glasses might be small or large, short or tall, as long as they are comfortable in the hand and easy to drink from. You might be surprised how many glasses go into production with the very serious flaw of dribbling all over the drinker no matter how carefully one tries to sip neatly. Try a few glasses before you buy a whole bunch of them, or take them right back to the store if they prove mischievous.

As it happens, you don't need to think too much about it. Water can be served politely in anything except mugs or empty jars. And even empty jars are sometimes perfect. Depends on the circumstances, and how much style you have. I've seen beakers work on occasion. A low, sturdy glass of at least six ounce capacity is good. It is enough water, but it won't tip over easily in the carnival of arms and sleeves and hands and flying porcelain which is how an excellent meal looks to the glassware.

Wine glasses might be any shape at all. You might choose some kind of stemware, in which case you need to add the quality "stable" to the other important quality, "easy to hold in one hand." There is a great deal of romance attached to the image of a tall, shapely and graceful wine glass, but you will have to weigh that benefit against the gracefulness of your friends. Wine can always be served in those little French cafe glasses produced by the billions by Duralex. Very continental and very hard to knock over. Harder still to break, for while you should always be prepared to buy new glasses, you may not want to make it a habit.

Be sure to have enough glasses that can be placed on the table without apology to serve your largest likely number of guests both water and wine with dinner. Plus, if there is even the barest possibility champagne will be drunk in your home, two or four or eight glass champagne flutes, tall and uncomplicated, should live on the shelf. Add a tall, fat glass or two which might not even be glass but which you enjoy filling with water and drinking to the dregs for all the water you and your darling should be drinking all day when you are nowhere near the table. Healthy and hydrated are excellent qualities in a lover.

SILVERWARE

If the dishes are good and the napkins clean and big it really doesn't matter what utensils you have as long as they are heavy enough and easy to use. Seldom is silverware so hideous to be worth remarking upon. And even when it is, it is usually in good humor and does not affect anyone's enjoyment of the meal.[28] Early pawn shop flatware, as long as it has weight to it, can be quite nice when paired with good porcelain or ceramic dishes and linen napkins, folded but not necessarily ironed. The pieces needn't even match. No one is going to be shocked by eclectic silverware on your table. Go for heaviness without going to extremes. There is something sensual and slowly provocative about eating with heavy utensils. God knows what, but there you are.[29]

Meanwhile, if your dishes are unfortunate to ugly and your napkins are in a duck design from Acme Paper Products, no silverware you choose is going to help.

Of course you might want to own real silverware. There is, in certain circles, an age you can reach where regardless of your marital status you will be perceived as disheveled and incompetent and very bad mate material if you haven't yet figured out your silverware and dishes sufficiently to set a table without apology. Only the potential partner who is hoping to leverage your incompetence into a position of power for themselves will respond warmly to this sort of thing.

Which is still not to say you must have conventional silverware. You might be the sort of person who has a drawer full of antique silver nestled in fine-grain crimson felt which you use as casually as you do linen napkins. Or perhaps you discovered your flatware while travelling in Romania. Unconventional, surprising even, but fine as long as they hold to the rules of utensils: Others must be able to eat with them comfortably and they must not be toxic.

Or you can go to the store and buy flatware. It is not difficult and not that enormous of an investment.[30]

---

[28] Except, I suppose, in the event that they were carved into some fabulously grotesque or cruelly offensive shape which cannot be digested kindly. I think I have actually seen such things, but I seem to be in denial about it. Can't for the life of me remember what they were.

[29] You can argue with me all day, but in the end, if you insist on light flatware, especially the kind that is difficult to hold because of some silly, possibly cylindrical, modern design that you thought was clever in the store, your dining companion is more likely to be aggravated and nervous than pliable and open-hearted at the end of the meal. You do the math.

[30] Unless you want something really nice. Silverware manufacturers, like plate and mug manufacturers, have in recent years chosen to design their products with the impulse buyer in mind. They have been very busy creating cheap, light, and fashionable designs in multitude styles, and have rather left off making the sort of stuff you can use and enjoy and pretty much not notice for the rest of your life. That sort of thing doesn't appeal to the modern consumer. Not interesting or romantic or creative or modern or something enough. Again, if this is not a realm in which you are naturally expressive, don't be. Reveal instead great affection for those who will use your utensils.

Some suggestions. Go to the fine silverware section of a good store and ask to see the casual designs in stainless steel or silver plate from the big, old, sterling silverware manufacturers. Or pick up the habit of visiting estate sales, antique stores and auctions till you find something you like. Or get on your mom's good side and inherit her set of silver early. Or only ever cook things that can be eaten with one's hands.

NAPKINS

Napkins are very important. You only need a few of them, they are not expensive, and you can throw them in the laundry with everything else. Again, being a rare chef means you are not required to have ironed napkins. More than that. You are not even required to have real napkins. Clean dish towels if they are not burdened with some embarrassing or cute pattern work very well as both napkins and as placemats. Actually, any kind of napkin works fine as a placemat in a pinch.

Here as everywhere, err on the clean and patternless side if you are unsure of your own aesthetic. No one ever notices a boring table setting, whereas napkins which clash dramatically with your plates can impede many a visually oriented guest from fully occupying themselves with the color of your eyes. Stick to the dull, and then kick in at the last moment with flowers and food which are beautiful and delicious and conversation which is compelling and full of laughter and warmth. Also, you won't feel as though everyone knows what year you bought your napkins because of the colors.[31] Of course, if your dishes are suitably plain, go wild.

For the occasional cook, especially if that cook is very young or in a non-profit job, there are better approaches to acquiring excellent napkins besides dropping dollars by the dozen at the nearest boutique of French home imports. If you know how to sew or would like to learn, making napkins out of cotton or linen fabric can be a wonderful exercise in executing straight seams.[32] Or haunt garage sales. Napkins made out of India cotton or madras that you can pick up for a dollar or two at the other sort of import stores are just fine and will be appreciated by your guests.[33]

---

[31] Did you know that fabric manufacturers get together every year and decide which colors are going to be fashionable two years down the road? This is why it is so easy to identify when something was bought by noting its color. A sort of carbon dating. Avoid the whole thing by sticking to white, natural, or perennially unfashionable colors that you happen to like. Good quality, uninteresting napkins should last forever. In fact, I picked up mine at a garage sale after someone died, which means they are going to have lasted for two forevers when they are buried with me.

[32] Cut out squares of fabric at least 21" x 21" and ask someone to show you how to finish the edges. Or just wash the pieces of fabric a bunch of times, pull off the loose threads, and be very modern and shaggy.

[33] I reveal my prejudice toward cloth napkins made of natural fibers and in generous sizes. The objection some have to such stuff is that they need to be ironed. I don't have that objection because I find nothing wrong in

In a very tight pinch where you must use paper napkins, make them be the large dinner sort. You may be forgiven for using lunch box napkins or paper towels, but your campaign will not be advanced.[34] Meanwhile, don't fuss over the napkins, making your guests feel as though they are putting you out by utterly needless extravagance. Use the most exquisite napkins as though they were merely rags. Behave as though the merest rags were most beautiful cloth. Have a darkly-dyed napkin option if you tend to cook things in tomatoes or curries. Otherwise, lighten up and don't fret if the white napkins get a little stained.

No need for truly wonderful napkins. Still, remember that whatever you give your guests as a napkin, it will lay there on their lap throughout the meal, now and again being caressed by an adorable hand and occasionally touching lovely lips. You give them what you think will be right.

---

not ironing them. I steer clear of napkins made of synthetic fabric or even what others find to be a tolerable blend, but I have seen them used to good effect on other tables where textures are different than on my own. I ask that you remember all the time the purpose of cooking as courtship and know that although it is very nice to have neat looking napkins, it is also important that they feel good in the hands of your guests. Fold cotton and linen napkins immediately when they come from the dryer and they will be quite neat, maybe even neat enough to persuade you from what seems to be a more sensible purchase of permanent press or synthetic napkins. I add, because this is a crusade of mine, that natural fibers are wonderfully absorbent which is maybe the point of napkins to begin with, but reluctantly admit that it is a matter of personal choice.

[34] Some people—and some of them are terribly delightful otherwise—will even try to argue that paper towels are the best possible napkin. Consider this: Someone who thinks paper towels are terrific is unlikely to be offended by the use of cloth napkins. Whereas the person who understands cloth napkins, when offered a paper towel is likely to wonder what else their dining companion thinks is best when disposable. And we'll just leave alone the possibility of insulting someone's environmental sensibilities.

REAL COOKS

An expression of absolute admiration and appreciation.

THERE IS NOTHING so wonderful as to know a real cook. It is having entree to the finest restaurant in the world and the right to enter and nibble at will. Better. You visit casually near dinner time and something appears which they consider humble but which makes one consider saying grace. Or you are invited ceremoniously to an event or a celebration or to Friday or Sunday supper or a dinner party on Saturday night, and you arrive, champagne in hand, to enjoy a meal which cannot be bought at any price. Food made by one who knows how to cook cooking for friends. No concessions to penurious owners nor intractable vendors. No nod in the direction of economy nor in the equally distasteful direction of high-priced flamboyance. The finest ingredients taken moments earlier from a dazzling garden, or purchased carefully from a myriad of stores, each providing only one aspect of the meal. Wine from the wine shop, bread from the bakery, vegetables not found in the yard chosen at the farmers market.

Real cooks don't always come home with what they went out for. Maybe a bunch of vine-ripened tomatoes or some especially slim and green asparagus at the market inspired them to change the menu. Real cooks write lots of checks and carry cash.

All the non-perishable ingredients, the things you and I and even the managers of very good restaurants buy in the condiment aisle of the grocery store, are found in strange and lovely bottles; herbed and spiced oils and vinegars, fruits and vegetables relished and pickled and preserved at some earlier date, maybe one afternoon while you were drinking coffee or wine or water at the table, gossiping or discussing all manner of things philosophic and politic and romantic and not really noticing your friend's constant movement around the kitchen, cutting and stirring and pouring and capping and otherwise setting things aside.

ODDLY, IT IS NOT real cooks who insist that the finest ingredients are necessary to produce a delicious something. No need to worry over making your own unless you want to. Real cooks know that as wonderful as it is to have and use fine ingredients, it is more important to feed hungry people hanging around the living room. Real cooks know that it is a very bad idea to ruin a romantic interlude with a too-fussy midnight snack, and yet know it is sometimes critical to have a midnight snack. Real cooks like making grilled sandwiches at two AM. Real cooks take stale bread and aging onions and make you happy. Real cooks love leftovers.

It is rather the amateur cook who has a little, very dangerous knowledge and wields it cruelly who makes the novice or non-cook feel small for making the very same thing a real cook would have been praised for. "What, you have no raspberry vinegar!" the amateur cook will exclaim, as though you had been found lacking in the milk of human kindness.

Real cooks don't expect their friends who cook to have a Cuisinart DLC anymore than real photographers expect friends to have Hasselblads. Real cooks don't expect regular people to be real cooks. Real cooks would like to be invited to dinner at your house more often. Sometimes they want to be the one who brings the wine.

Meanwhile, I apologize for suggesting that there is anything for me to say about cooking. I didn't mean imply that. Feeding people is not cooking. Courting people through food doesn't mean you must cook. It may mean sharing an invitation to dinner. Or pulling together something edible. Or knowing one restaurant from another. It might even mean letting people figure out how to feed themselves.

CLEANING UP

Could it be that people are friendlier when they are not afraid to touch things?

EVERYONE KNOWS somewhere within themselves that everyone is different. That nothing one learns here can really be applied there. The only thing one learns is how to better acquire experience, how to be less permanently injured and how to injure less in the process. Learning all the time the same things more and more deeply. Everyone knows this. They will be happy to tell you all about it. But then they gasp in the very next breath, "Can you believe she did that?"

Well, yes. I can. Nothing easier in the world than to believe that someone did something odd and incomprehensible at first glance, and maybe even at second and third glances as well. Nothing harder in this world it seems than to let it go at that. Live and let live. Forgive and forget. If it even requires forgiveness.

I mention all this because maintenance of one's self and one's space is in third place, right after money and sex, as one of the top arenas in which no one will understand why you do what you do. Nor you them.

Which is why we start off a discussion of clean-up with a tirade on patience and tolerance and forgiveness of the quirks of others. No sense in brushing away layers of defenses with food sublime and sweetly offered, then destroying the promise by refusing to arrange yourself comfortably near another until the whole kitchen is scrubbed clean. I don't care how important cleanliness is to you. In the time it takes you to turn on an overhead light and pull out a scrubby sponge someone could easily rethink the situation and decide it is more important than they thought a moment ago to get home to a good night's sleep. See you at the gym, Mr. Clean.

On the other hand, you hardly want to get up on a sunny morning that has been filled with kisses and caresses in a rumpled bed and find the kitchen too disheveled and disgusting to even make coffee. The table too sticky and cluttered to place the newspaper upon. And even if such a lovely scenario does not materialize, it can be discomforting for some people to leave their host, their friend, their would-be companion in the incandescent night with a forbidding clean-up ahead of them. At the last moment your great gift is broken in two by guilt and remorse on the part of a polite guest who hates the thought of leaving you to the chore, but who also knows it is time to leave. Go home! you think, or Stay. But they don't know what to do, and it is actually your fault.

A rock and a hard place, you say? No. But neither is there one right action. The answer is as usual to be sensible and considerate at all moments, and flexible and responsive to the concerns of others and particularly a particular other.[1]

TO CLEAN OR NOT to clean. You don't want to offend anyone with relaxed hygiene anymore than you want to drive them off during a cleaning frenzy. Where exactly is the fence to sit upon?

In the context of unknowing, which is the context of much courtship especially in the early moments, you may want to avoid the whole issue. Or resolve it gradually, almost imperceptibly so it is barely a problem at all. Washing things as you cook, for example. Not too hard, and very handy later on when you are trying to convince someone to snuggle when they might think you should be cleaning up. Imagine being able to look toward the

---

[1] This is also true when you are on the other side of the equation. You can court others by being an excellent guest as well, by not demanding that others adhere to your standard of cleanliness or other aesthetic. But before approaching the topic of how to behave when at the home of another, let's finish up the part about being a desirable host.

sink and stove and see nothing to speak of. "Darling, really, there are only the dinner plates in the sink." If they still seem anxious, say, "You're right. Go put on some more music and think about whether you would like coffee or cognac or Calistoga while I clean up the last few things." Then clean the kitchen as if your mother were arriving at midnight.

In almost every case a willing guest will forgive everything that is actually in the sink and below the level of the counter. Try not to pile up the dishes so the faucet won't work. You should always be able to get a glass of water or wash a single thing you need without excavating the whole sink.[2]

Another approach one can take during the making of the meal is to include your guest or guests in the fun. When they ask sincerely—which is to say, a second time—what they can do to help, if you don't have something that needs desperately to be chopped, respond "Thank you for asking. If you like, why don't you wash up that stuff in the sink." Or better yet, say something like, "Keep stirring this for me, and keep an eye on that simmering pot. It is about to boil over. I want to clean up that awful sink full of stuff." And then do just that. There you are in the kitchen, both of you with your hands full and nothing to do but flirt[3] with one another.

But perhaps you didn't keep the kitchen straight while you made dinner. It is a disaster and you are sensing a little too late that your companion will not take well to the idea of ignoring it whether the event goes till tomorrow or not. Their attractive brow is starting to furrow and their eyes twitch toward the kitchen. "Did you rinse the dishes," they try to ask nonchalantly, plainly made nervous by the idea of sauce drying onto a plate.

Don't fret. No reason why a sink full of soapy water can't be a lovely interlude in an exquisite evening. Make it ritual. Make it wonderful. Light the kitchen so you can see. Perhaps put on music, more for them but also for you. Quite loud if you like to dance about while you do dishes and if you don't have neighbors who will complain. The noise of water and the banging of pans will preclude most conversation anyway. Place a comfortable chair on the far side of the kitchen. Place your friend in the chair with a cup or a glass

---

2 Tracy adds that big pots which would never make it into the sink gracefully can be left on the stove if the stove is clean, if the pot seems clean from a distance, and if the pot is covered. In other words, one would have to go over and lift the lid to determine whether it needs attention or is just waiting to be put away. Any guest with a half a mind to be friendly will accept the charade happily and refrain from close inspection.

3 It's not that I don't trust you. But my blood does run cold at the thought of what some people think flirting means. All it means as far as I am concerned, and all I am suggesting, is that one's full attention and all powers of humor and wit and intellect and all sexuality and sensuality be directed only in the direction of the one or several others you happen to be flirting with. All of your most delightful you offered as a careless gift. It is an exercise in focus. And since it must be done with a light hand—it is only flirting after all—it is also an exercise in discretion and restraint. Just wanted you to know I am not suggesting anything racy or seductive. For heaven's sake, do you know how easy it is to break plates and glasses while washing them in that slippery soapy water? In the interest of the china and glassware, flirting only.

of whatever they seem to need or say they want. Or perhaps a conversation is in progress. Leave the music low and get the chair closer to the sink. Let them wander around while they linger on the political or the personal. Or arrange them in another room with a really big book of interesting stuff. Ask for the grace of ten minutes. Kiss them wherever it is appropriate. Then do the dishes. Wipe down counters. Without fanaticism, but also without oversight. Do not take more than fifteen minutes to accomplish the task. If your guest insists upon a chore, give them something you would give a seven-year-old to do. Clear the table. Dry plates. Mostly nothing. Get to the next thing with as much haste as the details of the situation will allow. Conversation, or whatever.

Of course, they might be that exquisite sort of person, that most desirable guest who insists on doing dishes after the meal. If they offer, refuse; but if they start in and seem to be perfectly happy about it, let them go. It is making them feel useful and giving them something to do with their hands. You know how nice that can be. If you are terrified of another doing dishes in your home, jump in and do them yourself, giving them something else to do, like sweep the floor or clear the table.[4]

But perhaps it is you, quirky and otherwise delightful you, who is made nervous by the carnage in the kitchen. Your own neurotic eye that keeps wandering toward the back of the house, while your intoxicating, although apparently slovenly guest is putting on music perfect for slow dancing and teasing you to leave the dishes alone. They are humming and swaying to Stardust, and you are thinking "Ten more minutes and I am going to have to scrub the plates." For heaven's sake. If you cannot find it in your heart to be flexible, if having a filthy kitchen will ruin your mood for the rest of the night and most of the morning, go to your guest and explain ever so humbly that it is a terrible habit of yours, but one which dies hard, and that you simply must take ten minutes to clean up the kitchen. Swear you will make it up to them, and then do. However much they may want you to join them at that moment, in the end they will be impressed by someone who likes a clean kitchen and is willing to make it that way themselves. Take care, though, and don't take more than ten minutes to soothe yourself in this. You are not what's important.

Again, if at all possible, wash things as you go along. This suggestion will be met with cries of dissent by many the excellent cook. But there are good reasons for going about the preparation of the meal in this way. One is that if your kitchen is sufficiently, but not fabulously stocked with the tools of the trade, you will probably run out of bowls and pans and knives and chopping boards if you don't recycle them for second and third use. If you keep up a steady pattern of washing things you are done using, you won't have to stop in

---

4 Don't, for example, ask them to dust the bedroom or scrub the bathtub.

the middle of a process a half hour from now to wash out the bowl you need. In another scenario, things used for preparation might also be used for serving and you will appreciate having them already clean and dry. Again, you will hear the cry of devoted chefs everywhere, frantic to think you might be using a mixing bowl for serving. They must shut up. It is just as likely that a splendid serving bowl has been used for mixing. Besides, one approach to acquiring bowls and pans is to consider whether they will be both functional and presentable, thereby avoiding the necessity of purchasing two large awkward things when one will do, and further avoiding the often Sisyphean task of finding a place for them in your kitchen. An excellent approach in many respects, but it does mean that vessels used in the preparation of a meal might have to be washed to be reused as serving vessels.

Another enticement for washing things as you go along is that it is much easier to wash something that has just been used than to try to wash it five hours from now. Still another is that dirty pots pile up in the sink and make it impossible to use. And they clutter up counters in such a way that even if you were to move them to the side, the surface is still difficult to use.

But the very best reason to keep things under control is to make the final chore of washing up at the end of the night less Herculean. Nice enough if it turns out that you do the deed. But very very nice if someone you adore decides they want to clean up. How horrible for them to walk into a kitchen which would require all the warriors of Sparta to make right in a single evening. A strongly built person might walk right out again saying they have changed their mind and do not care to clean up after all. Hopefully they will make their exit with humor. Unfortunately the kitchen is still a mess. Another of sweeter disposition will make a valiant effort to clean up, but you will have to help and their desire to do something for you will have been cruelly thwarted. Instead of it now being your turn to do something for them—and the imagination reels at what might have transpired in such a tennis—it is simply late in the day and everyone has wrinkled fingertips.

It need not transpire so badly. Find your best nature, your most optimistic self, and jump into the task. Behave as though it were nothing but usual for you to clean up such catastrophes and that you do not believe it will take more than a half hour. It shouldn't, especially not since you have help or at least companionship, and conversation will make any amount of time fly by as though it were mere minutes.

Still another reason to clean as you go is that you might have a partner or roommate who tires of those long hours when there is no way to make a cup of tea, and who laments that helping in the kitchen always means washing dishes, which is not so much fun for most people as chopping and mixing and stirring and tasting.

One good way to get things washed en route is to wash everything that can be washed every time you need to clean a particular something for reuse. So instead of only washing off that chopping board, wash everything in the sink as well. Your hands are wet and the water is hot, so you may as well do it all. It will take a very few minutes, if that.

Of course you might have acres of counter space, a deep sink, a kitchen outfitted in a conveniently redundant manner, and the very charming reality of someone else arriving in the morning to clean the house and do the dishes. In which case, be careless and make a reasonable mess as you prepare a meal. At the end of the day, no one is going to argue with the proposal that another do the dirty work for their daily bread. You have only to make sure a table is clean for breakfast in the morning and that enough mugs and maybe small plates are clean for coffee and toast or whatever. In this case, remember to turn the lights off in the kitchen and close the door if possible before sitting down to your meal.

CLEANING UP AFTER THE MEAL

The first thing is to get everything as close to the sink as possible. Certainly everything must be removed from wherever the meal took place. Clearing the table, we have always called it. Can't say exactly why it is important to clear the table but it is. Perhaps there is some symbolism having to do with how one leaves one's environment and naturally the answer is "How you found it." Since one eventually must leave the table and move on, it must be returned, at least symbolically, to its original condition.[5] And of course, if you are planning to wash the dishes the table must certainly be cleared first.

When everyone seems finished with their meal, and not a moment before, you can rise and begin clearing the table. The party might remain at the table for hours still, more things might be served, desserts and drinks of many sorts, but the bulk of the dishes and everything having to do with the main body of the meal itself should be removed. That would include all plates and utensils, all serving platters and bowls, and all condiments and accessories which were specifically for the meal and won't be required for dessert. Someone will

---

[5] There has been that night or two, always in the company of Italians, when we never leave the table, never really stop eating or drinking, and the table is never cleared. The metaphor is perhaps that the feeding, the nourishing, the love and sensuality of food and the warmth and dynamic of conversation never ends, never gets cleared away. Even when we move into another room for some good reason. Something about Italians, one can believe that the mess in the kitchen really doesn't matter. One forgets there is a room destroyed, and continues through the house or onto the terrace littering one's path with small plates, crumbs of biscotti, wine and liqueur glasses, and tiny little espresso cups and spoons. I don't think you have to be Italian to make this work, although it helps. What you do have to do is make your guests forget completely about the need to clean anything up. Again, a good way to do this is to have there not be a great deal to clean up. Dishes from preparation completely cleaned and put away so that the only stuff is that stuff which is still, technically speaking, in use, and so does not need to be cleaned up.

probably help you, or might even begin clearing the table before you do. If they beat you to it, rise to assist them or allow them the chore. It is a gesture of thanks and appreciation for all the work you have done in preparing the meal. Say thank you.

When clearing the table yourself, leave all the glasses, as well as carafes of water (which might need refilling) and bottles of wine, until people have actually left the table as you cannot know who will want more. If coffee, tea and other after-dinner drinks are served, those things too can be left on the table until everyone has adjourned somewhere else. When that happens, you would be very kind to offer new glasses for wine and water to anyone who is still drinking, as the glasses from the table are probably heavily finger-printed and coated with crumbs and oils from the meal and so will not glow as nicely in the light of the next room as a fresh glass.

If you did the worst part of the clean-up before the meal began, you may very well want to put off cleaning up the dishes from dinner until later or even tomorrow in deference to the rhythm of the evening. It might have something to do with the formality of the event. The more casual the event, the more likely you will feel like cleaning up during the course of things, and it will seem more natural to allow guests to help or watch. When a meal is more formally concocted, it often seems better to leave everything off till tomorrow or at least until everyone, or almost everyone has left. That last, lingering someone might be just the right person to help with the dishes, the task providing an intimate context for further conversation, a change of pace and attitude after hours of more formal socializing. Strangely enough, they might very well feel privileged to be included in the final ritual. They might even be so wise as to know it is an excellent opportunity to get to know you as they watch how you go about cleaning up in your own home.

Which suggests you do it in a manner which will not frighten nor repel, making them run home to pull their covers over their head; but rather will soothe and include them, making them eventually think about pulling your covers over their head.

Whatever you clean, clean completely, treat your things with respect, and if you are one of those compulsive persons (even if you do stop short of sterilizing your flatware in the pressure cooker), try to have a sense of humor about it and accomplish your cleaning without remarking that everyone is not so good at it as you. If you know you do not do a good job and that if someone sees you do the dishes they will be forever afraid to dine again at your home, you are in trouble. You can always make up reasons why the dishes can wait, but it is far better to learn how to do it right.[6] In any case, be sure to wrap up

---

6 At the end of this chapter there are a slew of suggestions on how to clean. I feel very puritanical having this chapter at all, and damn near Lutheran for having cleaning suggestions. Yet, I can't get around my under-standing that people get nervous when a place is too filthy and it is not their own filth and so they don't know

any left over food and put it away so it won't spoil, and otherwise clean up so that no ants or cockroaches or dogs or small children are tempted to come in during the night and have their way with things.

ON BEING A MOST DESIRABLE GUEST

A desirable guest will accept the machinations of their host without making it more diffi-cult than it must be. Surely you would never be one of those fitful guests who insist others be the way they would have them. If a filthy kitchen bothers you, or if you feel like being especially wonderful to have around, do the dishes yourself and do them as though you actually enjoy the chore. Remain part of the conversation. Keep anyone from thinking you are doing anything like work. Be sure to wash everything very well.[7] This is a particularly wonderful thing to do for people who have children and you should do it whether you care about clean kitchens or not. Unless they have a housekeeper, they might not have seen the sink completely empty in weeks. Pretend for those minutes it takes you to do all the dishes and clean off all the counters that it is you who are the host. Make sure your friend is com-fortable and has a drink of some sort to occupy them and keep them from trying to do anything. If they demure, insist it is your pleasure to clean up after such a fabulous meal. That it is the least you can do. If they seem at a loss but you believe that secretly they are thrilled not to clean up the kitchen, ask them to do something for you like put on some music or find a book they have been meaning to lend to you. Or tell them you will never come over again unless they shut up and let you do the dishes in peace. Grab their face with soapy hands and kiss them squarely.

Do not, however, be a freight train. Some people really can't bear anyone else in their kitchen. If they say anything like, "No, really, I prefer to do the dishes myself," instead of the more acquiescent, "You don't have to do that," you can ask once, "Are you sure?" but

---

where it came from; and that nervous people are disinclined to be comfortable, to open up their souls, to drink of new friendship, and rarely take their clothes off. At the same time, I have noticed people can also be nervous in a too-consciously clean place where they might be worried that their very breath will violate the purity of the space. It is not so much the degree of cleanliness, but the attitude of it. A fairly filthy place might have an aspect of formality, an affectation that it is cleaner than you are and you had better watch your step which is equally, if not more discomforting than an honestly squalid spot. And I have been in hospitals which have been warm and welcoming for all their sterility. The only thing for you to do is be aware and sensible and respect-ful and willing to look at yourself and be accepting of others and take care of what you feel must be taken care of. Arduous as it sounds, I swear to you it is the easiest thing in the long run.

[7] Doing the dishes badly at someone else's house is among the most nasty, non-criminal acts known in the civilized world. Not only does the host have to appear appreciative and thank you for your efforts, but they have to redo the dishes themselves after you've left, or surreptitiously if you don't happen to leave, or they have to pretend they are not disgusted when they have to use a grimy plate in the morning for toast.

probably it will be best to let it go. You made the effort. You were a good guest. Now accept their wishes without argument. They may be especially anxious about their dishes or glasses and don't like others to wash and possibly break them. They might be terribly picky about how things are cleaned and know they will have to do it over to please themselves. They might not like anyone in their kitchen. You can't possibly know. Don't let your desire to be a good guest and to do the dishes override your sensitivity to the quirks of another.[8]

A common possibility is right in between those two extremes. Your host cleans up the kitchen and you ask very sincerely, "What can I do to help?" They will say "Nothing at all. Relax and enjoy yourself." You look around and see what might be done. If there is an extra sponge or cloth, clean the table or the stove. Do stuff and keep out of their way.

If you err, err on the side of cleanliness and helpfulness.

SUGGESTIONS FOR CLEANING IN GENERAL

Follows are the things I can think of without thinking too hard about it. Too easy to become fervent, then evangelical, then lose entirely the respect and attention of readers who are already resenting me rather than admitting their home is a sty. Still I persist. If you would like to tend more toward clean than filthy:

HAVE THE RIGHT STUFF

Dish soap and sponges and scrubbing pads or brushes and gloves. Scouring powder to scrub the sink. In the bathroom, a long brush for cleaning the toilet. Feather duster or at least dust rags. Having the right stuff makes the job, which will happen eventually however you look at it, so much easier and faster and more pleasant. Not having the right stuff makes it a horrible task and you will be sorely tempted to simply throw out all the dirty dishes and start anew. You can do this. There are no laws against it, besides the universal ones against wastefulness. But in the end it will be more work to go out and find new dishes and pans than it would be to clean them.

Have clean dish towels available at all times. That means having more than one. Five is good. Some out, and some in a drawer so you have clean ones when you need them.

---

8 You know, this is not the only room in the house where what you want to do, what you think will please someone, might not be at all the thing for them.

Whichever ones are out will get used and so won't count as clean if someone is looking for a clean towel for any particular purpose.[9] Wash them whenever you do the laundry.

If you do not have a dish rack, spread a dish towel on the counter for setting things out to dry. If you do have a dish rack, place a towel beneath it to catch dripping water. If you have a dishwasher, use it with discretion.

WASH EVERYTHING WELL

Wash the backs of plates, the outsides and bottoms of bowls and cups and pots and pans. Wash lids to things.[10] Even though it may seem there is no reason for the outside of a bowl to have gotten dirty, be assured it is. Even though you cannot fathom how a lid to a pot in which water was boiled could have become worthy of your soapy attention, be confident it has. Filthy fingers pick things up, sauce splashes about, and there was probably something besides water in that pot at some point. You would be surprised how much starch from rice and pasta gets into the water which the boils and bubbles and bursts in broad blotches on the inside, and, miraculously enough, the outside of lids as well as their respective pots and pans. Be sure to have dish gloves if hot water bothers you.

Soak things that do not clean easily on the first try. Not for days. Just for the time it takes to do the rest of the dishes. That should get you pretty far and they should wash with ease in most cases. Scrubby sponges will usually suffice.[11] On this note, you will find that the better quality and the healthier the food you cook with, the easier it will be to clean up afterward. For example, you never have to soak the salad bowl.

Wipe off counters whenever you have a chance while you are cooking. Wipe counters well at the end of any meal with a clean sponge or cloth. Scrub them now and again. Don't forget to do this. It is a humor-eating event to set something down on what

---

9 No, I don't know what that purpose would be, but I was asked for one just the other day by a woman I happen to be related to and so know that when she asks for a clean towel there is some very good reason it must be clean. And no, I didn't happen to have one and so had to humbly offer her a towel I was mostly sure had only been used to dry vegetables. Is pesticide and garden dirt any worse than laundry detergent? I was asking myself. Paper towels would solve the whole thing, I know you are thinking, except they don't solve anything if you think about it a little more broadly.

10 One third of you will wonder why I mention this so obvious thing, another third will not understand what I mean by washing the outside of things that are only used on the inside, and the third third will cross their fingers in joy and hope fervently that the second third reads the rest of this suggestion, undergoes an epiphany, and joins the swelling ranks of the first third. I am guessing that most of the third third lives with a member of the second third and has just about reached some kind of limit.

11 Along with what was once called "elbow grease", but I haven't heard it mentioned in a very long time. Maybe it was discontinued.

should be a clean counter and to have it soak up some spilled juice or be firmly cemented to said counter by an imperceptible bit of jam. If cooking is not taking place, if there is no food being eaten or prepared within a few feet of a flat surface, most people will assume the surface is clean.[12]

Clean your kitchen table and chairs and any other tables and chairs used for dining. Wipe the chairs off after a meal or at least before the next one. Scrub the table with a soapy sponge and look from table height to see if it is in fact clean.

Clean your kitchen floor with some frequency. Sweep it for no reason. Mop and scrub more than once a month if you use your kitchen more than once a month. Or pay someone else to do it. Have them clean your bathrooms as well.

Pay attention to the tops and bottoms of things. The tops of baseboards are often neglected. As are the tops of hanging lamps. Again, remember to address the bottoms of dishes and pots and pans.

Clean the stove, the front of the oven and the front and top of the refrigerator. Wipe down small appliances and any parts you can't wash in soapy water.

Clean out your refrigerator and clean the surfaces with soapy water and a sponge.

Use a soapy sponge to clean the front of cupboards. Not everyday, but more than once a year. Try wiping down wall surfaces. People will think you repainted or that you replaced the light bulbs.

CLEAN THE BATHROOM

Walls, floor, mirror, counter, sink, tub or shower, and all the surfaces of the toilet, inside and out, upside and down. Bathroom corners and the top side of any trim or molding can become particularly vile and should be kept under observation. Have sponges and a toilet brush and some kind of good scrubbing compound, like Ajax or Comet, always in the bathroom. Hire someone for the task if it is simply too difficult or complicated for you to do. When you cook for others it is almost certain that they

---

[12] A silly assumption, I understand, just as one shouldn't assume that the ground is free of chewed-up globs of gum and dog poop and shouldn't walk about naively admiring trees and people and architecture instead of examining the ground where they are walking. But that is still what most people do, foolish optimists that they are. Or perhaps just absent-minded, the lack of evidence that food is being prepared allowing them to forget that flat surfaces are often covered in gook that you don't want to place your sweater or portfolio in. On the other hand, I am guessing you would not be too delighted to find that your friends have come to know that your counters are unsafe and have adopted the habit of checking them and cleaning them off before lingering in your kitchen. I am shuddering and resisting mentioning all the other things I hope no one has to check.

will experience your bathroom. Alone in that little room, they have little to do besides notice it. Lighting is usually good, if unflattering. Surfaces light and revealing. That your guests are exposing vulnerable parts of themselves might make them more critical of uncleanliness. All this is not so unforgivable. Far less forgivable would be your refusal to have respect for the frailties, both physical and emotional, of others and to leave your bathroom, the only convenient place available for them to bare their valuable assets, slimy and scary. Accept that bathrooms accumulate the detritus of our bodies, as well as the usual dust and dirt which grace the rest of the home, plus an additional outfit of molds and mildews which flourish in the warm dampness, and that few of your guests will really enjoy the company of all that.

DUST

That is a verb meaning to remove dust from objects and furniture in your home with either a short feathery broom, which is very fun, or with a soft cloth, which is very little fun. It is best to actually pick things up off of tables, dust the surface, dust the objects, and then replace them or put them where they actually belong. The feather duster is good for when you don't feel like doing so much work, as you can forego picking things up in most cases. The feathers will also extract dust from all sorts of places you could never approach with a cloth even if you tried which you won't. Tops of hanging pictures and paintings and the lower rungs of tables and chairs are easy to forget but just as easy to dust if you do remember. Sculpture must be dusted as well, which is nice since it gives you a reason to caress and examine the work as it was probably meant to be caressed and examined in the first place.

VACUUM

Another verb, this one meaning to use a vacuum to clean rugs and carpets and sometimes hard floors you don't feel like sweeping. If your vacuum is not working, do not assume it is broken. It usually only needs a new bag inside, and maybe the filter needs to be changed. Once you get it open, it will be obvious what must be done. If you don't have a vacuum but you do have carpets, get one. If you don't have carpets, sweep frequently and mop now and again. Scrub any non-wood floors with a brush when you have extra energy or aggression to dissipate, or if you just want to do something that will make you feel better right away.

MISCELLANEOUS

Wash your sheets and towels and fix your bed.

The idea is to make your home a place suitable for courtship, in the form of food or otherwise. Cultivate a seductive dishevelment if you must, but be very careful. There is a point at which the best sorts of people simply say to themselves, "I don't believe I will get naked here."[13] A good time to do cleaning is before a party, however small it may be.[14] You benefit from seeing your home through the eyes of others at that moment. Do things first which cannot be done once people arrive. Like cleaning the bathroom, dusting and vacuuming, making your bed (if there is any reason at all someone might glance at it), etc. Leave yourself and the kitchen for last. You can clean up the kitchen in the company of your first guests, and if people arrive while you are in the shower, they will enjoy knowing for those few minutes that you are naked in the house somewhere.[15]

EPILOGUE

Terribly troubling this topic, cleaning. There are so many cultural standards and expectations. People are so quick to condemn. And then there is that whole thing about godliness.

It is possible for both a sterile room and a grimy building that couldn't be thoroughly cleaned even if you tried to be comfortable and inviting; possible for either to be miserable places and for the degree of cleanliness to be blamed. Whatever your standard, make it be comfortable for others.[16] At the end of the day, all you can do is what you believe to be right and hope that others will be tolerant and accepting if it doesn't happen to exactly

---

[13] I am well aware that all my admonitions are ridiculous in the face of love. Lovers have been known to collide in all sorts of unthinkable squalors. But one cannot always count on love when courting others. Wise, if you would have love remain, to keep the house clean. I know house cleaners who openly claim to have saved as many marriages as a therapist might boast and for far less money.

[14] You may even consider planning a party just to inspire you to clean.

[15] Of course, the thought of you naked should be a pleasant one. Whatever body you have, it should be one you love and which delights in itself, which in turn will make others enjoy it—or the thought of it if that is all they get—as well. Spend more time naked if this is not the case. Get used to yourself, change things you want to change and can without misery. Stretch and employ your muscles. Use good soaps and lotions and fluffy towels if you can. Dress to please your body and your soul for there is no reason not to. Stop doing things you know are wrong. Dance and sing. Make love and sex part of your life. Your naked self will be a vision of loveliness, in reality or imagination.

[16] I am reminded of Jewish friends who astound me by their adherence to a thousand laws concerning cooking and housekeeping, most of which seemed designed expressly to exclude me from their midst, while at the same time going to lengths to assure I am comfortable in their homes. Likewise, I try less successfully to make it possible for them to join the occasional dinner party at my home.

match their idea of correct. They can't possibly know what is right for you, nor you them, so they can only condemn you for not doing what they think is right for you, which is no condemnation at all.

On the other hand, if they are disappointed because you are not doing what you know is right, then they have a very good point.

COFFEE & TEA

In which the rites and rituals, habits and hankerings surrounding such stuffs are considered & explained.

COFFEE[1] AS COURTSHIP. An ancient rite. A provocative, sensual, stimulating thing cloaked in careful propriety. To offer coffee is to offer nothing else and yet to suggest the potential for anything. All possibility presented with flawless politesse. A gift of time and substance so small as to be freely forgettable, and yet a gift nonetheless which is received and may be returned in greater kind. To share coffee with someone is to share nothing at all, so common and unthreatening is it. Yet to share coffee with someone is to share with them what you share with most treasured

---

1 By which I do mean coffee or tea. Coffee and tea. Infusions. Anything to drink out of a cup or mug. But mostly I mean coffee.

intimates. Shared casually and seemingly without purpose or agenda a hundred times until the critical mass of intimacy and knowledge is built and becomes something of value. A blank canvas prepared for the application of colors and forms, for new stories and themes to be drawn upon it, a foundation almost breathless in anticipation.

Or not. Perhaps just coffee or tea for an hour in an afternoon or evening to put someone off their more weighty desires. "No. I won't share a meal with you, or a night or a week or a life for that matter," the cups seem to say in your stead. Not food. Not nourishment. Nothing. A little brewed poison to help keep your wits about you. Taken at a table too small to support anything of substance, but still big enough to separate one body from another it doesn't want to brush against.

There are a thousand thousand ways and places and times of day and year and life to share coffee or tea and each of them is fraught with its own associations, implications, intimations. You can ignore them, you can abuse them, you can try to control and manipulate them. You can resist or relax. You can enjoy what you are doing or you can rush past and pretend it didn't happen.

Assuming you take part in this worldly ritual at all. As stupid as smoking this pleasant addiction, although not as immediately and broadly antisocial as that other sport. Infinitely social in an infinitely intimate way. Coffee in bed, at sunlit tables in homes and in cafes, after the most exquisite dinners or lunches, for breakfast, on couches and in armchairs in a thousand upholstered and lamp-lit rooms, on curbs of busy streets, on a hundred thousand patios overlooking as many vistas of shocking or serene beauty. Coffee or tea. Infusions of flowers. The occasional lemon and honey in hot water. Or chilled things, iced this's and that's, sipped under umbrellas and on porches and in the shade of big, leafy trees.[2]

Coffee can be anywhere. It may be horrid or sublime. It can satisfy or torment. You will profit by knowing your neighborhood and where better than drinkable coffee can be found, even if you don't happen to partake of the stuff. You might have companions less familiar with the area than you who will depend upon you to lead them to a tolerable cup. Notice which spots serve beer and wine in addition to coffees and teas for it is not infrequent that a variety of moods are thirsty. There is no need to be evangelical about it, dragging uninterested parties across town for that perfect coffee. Better to know palatable places in

---

[2] It sounds good, but we still have an unfortunate, recent period of coffee history to shake off. Millions of corporate minions slurping down countless, tasteless cups of coffee percolated from beans grown and roasted and ground up who knows when, all consumed in an effort to appear alert and interested in a proscribed task. Spouses doing the same at a million dinettes in a million kitchens with no more conversation or literature or pursuit available to absorb the frenetic energy of a caffeine-sparked soul than housework or the daily drivel of a morning paper or the hour-old gossip of an equally thought-starved neighbor. Not everywhere. In other houses there were dark-haired lovers making perfect espresso for their best friend before making dinner for children, slipping into familiar laps and offering and receiving the day's reports of a strange new land while drinking together the nectar of an old world.

several neighborhoods.[3] You don't have to try them out yourself. Friends and relations who drink coffee will be delighted to tell you where to go. If there is a spot with a particularly fine atmosphere in addition to wonderful coffee in a neighborhood worth visiting, maybe there are a few who wouldn't mind voyaging across town after all. A field trip.

At home, of course, coffee and tea should always be very good. Not necessarily complex, not necessarily espresso. Use good to excellent coffees and teas and prepare them with some care. Sugar and milk or cream are necessary condiments. You don't want to make coffee only to discover your guest can't enjoy it without sugar or cream or whatever you are missing. Honey is good to have around as well, and there are ways to feign steamed milk for special occasions which are better than all right.[4]

UNFORTUNATELY FOR THE financially or spatially cramped, it is not possible to make coffee with stuff already lying about the house for other purposes. Unless you have a home chemistry lab. And even then. People hesitate to drink stuff made in vessels which might have recently held toxic solutions. You have little choice but to succumb to the approved drug culture of our time—and many times before ours—and buy some coffee paraphernalia. Otherwise you risk disappointing a law-abiding junky. A scenario bursting with ugly possibilities, the best of which is they suggest adjourning to a cafe for their fix. The worst of which involves caffeine withdrawal, and possibly such deep sorrow as will make you cry yourself.

But why would that happen? Coffee-making equipment includes some of the most lovely things you can put in your kitchen. Certainly it is no more troublesome to have around than anything else.[5] No reason not to have it, unless you have some reason you don't want people to hang around your home.

You have quite a bit of choice in the matter—from the simplest of sculptural, non-mechanical filter contraptions to machines with valves and clamps you plug in and wrestle

---

[3] The rub, however, is those times when the only good coffee in town is across town. People in cities like San Francisco and New York don't want to believe this could be true. But there you are, in Wichita for example, and you know you are damn lucky to have only to cross town and not state lines for a cup of joe. Or a cappuccino rather. Don't think about it, don't offer alternatives you know will be disappointing if chosen. Pile your followers in the car or on bikes and get across town. Of course, you might have had the foresight to learn how to make coffee yourself. Then you would have at least had a choice. But still. Sometimes people need to get out. If your town truly has no cafe of worth, instate an exchange program with a friend. Both of you acquire what you need to make good coffee, and then when necessary drag guests over to the other house for coffee. They get out, the coffee is worth the trip, and the change of venue might do you some good.

[4] See Cafe Au Lait.

[5] Unless you bought something overly elaborate or ugly or difficult that you do not like using and that sits lurking on the counter or in the cupboard. In which case, give it away and get something that works for you. There are plenty of options. Seek the advice of people who know more than you, but who also know you.

with to erratic effect until you prove yourself to be the alpha appliance. Fortunately, you are not required to impress anyone with elaborate mechanical devices nor by turning out exotic and perfectly executed coffee drinks in the fashion of the day. In fact, such stuff is likely to undermine the greater purpose of courtship. The promise of anything should always be less than what is delivered. Far better to make something delicious and surprising with somewhat simple devices. Serve your guests what will be wonderful for them rather than invoking your own fascination with some new technology or your newly discovered understanding of coffee chemistry. Use rather than wield any skills or knowledge or technology you acquire.

Here follows a short list of coffee-making devices. Follow the directions that come with any contraption, or defer to someone who knows how to make coffee. Learn slowly while you watch others do it:

MELITTA

A cone-shaped filter and filter-holding device and something appropriate for the coffee to be filtered into. Water is brought to a boil in a separate vessel and then poured in increments through the ground-up coffee which you will have measured into the paper or cloth or gold metal lining of the cone. Making coffee with a Melitta filter requires your attention and a small amount of dexterity.

Melitta makes a white porcelain coffee pot and filter cone which is very nice and in wide use. It can be found in coffee specialty stores, which abound. Melitta also makes a version that can be picked up in the grocery store which is a glass pot and a plastic filter holder. Both the porcelain and the glass pots can and will break if left on the stove at too high a heat or for too long in an effort to reheat brewed coffee. The inevitability of this can be postponed by trying to remember to use a round, flat metal device designed to diffuse the direct heat of a stove.

Other manufacturers and artisans make Melitta-style coffee pots, which have various charms and respond variously to direct heat.

Some pots filter coffee directly into a thermos, which is very nice as coffee stays warm without getting burnt on the stove.

MELIOR

The most ritualistic of the coffee makers and considered by many to be the best way to treat coffee. Only devotees of the bean will be very willing to pay the required attention to this elegant and lovely thing, usually of glass and with a complicated plunge mechanism. It makes a very particular sort of coffee as the ground coffee steeps in the water like tea until it is filtered out and pushed to the bottom of the pot with the plunger. This device requires a particular grind as well. Not so fine that it pushes through the screen. Not so coarse that it doesn't brew well.[6] It is extremely important to take apart and clean the several screens which comprise the base of the plunger between coffee episodes. Otherwise you will soon be making very vile coffee.

Spoon the appropriate amount of coffee into the glass beaker. Generally an inch, but you will have to read instructions, get counsel, and then adjust to your taste. Pour in with some care almost boiling water. It gets a little foamy at the top sometimes. Stir slowly a few times and add a little more water if needed. The brew shouldn't come closer than a half-inch from the top and maybe a whole inch is a good idea. Place the cover on the beaker with the plunger drawn all the way to the top.

Now take the brewing coffee plus cups and condiments to whatever spot has been chosen and let it finish brewing, as one might with tea, while you settle in. Very nice courtship technique. No scurrying back and forth to the kitchen counter. By the time you are comfortable the coffee is ready. Press down the plunger slowly and firmly and with care and attention. Pour your friend some coffee first. Make sure that cream and sugar and a spoon are at hand for them before you pour for yourself.

Do not pour more water into the old coffee grounds. If you need more coffee, rinse the pot and the screen and start over.

Don't buy an inexpensive Melior or one that involves any plastic parts. Some cannot be disassembled and you cannot clean them. Nothing to do then but move on and leave the rancid thing behind. To be safe, get the traditional Pyrex and stainless steel model with a black wood handle which is made in France by Melior. It must be as strong solid as you are. It must stand up on its own to the force of the plunger.

Also the most dangerous of all coffee makers. Don't play with them if you are not serious. It can hurt you and ruin your rugs.

ELECTRIC DRIP COFFEE MAKERS

The kind where you put water in one side of the machine, coffee and a filter in the filter part, turn it on, and the water filters through the coffee into a pot. Some of the more elaborate models drip the coffee directly into a thermos pot, which keeps the coffee warm and fresh for a good amount of time. The filter might be shaped like a

[6] I try but never completely grasp the details of proper grind. Consult your coffee store.

cone or like a bowl with a flat bottom. The coffee, strictly speaking, should be ground differently for these two different shapes. If the coffee you use is very good and you get the amounts right, you can make a very good cup of coffee which no one will scorn. And you can turn it into café au lait which is not so hard as you might think. Make false steamed milk by heating milk and then whirring it in a blender or with the minipimer immersion blender for a moment. A tall, heavy glass filled half with coffee and half with this "steamed" milk passes for kindness, and on occasion, love.

STOVE-TOP ESPRESSO POTS

The essence of Italian coffee. Forget about those electric miniature espresso makers.[7] Get a real one and build a room for it, or just get one of these sweet little things. So unassuming. So solid and real. Water in the lower vessel. Strongest Italian fine ground espresso in the small, sieved cup which lives between the upper and lower portions of this transcendent piece of engineering. The two halves fasten together with precision and strength to withstand the steam as it is forced upward through the coffee, re-condensing as deepest brown nectar in the upper vessel, from which it is best poured into intricate and fragile porcelain or hand-built ceramic demi-tasses and served with sugar and tiny spoons suited to the purpose. Not silly, not pretentious. A very small amount of this potion is all one person should have in one evening. One tiny cup, or perhaps two, neither filled to the top, all together not enough to fill even a modest coffee cup. More than enough to fill you.

STOVE-TOP STEAMERS

Not for making coffee but rather for making the steamed milk so popular with coffee. A stainless steel vessel with a top which screws on strongly and tightly and which has a long spout and a valve. You fill the container two-thirds full, screw on the top firmly, and put it on a hottest stove. When the steam has built up sufficient pressure in the container, you open the valve and steam shoots dangerously from the long spout, which can then be used to steam milk or water or cider or whatever you like. Get someone who knows how to do this to show you how and to explain the intricate details of doing it well. Then share café au laits or cappuccinos or lattés or hot choco-late or steamed cider or steamed milk and any of a myriad of liqueurs in the company of friends.

---

[7] I am harsh and mistaken. It turns out to be perfectly possible to make decent espresso drinks with one of these contraptions. That's the thing about writing. You set a thought down one day and the next afternoon someone offers you a coffee and you think, Oh dear, do I have to go back and rewrite the whole chapter? The whole book? When does it end? Never, of course, if I continue to experience the world and learn new things. So this offering is incomplete, already inaccurate. But it is at least offered. Please move past it as I will.

ABOUT THE COFFEE you keep in your home. First of all, whatever it is it should be kept in the freezer or in an airtight container, and it should not be kept for a very long time. Over time, it will turn stale. Coffee should not come in a can, unless the can itself was packed in Italy. It might be bought as whole beans or you might have the purveyor grind it up for you. You must tell them what sort of coffee-making device you use. Grinding machines in grocery stores let you set the grind yourself as well. Ask the employees at your local coffee roasting store how much coffee you should use for how many cups of coffee. If you are the measuring sort, you can buy little scoops which will help you measure out the coffee correctly.[8]

If you want to grind your coffee at home, acquire a grinder, electric or otherwise, and take your chances at grinding coffee to the correct grind. In spite of the amount of time spent on the subject, it really doesn't seem to matter much as long as it is sufficiently ground. It matters much more that your coffee be of excellent quality to begin with, that it be fresh, and that you use an appropriate amount. Too much rather than too little, although preferably neither. Worry most about grinding the coffee well enough as it is almost impossible to grind coffee too finely with a home grinder.

It is also important when you are planning to serve coffee to have cream and sugar and honey on hand. Unfortunately for the good host who would try to make their guests happy, the health trends of the past decades have made it almost impossible to second-guess what someone will like in their coffee. Maybe cream, maybe half & half, maybe whole milk, low-

---

[8] You shouldn't be very surprised to discover that there is no advice for you here on that count. Honestly now, even if I did tell you how much coffee you should use for how many cups of water, would you believe me?

fat or non-fat. Maybe they prefer a non-dairy creamer.[9] No way to prepare for every eventuality. You might be able to discern what someone prefers from the way they fix their coffee in cafes and restaurants, and you might get it right. Don't bet on it, but don't worry about it. You will in any case learn very quickly what it is they like and you can get it right the next time. Ask them what they like before you start making coffee as some people won't even want to drink coffee if there is no cream or sugar available. They will feel badly that you went to the trouble and will try to be polite, but you won't be fooled.

TEAPOTS EXIST IN GREAT variety. Find one you like and like to use. If you don't like and don't like to use the teapot, your good purpose will be undermined by your own reluctance to use your pot.

In addition to a teapot and means to boil water, you might have either a tea ball or a tea strainer. You don't need either if you intend to only ever serve tea which comes in little tea bags. But since someone might bring you some wonderful and exotic tea which is not packaged for your convenience, you might like to have on hand one of these little devices. The tea-ball is a sieve in the form of a little hollow steel ball which is hinged to open in half and which is attached to a little chain with some sort of hook or other device at the end to keep the chain from falling into the teapot. It is unwieldy to use at first, but there are those who prefer it. You fill the ball with tea, fasten it shut, place it in the teapot, fill the tea pot with boiling water, and then let a few minutes pass. Tea will take less time to brew than other herbs will, and flower infusions take still more time than that. The timing depends as well on the tastes of the tea drinker. When the brew is to someone's liking, take the tea-ball from the teapot, put a towel or a cozy or something around the teapot to keep the heat in, grab the appropriate number of cups, the required condiments, which might include milk, sugar, honey and lemon, and cookies, and go linger somewhere comfortable.[10]

Many, for example most English people, prefer to use a tea strainer with a handle which rests on top of the cup you are to drink from. All you do is spoon tea into the teapot, pour boiling water into the pot, and wait a minute or two or whatever for the tea to brew. Then pour the brewed tea through the strainer into the cup. In England, those who take milk with their tea, which is almost everyone, put the milk into the cup first, thereby eliminating the possibility of someone pouring the cup too full to add the preferred amount of milk. Very clever. It does however depend upon the tea drinker knowing how much milk they want. The only problem with the tea strainer approach to making tea is the tea stays soaking in

---

[9] In which case you shouldn't be making them anything at all. Just send them down to the diner.

[10] This is an excellent occasion to have a tray. A tea tray, as it were. If you have a nice-sized chopping board that is not too heavy, you might be able to summon it to service.

the pot and the water that is left gets very rowdy. You can always add more water to the pot, but eventually you end up with tannin brew which is bitter. Rinse out the pot and start again when it comes to this, although preferably somewhat beforehand.

An interim solution, which falls between the strainer and the tea-ball and which is in some vogue, is the teapot which has a strainer as part of the design. In this case, there is some straining device that lives below the lid of the teapot. You place an appropriate amount of tea in this strainer container, replace the strainer in the teapot, pour the boiling water through the tea into the vessel, and replace the lid of the teapot. When the tea is steeped to someone's liking, you remove the whole strainer and the tea within it. Since most of these strainers are not so fine a mesh as the cheap little cup strainers used by law students in London, there will be more delinquent tea leaves wandering about in cups. What of it. You can pretend to know how to read them later.

Then of course you can just use tea-bags. Not very stylish, but not so bad. Treat them like the tea-ball, taking them out when the tea is brewed sufficiently. If you leave them in and add water too many times, you end up with the bitter stuff, the tannin from the leaves. You will know when it happens. If you are drinking tea you can taste the change, and if you are not drinking you will notice your companion stop.

If you are planning to only use tea-bags, and have sealed the vow by not having the means to brew loose tea at all, you must be very careful when you purchase tea. Nothing easier than accidentally coming home with loose tea. Nothing more certain than that the next time someone wants tea, that is the tea they will choose. And you will find yourself messing around ever so awkwardly with a full-sized colander over a tiny little cup. Not that this couldn't be an excellent occasion to display your sense of humor.

Yes of course you can make tea in individual cups or mugs, and should when someone wants a quick cup, should individuals have irreconcilable preferences for tea, or if, like me, you have never satisfactorily resolved the teapot issue. The important thing is to offer tea or coffee or something to anyone who would like some, and to all others as a gesture of hospitality and perhaps affection.[11]

---

[11] The social script varies from country to country, from town to town, and even from home to home. Claudia recounts the traditions of her native Chile where at least three offerings of food or drink must be refused before, finally, in response to a most humble offer of water, the guest may at last accept the earlier offered glass of wine or plate of food. It would be as impolite to not eventually accept something, even if it is only the glass of water, as it would be to accept the first thing offered. "Insincere!" some more blunt persons cry. I instead marvel at a custom which allows guests to assure their host that they have come for the pleasure of company and conversation without risk of going hungry or thirsty. People who have the habit of continually offering food and drink are often soundly mocked. Fine. Better that than risk not offering enough to a guest whose customs prohibit them from taking the first thing offered or asking for anything that has not been offered. Complicated and convoluted, in the opinion of forthright gringos who pride themselves on always saying what they think, or at least taking what they want. An elegant and direct means of communicating what is otherwise unutterable, in mine.

TEAS TO HAVE ON hand include: English Breakfast tea, or some utterly innocuous tea.[12] Earl Grey, which is more aromatic and preferred by many. Inexplicably, men are often fond of the smoky, perfumed Lapsong tea. One or two herbal teas or flower infusions are handy for those who do not like caffeine or do not like it late at night. Chamomile or some chamomile blend. Something infused with the flavor of some fruit, perhaps. Apples, oranges, berries. Maybe a decaffeinated black tea. If you do not drink tea, there is no reason to have an elaborate selection. Tea, like anything, can go stale. Discover what your companions like by noticing what they tend to order,[13] or just ask them what they usually drink and keep that on hand.

---

[12] Mind you, a good brand of English Breakfast is the vast superior of most innocuous teas.

[13] Do not suppose that because they ordered something once that they prefer it. They may have been experimenting in a tea house with a particularly broad and imaginative selection and have found that they don't like oolong tea at all. You must observe people for longer than a moment to learn anything of note.

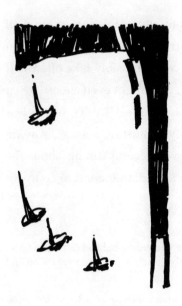

TABLE MANNERS

In which the idea of manners is questioned, contorted, disturbed and distilled, but remains intact.

IT IS NOT MY INTENTION that you should execute a meal meant to advance a campaign of courtship just to screw it all up the moment you sit down to eat. If you have wonderful table manners, and wonderful manners universally, you will also be able to take much better advantage of courtship opportunities when others are slaving away in the kitchen. Good food is good food, and while there is a certain amount of benefit to having been the one who cooked, there is plenty as well in being a good co-guest.

Why you? Because it has to be someone. Manners of any kind are all about being considerate of others and making social interaction as smooth and effortless as possible so you can attend to other things. The fewer manners others possess and display, the more important it is that you be well-mannered. Otherwise you will end up in a downward spiral towards the compost heap of cultural conversation.

Besides, why not you? It isn't terribly hard to be well-mannered and it in no way precludes being imaginative and doing pretty much exactly what you want to do. Emily Post and others might think there are a bunch of rules to memorize and follow,[1] but there is only one: Do the right thing on the right occasion. The "right thing" being that which is at once most considerate of others and not inconsiderate of yourself.[2]

You choose. Either you can memorize a bunch of rules and act according to the letter of the law,[3] or you can learn and comprehend what is always a very small number of laws, and then derive all decisions and action from that foundation. Walk and invariably stumble on the concrete, or revel in the freedom of the abstract.[4]

Back at the dinner table you will be able to listen to debates about this sort of thing all you want, happily eating your salad with any fork which strikes your fancy because you will be eating in such a way that none of your companions could possibly take offense. If your manners are deeply rooted in the rich soil of your soul, you might even choose to eat your salad with your fingers and no one would think less of you for it. Conversely, a less good you might use the right fork but in such a scandalously disgusting manner, waving the it about, chewing loudly and with your mouth open while complaining about the amount of dressing on the lettuce, that no one will want you for a dinner guest or companion ever again.

---

[1] I doubt it though. I'll bet they are all very aware of how simple it is to be well-mannered and just made up all those rules to fill books and to give people who are too lazy to digest the big issues something to chew on and harp about.

[2] People are not impressed nor honored by the consideration of one who is posing as a lower life form. "Obsequious", an ugly name for an ugly thing, is the word given to those who pander to others while appearing to denigrate themselves.

[3] The law itself works in this convoluted way, and not surprisingly so since the principles of fairness and protection are directly contrary to the aims of most people who solicit benefit from them. Turns out you can't derive most of our laws from the Constitution, let alone from any higher principles.

[4] For example, when studying physics or geometry or calculus you might work very hard to memorize a page of formulas and a few applications. More fruitful would be to study and understand the ideas behind the particular science or art. Then it won't matter what the particular application is. You will be able to derive from basic principles the appropriate formulas and see clearly how to apply them. Or similarly, in the realm of religion there are those who search their chosen document for rules and regulations to guide the daily form of their life, to tell them how to behave in each and every given situation; meanwhile, others digest a teaching or two from the philosopher of choice and base their actions on those principles. However, unlike in the more limited and incomplete arenas of science or math, neither approach to spirituality allows two people to come up with the same pattern of behavior. Which is why it is so very good to have tolerance be a daily directive as well as one of the founding principles of any life-guiding philosophy. Mathematicians and physicists, in contrast, are not well-served by striving toward tolerance of conflicting beliefs. Many religions fancy themselves positively scientific and fall into this same, limiting trap.

TABLE MANNERS CAN be summed up as follows: Be attentive to and considerate of others. Add to that general principles of courtesy.

Which is to say, your hand does not have to remain in your lap throughout the meal, but neither should it flop about in the lap of your neighbor. Elbows might be adorable on the table, but they might just as easily be as awful as your mother said they were if they in any way obstruct another from enjoying their meal. And I'd wager that no one outside of the catering profession really knows whether one is served from the left or the right. One might guess you are served from the left because it is easier for a right-handed person to serve themselves from that side.[5] But it would then be the height of courtesy and consideration, according to me, to serve your left-handed guests from the right. People more concerned with the display of propriety than with its purpose would of course vehemently disagree.

You see, it is at once so endlessly complex and unspeakably simple. How could I possibly list the details by which one behaves well at table? How could I list the ways in which one might behave inconsiderately and with what one might call, "Bad Manners?" The workings of the incomprehensibly vast physical universe can be derived from the simple equation, $E=mc^2$. How much more vast this non-corporeal universe of perception? Encompassing all, how much more simple the defining law? Don't make me tell you which fork to use. In the scheme of things what does it matter? It is but a delusion, a desired illusion that there is any difference at all between forks, or even between you and me. Use whatever you like, but use it in such a way that your companions do not notice and are not in anyway disturbed by this necessity of mortal existence. Eat and enjoy the food and all that surrounds it, and then be done with it. Other things await your attention.

AND YET...

Aren't there just a few specific elements of tableside behavior that might well be discussed? Aren't there a small number of places where one can really mess up, and in the spirit of learning, would it not perhaps be a good idea to explore them? We could see how things work in the specific, see how they follow from the general, and therefore be better at the whole process when sent out on our own with those vague and elusive axioms of Manner.

For your benefit, I asked around to find out what might be some of the big pot holes you could fall into. This is what emerged:

---

[5] This formula might also be derived from the arbitrary notion of our culture that "forward" is from left to right. I don't actually know what the rule is, and to prove to you how little I care, I am not going to bother finding out for you.

DON'T CHEW WITH your mouth open. No one will tell you you do this, and it will ruin your chances for any success in any courtship, romantic or not. A corollary: Don't make a bunch of noise when you are eating. Not slurping, not crunching, not chewing loudly. Even physiological things like a jaw that cracks when you chew will not be forgiven. Get it fixed, or apologize to your dining companion so they do not sit there wondering if it will stop or if they should say something. In a similar vein, try not to have food in your teeth nor on your face for any length of time. Use your napkin frequently and visit the washroom when you are done eating if you are not comfortable asking your companion for an inspection.

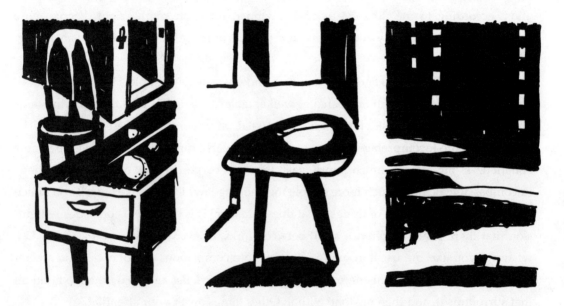

DON'T SCRATCH YOURSELF at the table. Or in public for that matter. It is immaterial what you think. Others find it repulsive, will reject you out of hand, and there is nothing you can say to dispute them.[6]

IF YOU ARE ASKED to serve yourself, do not take more than one-half X of any particular dish, where X is the number of people eating.[7] Or, if you have adopted the

---

6 I'm sorry if this does not correspond to your political beliefs or to your view of the world. In case you forgot, we are discussing Courtship, which is as cruel and unforgiving an environment you are likely to encounter.

7 This is an extremely conservative estimate which would have you taking no more than one-tenth when there are five people eating. Surely you can be more liberal to yourself. Although taking one-fifth sounds appropriate, it is not. It does not leave room to flatter your host by asking for more. It assumes you are at least as hungry as everyone at the table. It eliminates the possibility of extra food for a late or surprise arrival. And it tells everyone you are always ready to help yourself to what you think is your share. In the case of dishes constructed such that you must take your full portion or none at all (for example five chicken kievs or five fish in parchment) Go ahead. The host is in complete control of the situation.

clever device of general awareness, sensitivity to others and social consideration, take as much as you think is appropriate. In any case, do not be the subject of conversation the next day when the host recounts to a rapt audience how they managed to save the evening after one guest helped themselves to almost half of the main entree.[8]

DON'T INTERRUPT. Not exactly a table manner, per se, but since it is so often at a table that one finds oneself in conversation, it is worth mentioning. Interrupting people gives them the impression you either are not listening to them or are uninterested in what they have to say. Neither impression will get you very far into their hearts.[9]

USE YOUR NAPKIN. For all sorts of things. Wiping your mouth is one thing to do with it. If you have the unfortunate occasion to remove food from your mouth, use your napkin.[10] If you are in a restaurant, ask for a new napkin. If you are in a private home and cannot discreetly ask for a new napkin, or just don't want to bother the host with your little issue, excuse yourself, taking the napkin with you, do what you have to do, and come back to the table with or without a napkin. Or lay low. Mind, we are not talking about fish bones and fruit pits and other things one expects to have to remove from one's mouth and which are expected to show up on the plate in some discreet manner.

DO NOT REACH OVER others or across the table. Ask for things to be passed to you and then say thank you to whomever hands the desired dish to you.[11]

---

[8] I am kind. This sort of brutish behavior will be the topic for conversation at parties—to which you will naturally not be invited—for years to come.

[9] Interruption and how it is not a simple matter of stepping into conversation while another is speaking is discussed at length in Deborah Tannen's book, *You Just Don't Understand*. In short, she outlines how people have various conversational styles and will recognize different things as interruptive. My synopsis: If your companions seem to become more and more quiet over the course of the evening, if they make increasingly feeble efforts to offer or join conversation, you are probably interrupting them. Figure out how to stop.

[10] A controversial point for some reason. Please side with me and do not, as others have suggested, take the morsel out of your mouth with your fork and try to return it to your plate. First of all, the whole table will be captivated by the suspense of watching you get it to the plate without dropping it. And then, who wants to look at for the rest of the meal?

[11] This one is so easy and so obvious I find it remarkable I think to mention it. But you know why I do and it makes me sad. What is with these people? Do they not notice you are sitting right there and that with so little effort it is an insult not to request it, you could pass them the snow peas? Are they so loathe to speak to you that they would prefer to dip their shirt sleeve in several sauces rather than ask you to pass them the potatoes? Do they not understand that to refuse to ask a small favor of someone is the height of inconsideration? Certainly they pay for their boorishness instantly if unbeknownst to themselves, losing in a breath a myriad of opportunities for courtship. Nestled in every request for someone to pass the tamarind sauce are valuable opportunities for changing conversations, for bringing others into camaraderie, and for the most sublime and fleeting flirtations. Objects change hands, eyes meet and look away and meet again. Only a fool would sight what

DON'T SALT YOUR food before you have tasted it. Besides being an insult to the cook, you show yourself to be the sort of person who prejudges. Very bad courtship strategy. Rumor has it there are corporations who use this as evidence of the sort of unthinking person they are loathe to hire.

IF YOU ARE THE COOK, be sure to have an opportunity to display your excellent table manners. Which means do not serve dinners so labor intensive you never sit down to eat with your guests. Join your guests for more than five minutes and feign you are relaxed and in sufficient control of the meal to enjoy it.

IF YOU ARE THE COOK, do not fish for compliments. Beyond, "Is everything all right," you should not mention the food at all.[12]

IN THE UNITED STATES and its provinces, take corporal expressions outside.

HELP CLEAR THE TABLE, unless there are three people who have beat you to it.[13] In which case you lose and have to offer to do the dishes. In either case it is part of the continuous exchange of gifts between friends. Certainly there are occasions when you can sit back and receive at length. Those are wonderful moments to have earned. I have done it once or twice. But in general your eye should be out for the occasion to give in return. The trick is to not simply parrot someone else's gift. If there are already enough people clearing the table, you are not giving anything by helping. Find another way to be useful or do nothing at all for the moment. I do not know why this is such a difficult thing. There is almost always plenty to do, and if not, there will be something that needs to be done shortly. No shortage of places to contribute. Leap into the fray right after you ask yourself, "Will this be of real assistance?"

A MEAL

You arrive at the table or whatever is serving as a table. If there are name tags, you should sit at your designated place setting. In general, there aren't. Please sit down anyway, serving yourself from a buffet if that is the style of the meal. Jump right in and be the first to go

---

they want and reach directly for it, choosing instant gratification over intercourse and its infinite potential. For that they might have stayed home.

12 Unless, when you taste it it is horrible. Then you should say, " Oh dear, this isn't very good at all." If you can fix it, good. If you can't, offer something else. Anything will do. It's good to have something on hand if you are trying a new recipe.

13 Unless you are a man and the three people are all women. Then you should get up and help just to make a point. What point, I'm not sure exactly. Or take care that you succeed in doing the dishes.

through if the rest of the party is reluctant. Someone has to and it might as well be you. Alternatively, if the rest of the party is ravenously approaching the buffet, wait your turn, allowing others to go ahead of you. Serve yourself discreetly and do not make anything but positive comments about the food. Sitting down, put your napkin on your lap. Make sure you have not taken someone else's seat. Observe who is sitting near you and note whether or not they are comfortable. If there is something you can do to help someone, do. Pour wine and water for others and then for yourself if no one else is taking the initiative. Say thank you if they have. When food is in front of you, whether placed there by you or by someone else, notice it. I don't care whether you like it or not.[14] Some small expression of appreciation at this point, even if it is under your breath, is in very good taste and will be heard or felt. No expression of discontent or disappointment, regardless of the reason, is in order. If something is wrong, fix it yourself, or address your host with discretion.[15]

Eat. Use your utensils and your fingers gracefully. Use your napkin regularly. Listen to conversation. Follow the rules of conversation as taught to you by your mother: If you don't have anything nice to say, don't say anything at all. Don't interrupt. Don't talk with your mouth full. Don't talk about work or money.[16] That should get you pretty far. Once your host is seated, if they need something get it for them. Especially if you are courting the host. The smallest gesture can count disproportionately at this point when a cook might feel misused and disoriented, or perhaps just spent. Wait until everyone has finished their meal, and then be the first or second person to start clearing the table.[17] Return to the table and continue enjoying your wine or whatever. Let the host continue doing what they need to do. If you have been effortlessly helpful, the host will feel comfortable asking you to do something if need be. Let others come to you. People are not so unlike animals, if they are unlike them at all. Be or don't be the last person to leave. It depends upon so many things. When you do leave, thank your host sincerely for a wonderful evening or whatever it was. The next day, send a short note saying the same thing in ink. Or if you are something like friends with the person who entertained you, call and tell them what a fabulous time you had. An underrated and frequently neglected bit of mannered behavior, so very important as the next day can be anticlimactic for whomever threw the party. Note as well that it gives you a chance to get any good gossip you might have missed the night before.

---

14 No one cares at all what you think. The subject is Table Manners, not Art.

15 Does everyone know what discretion is? It is that thing which restrains you from calling across the table to your partner that they should meet you in the bathroom for a quick fuck in about five minutes when a note or a glance would do. It is something a little to the side of modesty, but not utterly unrelated.

16 Sex, Religion, and Politics, on the other hand, are fine topics. Try Art or Gardening, Education or the Reality of Childcare in the USA for a change of pace. Unless, of course, any of these topics qualify as Work for you.

17 Don't be the first person unless you are very confident of your sense of timing.

By the way, all this applies to the most intimate dinner for two as well as to the most formal dinner for fifty or the most raucous festival for hundreds. Manners, since they all derive from the same principle of consideration for others and for self, do not change from place to place. Your demeanor might, the specific language you employ or the tone of voice might, but the manners themselves do not change. You should be as considerate of your oldest love as you are of your newest and most honored acquaintance.

We are not, of course. But we should be.

Not Cooking as Courtship

In which hideous crimes are defended, justified and even encouraged.

surprisingly, there are a number of occasions when to further a courtship you might choose to cook very badly or refuse to cook at all.[1]

---

1 This is not about simply not cooking tonight. This is not about how to order out effectively, nor how to make reservations in fine restaurants. Neither is this about inadvertently cooking badly when you are sincerely trying to cook. That of course is tremendously charming and counts wholly as Cooking as Courtship. This chapter is about not cooking and cooking badly, intentionally and to some purpose, though never maliciously. No, it is not a pretty subject, and everyone keeps asking why this chapter can't be sexier. It can't be because the only time I can think of that anyone would intentionally not cook or cook badly is when there is a problem; the possibility of being taken for granted, the heavy burden of former abuses, sour humor, the presence of sadly twisted quirks of a personal nature, unhappiness, imbalance, etc. In that light, you will be thrilled to find it not nearly so depressing a chapter as it could be.

Perhaps you don't much like to cook and know that the only way you will ever want to cook is if you are never required to.[2] This is no reason to not be able to cook, but it is certainly easier to plead that you want to bring the wine yet again if everyone believes that they too prefer for you to bring the wine. Then once in a bluish moon, you can cook something for your friends, offer it to them in silent thanks and, taking Camille as your model, appear to have been half-devastated by your effort.

Or perhaps you cook poorly because you are unhappy, feel cooking is expected of you and think that if you cook very badly someone else might take over the task. Unlikely. More likely they will continue to take bare sustenance from your table while proclaiming loudly to all that you are a terrible cook. This might be a good time to switch your tactic from Cooking Badly to Not Cooking.

In stark contrast to these whiny, selfish reasons, you might instead cook badly in order to heighten the dramatic impact when you do eventually cook something very delicious. Barely evil and reasonably manipulative. Make others believe you cannot cook simply by not cooking very often, and then only for people who are unlikely to rave about it to others, who appreciate it quietly and who respect your right to toy with others on this point. Or cook very badly once or twice for a few particularly loud people, preferably some of those insufferable amateur cooks. They never forget and will tease you ad nauseam in front of everyone important about your poor culinary skills. Don't defend yourself but rather look a little sheepish as though you have been revealed in a forgivable shortcoming. There is no need to be a bad cook. No reason to cut off your options. No reason to guard your inability to cook as you might your integrity when cooking skills, unlike a lack of integrity, can be so easily hidden from public view.[3]

However you do it, hold off revealing your cooking skills until the moment is ripe. Wait until the one whose attention you seek has long relinquished any hope of being fed by you, has accepted that you are intoxicating and irresistible for other reasons and has become lazy and entrenched in their judgment of your qualities. Wait patiently until they are confident that you have no conversation with anything in the kitchen.[4] Allow a world to come into being which does not include you making any meals. It will take more than six days.[5] Then, when your opponent, your target, your mouse, your love, your soul is absolutely

---

[2] Lots of things could be described this way.

[3] I sadly point out that a lack of integrity might very well profit you in some situations, as will being able to cook, while an actual dearth of cooking skills will never benefit anyone.

[4] Once again, no need to be belligerent about it, loudly refusing to cook, nor making political issue of it.

[5] A brilliant woman reports it takes a year after the actual date of commitment. "Do not do anything, and I mean absolutely nothing, in the first year of marriage you do not intend to do for the rest of your life." That is her advice to young people about to be wed, for better or for worse.

sure of you and sure they adore you and have forgotten entirely that you do not cook or at least not very well; when they have taken to complimenting your offerings of toast and sliced fruit, admiring your ability to find the best restaurants and your skill at ordering from menus, this is exactly the moment to spontaneously and effortlessly cook something which feeds the soul with scent alone before it even begins to seduce and satiate first the mouth, then the stomach and, finally, the self itself. Nothing worthy of the Cordon Bleu, nor even Tante Marie's, but magnificent nonetheless. The equivalent of a bias-cut and barely there silk velvet dress that falls to the floor.[6] No pleats, no ruffles, no buttons or zippers, no interesting seaming techniques. And no elaborate undergarments beneath. None at all. Just what's required, but manifest as the surreal. The dramatic impact of an at once casual and opulent offering. The effect on the unsuspecting victim can be very rewarding. "You can cook!" their eyes and perhaps their lips as well exclaim. You demure as though you had not noticed. The very same quality discovered earlier on might have been taken for granted as something you do as a matter of course, valueless, standard and barely considered. Now it is a jewel in the crown.

Who ever thinks to continue courtship so far past courtship's apparent end?

By the way, you are not done. You risk falling into the trap of becoming the default cook in a household or friendship now that your talents have been exposed. Unless cooking is like breathing to you—in which case it is very surprising to find you here—do not succumb. Do not allow cooking to become On Request, much less De Rigeur.[7] No need to get uppity about it. Simply don't rise to the occasion. Return to your former self. Allow them to sink, however ungently, back into that unknowing bliss, forgetting all, thinking perhaps that the meal was but a dream. Then, cook again. Confused, distracted, unable to fathom this angel of erratic mercy, and yours to do with as you will.

NATURALLY, AND I hardly need to mention it since it generally happens on its own, you should absolutely cook badly or not at all as a means of courtship in the same way you should stand and fight for topics of strategic, if seemingly tiny importance: To make a point, and to show what kind of response the beloved can expect when they behave

---

6 Russell howls, "Anachronistic!" Bias cut silk. The sort of thing Jean Harlow wore while slinking through a dozen movies. It is best in silk, although it is done in almost every fabric. The garment is cut so that individual threads in the cloth run diagonally across the body rather than vertically and horizontally. The fabric drapes and slithers over curves. A technique explored and nearly perfected by a Frenchwoman named Vionnet, and later used by just about everyone. Grasp opposing corners of your handkerchief or square scarf and pull gently to see the flexibility available from the bias. Is the metaphor beginning to make sense, or shall I retire to academia?

7 Again, unless that is the arrangement for which you have contracted. Only you know for sure.

horridly. No good pretending to be tolerant and indeed to tolerate those things which you know will not fly over the long haul.[8]

It is not so hardened a thing to do. Just because people have to eat does not mean the food must come from your hands. Cook hideously the moment anyone behaves badly toward you in the context of cooking, or in any context at all. They cannot believe that they can misuse you and still expect you to feed them, even if you had intended to moments earlier. Training. That's what it is, and it is not unlike what you do with a puppy or a child. It is no good to discuss things with them. They must see the repercussions of their actions. Throwing tantrums and positing ultimatums won't work. People and dogs, it would seem, change their behavior only when they believe such a change will be nicer for them in the end. Sometimes you teach this by showing them that life is nicer or less nice not in the end but right away.

Cook inedible meals, or simply nothing at all for persons who are monstrous. And don't pout.

Of course if they are very very bad, and you no doubt have your own image of what this is, not only should you not-cook, but you should not be there at all.[9]

WHY WOULD YOU not cook at all as a means of courtship? Not cook, even when it is common knowledge that you know how to cook and how to cook well?

For the very same reason you might not polish someone else's shoes or clean their room for them even though you are perfectly capable of doing such things.

There are those people who believe cooking is a menial chore. Who find it extremely difficult for reasons which are not entirely their fault to have respect for anyone who spends time cooking. These people are difficult because they are often quite attractive in a few very straightforward ways. But there is something odd about them. They do not recognize communication in this form. They are instead impressed by someone who is too busy to cook or who prefers to mindlessly and without appreciation for the art consumed spend a great deal of money in restaurants. I don't understand them myself, but I do know you must not cook for them if you are determined to court them. At least not at first. You can

---

[8] This is the easiest of all things to execute, as it is practically impossible to cook well when one has been insulted.

[9] Naturally, we are talking about adults. Children and puppies you cannot leave, but you can banish them briefly, if only to remove them from your anger. How does one make the point that another's behavior is intolerable without making any universal judgments nor accusations? I have come to believe all one can do is not-tolerate, as opposed to being intolerant. Not-tolerate and be clear about what you are not tolerating. That another behaves in a revolting fashion, out of fear or one of its many manifestations, does not give you the right to behave badly in return. This is an extremely large topic and one I am even less qualified to discuss than the one at hand.

still make headway into their hearts via food by arranging for meals that are and appear to be effortless, preferably ordered from some outside source, but which you know to be the stuff that feeds the spirit and soothes the mind at the same time it fills the belly. They will claim and exclaim often and in your company that they care nothing for food, that they would as soon have a bowl of cereal as a marvelous meal. But after you have fed them you will notice they have been fed. Enjoy them, revel in their dumb contentedness. Don't mention it to them or they will scrape it off themselves just to make a point.

It is tempting to ask, If you have to go so far around the block in order to feed someone so that they are fed, why would you be courting them? Good question. Sometimes people need to be drawn toward something slowly and unbeknownst to themselves. They may not be evil people, but rather people who have forgotten the world was not created for them to exploit. Enjoying the world in such a benign way as eating well seems wrong to them. But that does not mean they cannot be fed and warmed and that perhaps one day they will calm down and stop breaking things. Meanwhile, do not cook for them because they will then be forced to look down upon you as one of those earthbound creatures it is their burden and birthright to exploit.

You also want to be sure to not cook in the event that you are feeling put upon by cooking. Never mind how your other may perceive the situation. For yourself it is beyond important to not do things which make you feel misused or which you resent doing, whether or not anyone actually requested you do it. This is true in every room of the house and at all the off-site locations as well. Surest seeds of strong, weed-like bitterness that is only uprooted traumatically. Don't plant them. Be aware of what you are not thrilled to do, be supremely honest with yourself about why you are doing anything you don't really want to be doing, and unless there is someone else whose well-being in actuality depends upon your doing the hateful thing,[10] stop it. Stop stop stop. No one will notice, unless they notice your mood has improved. Whether or not anyone notices, courtship will be served. Get out or stay out of the kitchen if it makes you unpleasant to be there. You will cook badly if you are unhappy or resentful so no one will be sorry to see you stop. Oh, they

---

10 It is hard to come up with an example of this, it is so rare. Certainly it is even more rare for it to occur regularly and in the same fashion. Generally it is delusion on your part that their well-being is at stake since healthy people do not require sacrifice from others. But perhaps your brother is invalid and someone needs to feed him. You might have do it, or if finances allow you can hire someone to do it, but there is no guarantee you won't resent writing a check as much as roasting potatoes. Best in these cases to find a way to feed him which you do not resent. Be creative, be generous, delve into Confucian thought to help you through this trial of filial piety. Mostly, if you must do something which is that little bit too difficult for you to do graciously, circle yourself with friends who support you in your endeavor, who can help you achieve, temporarily, a degree of grace unnatural to you. To be sure, this situation doesn't arise all that often and not for all that long unless you are particularly selfish, in which case it happens every day and in the same ways.

might complain at first as people will, initially annoyed at having to figure out a new solution to feeding themselves besides taking advantage of your sense of duty. But that temper will pass.

It is not impossible that one day you might wander back into the kitchen and cook something spontaneously for others or for yourself, the shrouds of oppression having fallen from the kitchen and again it is a playground, a sanctuary, a theater, even perhaps one of those holy places where affection and regard and those deep and nameless emotions take form and are expressed. Not-cooking having run its course.

Then, and only then, can you re-consider using cooking as a means of courtship. A language returned to you, a restored means of communication. How nice for you. Many people never regain this tongue once it has been torn from them through abuse or misuse.

NOT COOKING MIGHT be a very advanced and enlightened means of courtship. One which others might not always understand, thinking perhaps that you are contrary or ungenerous. In some cases others might believe you are instead plain crazy and possibly stupid or incompetent. You know better, and if it becomes a point of contention you might try the most wily of all devices: Tell the truth. No one will believe you, you may impress with your imagination, and later when you are found out, no crimes will have been committed and therefore there will be none to regret.

THE TECHNICAL
PRODUCTION

*In which set, lighting, sound and costume are considered for
their dramatic effects.*

FOOD, FOOD, FOOD. What of the myriad of
things not food that your guests and you will see and smell and hear and feel? Hoping
others won't notice nastiness is not an answer. Imagining they won't respond to things
simply because you no longer notice them is a careless approach. You can't want their
senses to be in any way blunted. Heaven forbid they forgive and ignore too many tres-
passes out of a well-meaning politesse. Deliberate action gives rise to real sentiment, and
enforcing indifference to their senses soon they will not care at all how anything about you
smells or tastes or feels or sounds. What if your courtship is successful? What will you do
with someone who has turned off their sensibilities and has no inclination to re-find them
until they have walked a mile from your cave of horrors? Let alone the terrible possibility

that you are courting someone not in communication with their senses in the first place and so cannot be offended, and so cannot be delighted either.

Eventually in any romantic and intimate entanglement there must be so much occasion for forgiveness, you would be foolish beyond explanation to start off in the red. Which is not to say courtship should be staged in a false or extravagant manner. No no no. Humor and generosity, disingenuousness and compassionate honesty should prevail. That which has the greatest effect can be the thing which is not noticed immediately or even ever.

Reckless to ignore and neglect and leave absolutely to the whim of chance those things which speak to the senses. All the time,[1] but all the more if courtship is possible.

With all that and far more in mind, apply yourself lightly but without oversight to these several areas:

SET

Which is usually to say your home in general, its furnishings, decoration, state of repair, state of cleanliness, its location in the world, its entrance, its inhabitants. Few things will escape the notice of strangers, and even unnoticed can still work their destruction. In fairness, plenty of elements will not be noted but will have their good effect or no effect at all. Very nice, but do not count on such stuff to offset even one single awful thing.

Regardless of how little you care, your surroundings will affect anyone who comes into them. Regardless of how thoroughly you neglect them, how diligent you are in refusing to express yourself through interior design and decoration, people will notice what is there and know it is what you live in. They will notice what is on the wall, even if it only nails or markings from nails from paintings long gone with a former occupant. They will notice your furniture and whether or not it is clean and comfortable because they are not accustomed to it. You have long ceased seeing that which is ugly or needs repair. Others haven't. Perhaps you have also lost awareness of what is beautiful and worthy of appreciation. Others will notice and bring it newly to your attention.

Art will speak to your taste, to your many selves and possibly to your pretensions and ambitions. Books and magazines reveal your interests and your education, the breadth of your curiosity. Tchochkas, brick-a-brack, souvenirs, whatever is lying around might be picked up and asked about, played with and considered. The quality and size and placement of your television if you have one, your stereo, your music collection, a piano or some such

---

1 Oh yes, all the time. It is a matter of some debate, but I've no idea why. Even plants prefer their certain amount of sunlight, breeze and gentle noise; dying when it is all too wrong. How much more responsive to scene the unbearably sentient, shoe-footed being?

large thing, the portrait of your mother, photographs of friends and family and where they are, the dining table, your home office and a thousand other things will give others very good clues about your character.

Not that you should alter or arrange your world to create an impression of something you are not. You probably couldn't anyway unless you were a gifted set designer with astounding powers of objectivity. But you might choose to be aware of what your surroundings reveal to others, checking that it is what you would have revealed at first and then second and third and thirtieth sight, and that it is mostly true to you. There are no doubt a number of things in your home which are not: the odd inherited armchair, a painting by your cousin, a dining table you have not been able to replace quite yet. Don't worry. You only need to keep at bay those villainous things which will undermine you falsely and without remorse.

Besides, it may not even be wise to have everything in your abode be an honest expression of yourself. More you than you. An unrelenting museum of youness. Resist the temptation to surround yourself with souvenirs of past moments. It might push you accidentally into the ranks of those living off memories. Age has nothing to do with it. There is a suffocating stillness. Nothing is experimental or expressive or offers more than recollection. Nothing has moved for a long time. Only the person who created it and who lives in it can stand it for any length of time. A poorly curated retrospective of their life. Often even they are not comfortable there. A thorough housecleaning in the company of a ruthless and tactless friend will fix you up if you are mired here.[2]

In another scenario, one might finish their home in a fell swoop, designed and decorated specifically to express themselves through every fiber of fabric or wood or whatever. This can work to create a comfortable environment if the person who creates it is a comfortable being. Or it can make people nervous to see surroundings which are too full and apparently finished, especially if very many things match. They might jump unwittingly to the conclusion that the life is similarly complete, that there is no place for new friends or thoughts or that growth has stopped. The expression might allow change, but still reveal a character which is uncomfortable around things alien to itself. It could suggest to the casual observer that the resident is a bit controlling, has decided how the world should look and has imposed that view on their surroundings. The foreign and unfamiliar and perhaps fleeting are not welcome in the space. Everything is edited and approved by the resident monarch.

---

[2] I recently heard another suggestion: One evening when you have nothing better to do, dress up like a snooty interior designer (perhaps employing a tablecloth as a cape) and go through your house in character, pointing out everything that is dreadful, dreary and simply must go. This is from the Girls who wrote *Free Advice*. They recommend that you then open a beer and forget about the whole thing. I would suggest instead that you return to your original self and think about what the designer told you. My guess is that you could probably follow every word of advice from your fictional character and not go too wrong.

Such a space will impress some and is in any case wrought with evidence of the inhabiting soul, both in the specific and in the fact of its fullness. But a visiting human might easily fear they do not match or complement the furnishings and they could feel out of place. A Cezanne still-life lost in a stiff frenzy of Louis Seize. A Mies van der Rohe chair dumped unceremoniously in Martha Stewart's sun room.

The danger of a less fiendishly controlled environment is that something lying about might tell lies about you, might suggest to your guest that you are something you are not. The advantage is that when your truer self is slowly revealed it will be something of a surprise. A pleasant one, it is hoped. The disadvantage is that a lie might be told which is so compellingly against you that without inquiry you are designated disgusting and that is the end of that. Fortunately you are allowed to glance about your own home and judge for yourself if there are things which are both vile and inexpressive of any facet of yourself and dispose of them.[3]

You might also consider that it is within your power to change things you don't like and possibly alter that thing within yourself which gave rise to it. Confucius, again. Enforced habit gives rise to real sentiment, or something like that. For example, if you find you have a bunch of Nagel portraits on your wall, and with an objective spirit you look at them and consider what they might reveal about your views and images of women as well as your taste in art, you might just take them down. Then they will not be there to speak to your guests about your psyche, and not seeing them everyday you might grow beyond them. Similarly you might also put away somewhat permanently those violent and violently exploitative comic books and your copy of *Penthouse* and anything worse.[4] Depends what you are courting. If you have a *People* magazine, make sure it is not a subscription copy.

Perhaps your home was designed and furnished by a paid professional. An odd thing. If the designer was psychic and communicative, they might have furnished you better and with more honest complexity than you ever could have done yourself, plus left you with a comfortable bunch of connected rooms which do not strangle you with your own tastes and experiences. More likely, a designer lived out one of their fantasies on your dime and you now have a home which is as comfortable as a hotel parlor. Which can be good or bad, but mainly indifferent. People are affected differently by professionally decorated rooms, know they are the expression of a contracted commercial artist, and do not generally draw conclusions about you except that you had the money to employ one of them. And perhaps

---

[3] For those of you who slept through Logic 101, this implies that things which are vile but also expressive of something about you can be left lying about if you like, as well as all those things which are not you but also not vile. For most people, the latter category includes most things.

[4] This is not entirely about pornography and things erotic. You probably also don't want to leave out the personals column with various ads circled in red.

that you were too lazy or indiscriminate to remove the Nagel some misdirected designer placed over the commode.

Whatever. No one worth courting really cares what style your home is furnished in, and they care deeply. Whether you collect and meticulously upholster Austrian antiques or whether you whimsically slipcover stuff from the flea market—it doesn't make a spot of difference, and it is of enormous weight and importance. Others will accept or forgive or excuse nearly anything, but they will be unfathomably and irrevocably affected. If you choose to challenge your friends and acquaintances and potential loves with the state of your home, fine. Just know that is what you are doing. If you wish to have a comfortable place where people forget time and space and stay without thought, clean your house, go outside and re-enter imagining it is the home of another. See what you see and make sure none of it bothers you.

For safety's sake, always be aware of your guests, their humor and whether anything in your home seems to be disturbing them. Make them so welcome and so comfortable that they will tell you if a painting makes them nervous or if the television is distracting them, tease you about your magazines and ask you about your books, move lamps to better spots when needed. It might spark conversation, and it might keep people from simply not returning to your house and never knowing why.

Don't forget to clean your bathroom and fix your bed[5] and put the porch light on.

LIGHTING

The importance of light cannot be over estimated. So powerful and evocative that some theatrical productions will forgo sets altogether and summon their locations and moods through lighting alone and the skills of the performers. Never would a competent production neglect light, concentrating instead on the furnishings and props for a scene. To what purpose? Who will see them? Or in what glaring or insufficient or distracting light? Not that lighting necessarily needs to be elaborate and complicated. It just needs to be whatever you want it to be and not whatever it is because of the budgetary concerns and lack of imagination of some long-dead building contractor. Even the most unappealing abode, as long as it is clean and smells fine, can be made comfortable and inviting, even sultry and magic with lighting. A trick at times to execute because so many people are unaware of its power,

---

[5] And don't display pictures of anyone in your bedroom. Others will wonder whom you are looking at. As an aside because I really don't want to discuss your bedroom here. Just make sure it is clean and otherwise follows the guidelines for the rest of the house. You do reveal your regard for yourself by the way you treat yourself when no one is around. Your bedroom holds many clues to this reclusive being. Just so you know. We can talk about it later.

or are uncomfortable at first glance in low or unconventional light, or think that more light is always better.[6]

People respond to light whether you or they are aware of it or not, whether or not you have made any effort to make that response be one of delight and contentedness. You know this because you know that in severe interrogation a light is placed directly over a table, perhaps even directly over the head of the poor creature being questioned.[7] It is not there to make them comfortable nor encourage them to flirt with their interrogators. While it may be confessions you seek, they are likely of a different sort and will probably be pulled from the hesitant soul with greater ease in more kind light, be it bright or dim.

The best policy often seems to be to err towards less light rather than more, but perhaps eventually and not suddenly nor suspiciously. Lights can be lost slowly throughout an evening as they become more distracting than useful.[8] Though they might not become either. Who's to say an evening won't end up being one of those glittery, bright affairs where light surrounds and sculpts precisely and in peculiar context the human form? Who's to say that tonight won't be a night to see every glint in every eye, every tweak of a half-smile? Who's to say the light will ever go off? Who will care if the lamps stay on while

---

[6] I am not prepared to browse about the psychological profile of someone who cannot stand to be in a low-lit place. By which I do not mean suspiciously dark. Easier for me to explain Blanche Dubois who doesn't want to see or be seen too clearly than someone who must see and be seen. Or to the degree I can explain it, find it lamentable.

[7] A configuration strangely and sadly similar to that of many kitchen tables.

[8] Perhaps you understand, and so you should skip this footnote for it is long and remedial. But perhaps you are blind to the effect of distracting lighting. Perhaps it never even occurs to you to alter the lighting in your home. For my part, I do not remember to adjust the temperature. I implore you to take note. For the brightest and most common example, once dinner is served, the kitchen light might be turned off. Even when there is a closed door, the bright kitchen light glaring around the edges distracts and makes imaginative minds wonder what might still be going on in there. (Ironically, since in my experience it is much more likely that something interesting is going on in a darkened kitchen.) Certainly when there is no barrier, the lights in the kitchen should be turned off. If you remain in the kitchen for the meal, the lights over the stove and sink, if possible, are wisely extinguished, attention brought to the table or wherever you are now about to dine and converse and otherwise attend to anything but sinks and stoves. Really, I do not like to talk about such fussy detail. Only you can know which lights in your home should be on or off at any one moment. Perhaps you can think of it instead as economical and considerate of energy to turn off most of the lights in areas where you are not. Leave on low, small lights where people may have to walk so their experience of your home is never scary, dangerous, or frustrating. Some small, but in any case not harsh amount of light in hallways or rooms that must be nego-tiated. A nightlight or candle in the bathroom for particularly raucous events so no one is forced into a cruelly lit encounter with their own face or thighs. Kindness and care of others. Thinking of things they wouldn't have thought of for themselves. Never obsequious, and never at your own expense, as all that you offer others is equally lovely for you. Further a gift to yourself as the pleasure of others, their happiness, can only be paradise for you. Please let me know if you need to know more about this. Or ask friends for advice on the matter. As usual, take of advice as you would a plate of bon bons, which is to say don't gobble it up all at once. Consider and appreciate all that is offered, then politely ingest what is right for you. Taking it all in over the course of time, if that is what you need.

you pull a loosely woven blanket over your heads and let bright light filter and bounce about you?

Back to darkness. It can work a sorcery. Once upon a time there was a room full of people standing around awkwardly with glasses in hand. Candles were lit, lights turned off and a thousand conversations sparked and flamed. Another time when a whole neighborhood dissolved into darkness at the hands of poor utility management, a small restaurant placed candles on the tables and kept cooking on leaping gas flames brought into view by surrounding darkness. Hands were taken that would have never been taken in bright light. Throughout the room voices descended perceptibly into chests, then abdomens, then finally, within minutes, settled into those spots of great resonance below the belly. There was no reason to be anywhere else that night. Another time a fractured family reunited for a single evening when a daughter refused to turn lights back on once candles had been lit on the holiday table. The chandelier stayed cold and the room warmed and was lit by things which burn more brightly than filament.

It is not only candles (and candles, as you see, are not only for lovers). Light from lamps is as varied as the people who turn them on. As seductive or as off-putting and with as little evidence as to why unless you are a trained and talented lighting engineer. And even then. I wish I had some simple and simply expressible tips or guidelines to offer you about lighting. How could I? Not only can I not know what kind of space you are lighting, I do not know your motives, your desires, nor the quirks of other characters who will be playing in your scenes. It is for you to be aware of the many elements which are being perceived, however not consciously, and to design and alter them accordingly. Nothing will work in every case.[9]

It is a narrow distinction between forcing people into something with which they are truly and irretrievably uncomfortable, and pushing them past a curve of discomfort which is obstructing their acceptance of new experience. Certainly one can ignore first and fast complaints. If ten minutes have passed and someone is still noticeably uncomfortable or complaining that they cannot see in the low light or flame-lit darkness, give them light. No need to return to shocking incandescence, but do something to assuage.[10]

---

[9] Like that's big news. But I will offer a rule of thumb suggesting that pools of light combining to create more or less even light throughout a room, whether it is brightly or darkly lit, will in most cases give a good effect. As opposed to a single source of light. This, by the way, is how stages are lit. Many lights combining to create an atmosphere, reducing shadows, suffusing the stage with an amount of light rather than lighting a particular thing, although great care is taken to assure that particular things are indeed lit. People with excellent collections of art have the glorious option of lighting the works themselves which in turn light the room with richly reflected light and color. A simple solution, if you don't count the difficulty of choosing art worth lighting or the cost and complexity involved in lighting art well.

[10] Preferably something which is not back-tracking, i.e. do not simply turn lights back on which have been

Enough already with the night. In daytime light is as powerful. How light comes in through windows or is filtered through leaves, the time of day, the shadows cast, the quality and texture of the light, its warmth and where it falls, what filters it, what reflects it: all this and more combine to create light which is either inhabited or not. People will go and be where they are most comfortable. If they haven't a choice because of space or weather restrictions, it is for you to observe and manipulate light to make your guests comfortable where they must remain. Or they will leave early. Which might be fine with you. But if you would have them remain, all you need to do, since the sun will throw what light it will, is glance about from time to time to make sure no one is struggling to keep sun from their eyes nor shivering in its absence. Pull shades, rearrange furniture, offer hats, sweaters or whatever to make them more comfortable. Then as daylight fades, light lamps as needed.[11]

Regardless of the source, do not ignore light. If you become proficient in this arena, feel free to adjust light, with permission, in the homes of others. It is no coincidence that there is such a myriad of light bulbs on the market. No happenstance that lighting stores abound. Small wonder people travel far and uncomfortably for glimpses of gorgeous light reflecting off exotic oceans. Why should you think that suddenly, in your living room, people would become insensitive to light? Trust that they don't, and if they appear to, you are racking up debt.

SOUND

Not just music, although music might be part of it. The sound of your house, the sound of a lake or an ocean or birds in the very early hours of the morning. The sounds of your neighbors or neighboring industries. Cars and buses and trains and planes. You are used to it and have long since ceased noticing, but a visiting other or others will be as pleased or as jolted as you first were. Not that you must do anything about it. Just be aware it is all new to them. Or if not utterly new, at least not forgotten.

The sound of your voice, sounds you make while preparing food, while eating, while cleaning up, while you do anything at all will be heard. The clamor of cooking can be angry

---

turned off. This is such sticky stuff. I want to add that while you try to encourage another to accept a new way of being, I encourage you to learn a new way of lighting so that others are comfortable. If you can't figure out a way to make a fussy other happy with some haste, compromise for the moment your own comfort and figure out a better solution later in your own time. Rearrange your lamps, acquire better ones and dispose of bad ones. But perhaps the lamplight is not at fault but rather everything it touches. Is your home so dark or dingy that any source of light is swallowed whole by the first thing it touches? So bare and spare that light beams bounce endlessly, never finding a resting spot? Fix it.

11 Please don't do anything sudden and without warning. It is a horrible sensation to be suddenly thrown into relative bright or darkness without having been forewarned. At least for me.

or petulant and drive people away, or it can draw people from all parts of a house to be near it. In the kitchen and at the table, the noise of tools and utensils might be horrible and forbidding and excruciatingly lonely while in another time and place it is a backbeat to conversation. Who doesn't have some memory of a nearly silent dinner at the end of something when laughter and speech were gone and all there was to be heard was the sound of steel scraping against steel and porcelain? Who doesn't also remember joyous meals, steel clattering against steel and tapping against porcelain.

Recorded music might add to the scene or subtract. Waves of sound weave and work their way through the flesh and non-flesh of your guests, for better or for worse. It might offer a rhythm that resonates through them, setting the evening careening forward and outward and inward and everywhere it can go. Or it might instead counter and damp a rhythm trying to gather strength, undermining and poisoning what could be. In the case of a lost and hesitant crowd, it can set a pace, giving clues and cues to stage-struck guests grasping for lines.

Don't forget you are free to commission live music for any event. If you don't know why it would make a difference, if you think to yourself that recorded music is much superior because the musicians are better and one has more selection, you are overdue for an evening of living music. It is a stunning difference. Not always appropriate, but it is a neglected source of magic. If you do hire musicians, be sure to treat them as honored guests and not as servants.

Normally, it must be admitted, you will be negotiating recorded music. Few choose to commission live music for dinner for ten. Unfortunately for you, if you are looking for a quick guideline for choosing music, it remains ever a great mystery what music to play for a particular gathering of any number. It can be a nice idea to ask another to select the music, but you must remain arbiter of the atmosphere. People can easily choose stuff that is wrong and that even they decide moments later they don't want to listen to. Not everyone is so bold and careless of their ego that they can easily change the music they have just chosen. Not many would even notice it is wrong. Others will put on music especially designed to challenge you or the larger group of people. "Take this," they seem to be saying. It could be anything. In a single week in a single home, recordings of both Maria Callas and Courtney Love were put on with the same challenging agenda and with similar effect. Most people will put on music they want to hear or which they think will impress others with their sophisticated or quirky tastes without regard for what the selection will do to the nerves of the larger group nor to the rhythm of the gathering. Since you are director and producer, it is up to you to make sure the selections of others are working to good purpose. The point of letting another select the music is to coax them into choosing what will make them comfortable and maybe to give them something to do. If they use the opportunity to grind axes or chase some other anti-social agenda, you must step gently in and fix it. Experiment only with care and attention, always aware of how the music you or another has chosen is affecting the gathering. Change it without remorse if you think it is creating a mood which is not conducive to courtship and camaraderie. Turn it off when it adds nothing.

It is a minefield. What is soothing and sauce to one group is grating on another. Windham Hill artists are played and some people are happy while others are climbing the walls. Lynyrd Skynyrd is lullaby to some. It is only of the smallest importance what kind of music you prefer. When you are pursuing the affections and admiration of another, the right thing to do is what is best for them without being bad for you. Not surprisingly, this often leads to standard sorts of music. But it needn't. There are a million other recordings which are anything but standard but which have various good effect. Better even and possibly less dangerous as you have less chance of playing music which reminds them of another time, another place, and another person entirely.

Not that you should spend any time worrying about all this any more than you should spend time worrying if your buttons are buttoned. If humor and good nature hold sway in your home, you should not have a problem with the ominous chop chop chop of mad knives nor the odd minute of horrific music. On the other hand, if an evening seems to be wandering in a rotten direction or appears mired in some squalid heap of bad moodiness, check for sound. Are you chewing with your mouth open? Is anyone making sickening or nerve-shattering noises? Is the music frantic or dissonant or overly or underly intellectual or philosophical or simply too squirrely and spineless? Are the neighbors fighting or making a more affectionate racket?[12] If you cannot repair the situation, at least be sympathetic by mentioning the unmentionable. A sense of humor helps.

COSTUMES

Clothing should be clean and in good repair down to the tiniest and most intimate article. Unless you just came in from the garden and there is mud on your clothing. Real dirt from the surface of the earth doesn't bother anyone as long as it is not on your hands and face, which should be washed soon after your return from the garden. Neither does paint from painting nor spots and splashes honestly acquired during the course of cooking offend. Just be sure the fabric which forms the stuff of your clothing was once of great quality, fine or substantial to the touch, and that it was fashioned into clothing with wisdom and care, or at least not with vain carelessness. Down to the tiniest and most intimate article. You decide when it is time to change your clothes, remembering that disappearing briefly to take a shower and change can be a powerful move when well executed.

Clothing as courtship. Dressing for a different kind of success. A large topic few are bold enough to address, and even then stay scholarly and useless.[13] So you are on your own. Tips? Fabric should feel even more wonderful than it promised on sight. Design and construction should neither restrict movement nor recarve the form. I don't care what Dior thinks. Chanel is on my side. It should not present the flesh or form as though on a platter, but rather cover and protect and caress and honestly and proudly reveal the body as the lover would themselves given the chance.

There is no fashion. There is only your body and its need to be clothed for whatever reason: Warmth, modesty, discretion, safety, habit, law, etc. Your body is both unlike any other body which has ever existed, attached as it is to your head and heart and all, and it is no different than all the bodies which have been clothed for thousands of years. There are no requirements, rules nor social considerations special to clothing. Your manner of dress must only follow the guidelines outlined in every other arena. It should be what is most considerate of others without being inconsiderate of yourself. Others should not

---

[12] In which case there is little to do besides dissolving the embarrassed discomfort of modest guests through humor, letting them know that they are not alone in their chagrin, apologizing for the awkwardly thin walls, and possibly suggesting that you should all adjourn to another room, even if it ends up being the Lanai Room down the street.

[13] For insight and humor into the topic, read *Femininity* by Susan Brownmiller. Concerning primarily women but men might want to know what women fight when they fight with themselves and will be able to extrapolate easily from her very personal account to explore on their own the equally silly and time-consuming dictates of Masculinity. She is not so creative sometimes in finding solutions to the hard problems, but solutions are elusive and perhaps will prove to be individual.

have to look at you and wonder if you are comfortable. Nor should they need to avert their eyes out of discretion, respect nor aesthetic. Nor should they be compelled to stare. They should not have to make special allowances for you because you have hobbled yourself with bad footwear or narrow or fragile or insufficient clothing. They should not have to alter plans or forgo adventures because you vainly neglected to put on enough clothes to keep yourself warm or safe. They should not have to suffer your complaints nor forgive your untied self because you can't figure out what your shirt size really is. Your clothing should not make them question your regard and respect for them by being so haphazard and thoughtless as to be an eyesore. Neither should you make yourself uncomfortable in order to please others.

Have respect for yourself and for others when you decide what to wear. Be honest when you buy clothing and ignore sizes. Imagine what the garment will look like after it has been lived in for eighteen hours straight, escaped briefly and then donned again, which is a common and sought after situation in the most enviable of courtship circumstances. Good clothing repels dirt and creases and looks better after it has been worn for awhile, the excellent fabric taking its clues from your form, rather than becoming misshapen through contact with your body and movement. It should feel strong and good against your skin, keep you warm and keep you cool and shade you from the sun and wind and rain and sleet and snow. It should flatter you and make you feel beautiful and comfortable with yourself. Again, as a good friend might do. And like that good friend, it should not require frequent maintenance nor constant attention. Unless dress is a means of expression for you, there is no need for your clothing to be interesting at first glance. Better for it to draw the eye slowly if at all. Better for it to be staid and conventional in comparison to your own brilliance. Sad always to see a lovely person in fruitless competition with their own clothes. Sad as well to see a person of brilliance dressed in drab and flimsy fashion.

It is a big, hard problem, dress, and one which has been worked on for many centuries with little success. There is so much to say about clothes and what they mean to people and how they might be interpreted. The history of fabric and the human body is only partially documented in the hundreds of fat books published about it. I am not even going to touch on Bodies.[14]

You are largely on your own. Broad and abstract admonitions are all I can offer. Judge articles of clothing as thoroughly and harshly as you would a potential friend before adding them to your closet, and then do what you must to acquire them. Most commonly, you may have to pay more money for a better quality thing than you are in the habit of

---

[14] Although, as you might surmise, the same, oft-repeated guidelines for behavior hold which, typically speaking, lead to those lovely, healthy bodies very appropriate to courtship activities.

buying and wearing. Or you may need to learn how to make clothes and then make what you need. Commission clothing if you can find a good clothing maker. You will almost certainly have to find a way to transcend your current conceptions of what clothing should look and feel like. You might have to feel strange in something for a few hours or days. It is not so easy as the magazines would suggest to dress yourself well. And much easier in the end.

Only wear things you feel like wearing. Always be able to walk a mile in your own shoes. Don't wear anything sheerly for decoration.[15] Don't make too great of a first impression. Don't wear anything of extreme value outside of ceremonies. Don't wear anything which is brighter, more attractive or more interesting than you are. Don't wear anything of lesser quality than yourself. Don't ever wear anything a little bit of olive oil will ruin.

YOU WOULD BE EXTREMELY foolish to ignore all aspects of the technical production, and equally foolish to slave away at them. In theater a good rule of thumb, which hardly anyone follows, is this: To the degree you execute anything at all, execute it well and to a degree commensurate with or complementary to the execution of all the other aspects. For example, it might be unwise to appear at the door in Lacroix formal wear when your home is decorated in early garage sale, your lighting cruel and inconsiderate, and the menu barbecue. On the other hand, you might impress just the right person with your extremely sharp and purist priorities. What do I know? If your home is clean and comfortable though second-hand, if you could find it in your heart to adjust your lighting scheme so your guests do not feel as though they have been caught on a B-movie set, and if the barbecue is good at being whatever it is, the Lacroix might be very very appropriate, charming in its unlikelihood, its elaborate and exotic aspect set off delightfully by the simplicity of its context; the simplicity of context made still more delightfully disingenuous in contrast to your elaborate costume.[16]

---

15 I did not say never wear jewelry. I did not say never wear all colors at one time. Just that if you do, there had better be some other reason to be wearing that item besides decoration. Jewelry can have meaning, it can complement you, or it can create a particular sort of effect unavailable without the flash of metal or the glint of polished stone. Colorful clothing might also be something wonderful to wear and make you feel as though you are wrapped in the arms of a great love. It might capture attention at first sight as long as it is still more wonderful upon closer examination. I did not say you should dress to look like a field mouse.

16 Conversely, cotton pajamas have been worn to formal events with great élan. This last is an extremely hard trick, however, and should only be attempted by a very advanced student of clothing courtship, or a sincerely naive one.

Similarly you might perfectly light a very casually furnished home. Complementary because exquisite lighting can show off a mediocre interior to its best effect, even improving it. You might play music or serve food that transcends all the visual elements of your home. Your art collection might surpass by orders of magnitude your neighborhood, your wardrobe and your menu.

Be reasonable, be sane. Ignore what others think of you and be conscious of how your surroundings are making them feel. Again and again and again, you needn't change things just because others don't like them. Nor should you refuse to change things just because others don't like them. Both choices are reactive and hold rare success. Whatever it is you decide to do, or do without deciding, it will have its effect. You might as well have it be the one you desire.

DINING OUT

*In which you do not cook, and courtship
continues.*

OUT TO EAT. WHAT flawless pleasure. Someone else cooks, someone else cleans up, and you don't even have to say thank you much less offer to help. Just pay the check and head out into the anonymous night. If the food is no good you don't have to feign having enjoyed yourself. "The eggplant was soggy, and the salad awfully salty," you can cheerfully inform the waiter without remorse, removed from compassionate responsibility by the maze of walls between your table and the second-rate chefs in the kitchen. Spill red wine on the tablecloth. Drop your silverware on the floor and don't retrieve it. Pick all the mushrooms out of your salad and feed them to your companion. Order coffee and don't drink it. Not that you should do any of these things. But you absolutely should not do them anywhere but in a restaurant.[1]

Still, you first need to decide where to eat and with whom. An art practiced by few. Most eat with the people they are used to eating with, whether they enjoy them or not, and they frequent restaurants they are used to, or more unfortunately restaurants sanctioned by popular culture, which are too reliably either the worst places[2] or the among the most expensive ones. Fear of food. So many people will explain gently and reasonably that the best, even the only rational thing to do, is to eat at McDonald's. You know what you are getting—at least you know what it will taste like—and you can sue an enormous and wealthy corporation if you ever happen to get sick from their food. Can't say that about the inventive Egyptian falafel place out on 28th Street. Unfortunately, nothing that can be recognized as courtship can take place in a fast food restaurant. The tone and pace are all wrong. Materials are chosen for practical reasons and do not encourage fingers to imagine what they might touch next. You would have to already be in love, or so young your hormones are louder than the molded plastic, to escape with interest and imagination intact. Never mind provoking anything new. Independent and obscure spots may be just as inconsiderate of the senses, but at least they are new to you and there can be an element of discovery, even if you only discover how awful the place is. You never have to go back.

When choosing a specific place to eat, you will probably have an idea of the sort of place you are seeking. In France the various genres are clearly labeled and there are strict guide-lines as to what can take place in each of them. You can choose from the main menu of Cafés, Tea Salons, Brasseries, Restaurants, Wine Bars, Pizzarias, and all of the non-French places which are like normal restaurants to the rest of the western world. And fast-food, of course. The official classification of a place will largely determine the attitude of the meal. Cafés are non-committal and casual, open to the street or park, generally serve wine, beer and some other stuff along with the coffee drinks, and you can always get a toasted ham and cheese sandwich which will always be called a Croque-something or other. Tea houses are quieter than cafés, less open to the street, and serve more desserts than savories. They too serve coffee. Brasseries are loud, bright and fast-moving, waiters have even less time for

---

[1] There are a few things you should remember when choosing how to behave in a restaurant mentioned some-where near the end of this chapter.

[2] By whose standard? you ask. Mine, naturally. It seems the United States has poisoned the earth with the idea and the reality of fast food. So much meat to begin with, which is a political problem on every scale, from global reduction of old forests and indigenous economies to the very personal tragedies of heart disease and colon cancer, back to the national burden of poor health and the complete destruction of whatever cultural ethics and aesthetics we might have once possessed, gifts from our ancestors in every part of the world. Fast food is incompatible with respect for food and for the land and the creatures that feed us. We all suffer from this care-lessness, except maybe for the owners of the fast food chains. They too will eventually find there are no more beautiful things to spend their money on, no more food worth eating, no more tranquil places to relax. Then perhaps they will be sorry.

you than in other sorts of places, and you can order whatever you want or nothing at all. Restaurants are leisurely even when loud, courses are followed, and you are committed to having a whole meal, even at lunch. There is some overlap between these places. For example, for lunch one day you might choose between one of the more casual and affordable restaurants and a cafe that happens to have a particularly complete menu.

But you probably aren't in France.[3] In the USA, dining establishments have similarly different characters but are not so clearly labeled. Once you branch away from the Cafes, Family Style, and Smorgasbord places, which you should certainly do, discovering which is which can be more difficult than in a more regimented culture, and it is easy to find yourself unfortunately seated at exactly the wrong sort of place. Something that looked like a cafe can reveal itself to be a high-end restaurant only when you open the menu, and vice versa. When that happens, you can either enjoy the sudden change of plans and laugh about it later; or you can admit to your companion or companions it is not the sort of place you had expected and see if any of them are also unhappy about it. They may all be fine, or they may be thrilled someone was so bold as to say something and you can, after apologizing for the misunderstanding to the waiter, make your sortie en masse and adjourn to a more appropriate spot. A clumsy moment the entire price of a delightful evening.

It is maybe a better strategy to get proficient at discerning the character of a place before you ask for a table. Look at the menu. In fact, look at menus all over town. Drop by restaurants when you walk or drive by and have a minute to spare, especially around meal times. Walk in and see what the interior feels like, the atmosphere created by the clientele. Ask to see menus for lunch and for dinner. Make an especial effort to do this if you are contemplating asking someone to join you for a meal at a certain spot and you have never been there before. If you choose to depend on the opinions and experience of others, don't neglect to factor in the sorts of things they tend to like and not like and adjust accordingly for your own tastes.[4] If you are calling for reservations at a place you do not know much about, ask what sorts of things are on the menu and what their prices are. Listen to determine if it sounds like a loud or muted place. Ask how one should dress. All these answers will give you good clues as to the atmosphere of the place. Tell them what you are looking for, be it a place for conversation, for celebration or for inebriation, and inquire as to whether their restaurant will be a good choice for the occasion. They should be honest.

---

[3] I can tell because if you were you wouldn't be reading this book. You would be lingering in cafes and on bridges and in museums, holding hands and sharing kisses and glasses of warm and cool things. You would be watching carefully the manner in which French people prepare and serve food and learn ever so much more about food and courtship than you ever could with your nose in this book.

[4] You know how to do that, right? It is an elaboration of critical thinking, listening to and interpreting criticism for yourself.

Restaurants don't want unhappy people moping about any more than you want to be in the wrong place.

You are still left with the burden of decision. So what if you are familiar with every restaurant and cafe in your town and have eaten at all of them many times. You still have to think about what is right for today, for the people you will be dining with, and make a good decision. More than that. When someone else makes a decision you know to be a poor one, you have the unenviable opportunity to say something early on and avoid an awkward situation later. Imagine, your good friend's parents are in town and their child has invited you to join them for dinner at a restaurant which you know to be loud and filled with professional people performing that ugly mating dance of the Homo Sapiens Sapiens. Your friend has heard from other friends it is a great place, but has neglected to notice that the people who recommend it consistently favor the boisterous and bawdy over the discreet and delightful. If you go passively along you can expect an infernal evening of shouting into his father's hearing aid and hoping none of your acquaintances from last weekend come over and say hello. This would be a good time to think hard and come up with exactly the right place where everyone can enjoy the meal and visit. You must present your suggestion diplomatically, which is never easy but it will be worth the effort.[5]

Think about your dining companions and what they like. Not just what they say they like and think they like, but what you know they like from being with them and watching them and knowing things about them they don't even like to admit about themselves, which you probably know about everyone you have ever met even for twenty minutes four years ago at a garage sale. Think about what sort of atmosphere will be appropriate. It will be different today than it would be tomorrow, which makes it very difficult to plan where to eat next week. Festive and celebratory, quiet and protecting, airy and bright or airy and dark. Stuffy is almost never the right atmosphere but sometimes it is. There are restaurants which design their atmosphere to preclude conversation and so are very popular with people who don't have anything to say to each other. There are other places where if you are not engaged in conversation you will be compelled to listen to that of another table. Consider whether you want to spend a good deal of money, or very little, or if you do not care and know your companions don't care either. Is it a beautiful evening and do you want to eat outdoors? Is it important to you or to another that the food be very good, or could the quality of the meal be compromised in favor of the perfect setting? Was anyone formerly married to the chef or currently dating one of the waiters? Is it a long way from home? Does anyone have food allergies or preferences which must be considered? Delicate

---

[5] It will also be worth the effort to hold your tongue if you don't want to go to the restaurant because you don't like it but it is a perfectly fine choice in every other way.

stomachs? Is the smoking or non-smoking section more desirable, and is that the section you will be choosing? How is the wine list and does anyone care? Likewise, is there a full bar and does anyone care? How close are the tables and how comfortable are the chairs, and does anyone care? Obviously you must consider handicap access in some cases. And the hours and days of service. Certainly there are myriad elements to think about, and you can't possibly remember them all. Habit will form as you discover how a moment of thoughtfulness can make a meal at least twice as likely to be a lovely one.

As you get good at choosing a place to dine, you will feel more comfortable disagreeing with someone's initial suggestion. Take care. Just because you are good at something doesn't mean you get to do it all the time. Sometimes there is a very good reason a friend or associate or beloved wants to go somewhere that seems wrong. You can steamroller someone's hopes and plans for the meal without even noticing, perhaps thereby steamrollering some of your own bigger plans. Remembering you are probably dining with that person because you like them and like to spend time with them and are maybe even hoping to have the opportunity to spend more time with them, don't do that. Try to discreetly ascertain why any establishment has been suggested. "Is there some particular reason you want to go there?" asked in a sincere and not snide manner will usually do the trick. Offer in an authentically deferential fashion any suggestion you might have and your reason for thinking it might be a better choice. If your suggestion is not taken up, don't worry about it. The point is to spend time with people and to enjoy them, not to get your way all the time. You can do that quite easily by dining alone.

Take care in choosing where to dine for the additional, very good reason that it is easier to behave well and attractively in places which suit you, or at least aren't in violent or awkward opposition to your character. Still, wherever you are and however difficult it might be, good behavior is a good choice.

RESTAURANT COMPORTMENT

All Table Manners apply, except the part about helping clear the table. Plus:

BE RESPECTFUL OF the people working in the restaurant and of the space and of other diners.[6]

MAKE RESERVATIONS, and cancel them even at the very last minute if you

---

[6] If you are unsure what "respectful" means, ask five friends and listen carefully to their answers. Then read several essays by such philosophers as John Stuart Mill or Ralph Waldo Emerson. Then read Dear Abby or Ann Landers for one week straight. Then think hard about what it might mean to act with dignity and to treat others and yourself with respect. Look up all these words in several dictionaries. Figure out who it is you admire

change your plans. If for some odd reason the restaurant asks why you have changed your plans, say you don't know exactly why, but that you thought they would like to know. For the most part though they will simply thank you.

PUT YOUR NAPKIN on your lap immediately upon sitting down. Unless for some reason it would be disruptive, as when the silverware is wrapped up in the cloth of the napkin and unfolding the package would make a badly timed racket. In that case, wait until your companion has finished their thought, and then make minimal clatter as you remove the utensils and place your napkin on your lap where it belongs.

IF YOU DON'T CARE at all what you have for dinner, consider asking your

companion if there is a second choice they wanted to try on the menu, and order that.

IF YOU ARE THE HOST of the evening, or in many cases if you are a man,[7] make sure the rest of your party is seated comfortably before taking your own seat. Partly a gesture of consideration, and partly a strategy to avoid looking like a self-serving nincompoop when you have to rise again to help sort out some difficulty or confusion. As they say in the navy: "I got mine. How y'all doin'?"

SIT PROPERLY at the table. Which is to say in your chair and facing the table and

---

most in the world that you also have access to, and ask them to talk to you about what respect means to different people in different situations. From all this derive your own sense of what it might mean to treat others and yourself with respect, and then do.

[7] I know someday I'm going to have to discuss this man/woman thing, and I'm not looking forward to it any more than you are. For now, forgive me for acknowledging that many people continue to nurture expectations based upon gender.

the others at the table to the degree your legs fit under the table. Which is to say, not perched as though ready at a moment's notice to run off to something more interesting.

YOU MIGHT ORDER for your companion if they have told you what they want.[8] Especially if their mouth is full of bread when the waiter asks them for their order. Ask if you may and then be sure you get it right.[9] Be as though a translator. "He's having the eggplant masala," you tell the waiter then adding, "You know, I think I'll have the same thing." Don't try this for more than one other person.

IF YOU DROP SOMETHING on the floor, don't pick it up. Ask for a new one.

Or if you pick it up before thinking, put it to the side and still ask for a new one. Even if you don't really care, there is a good chance someone at your table will be profoundly disturbed by your continuing to use a utensil which has fallen to the floor. Old, ingrained repulsion that will be difficult for them to shake on such short notice and you shouldn't expect them to. If you drop food or drink on the floor that would be well-served by immediate attention, let your waiter know.

DO NOT COMPLAIN about the restaurant, the atmosphere, or in any way suggest you would rather be somewhere else.

DON'T CHEW WITH your mouth open. Not here and not anywhere else. You

---

[8] If you are a man and your companion is a woman, these waters are choppy from old storms that have yet to pass completely into calm. Sorry. Tread softly.

[9] Check as well to see if you are irritating them terribly by ordering for them.

would be surprised how many people cannot stand this particular habit, and how very few would ever say anything to anyone about it.[10]

DON'T MAKE NOISE while you are eating. If you seem to be unable to eat in relative silence, you should probably consult a dentist or one of the many variations of mouth experts available to you. There is probably a problem which could be destroying your teeth or jawbone in addition to destroying the humor of your dining companions.

DON'T EAT OFF ANOTHER'S plate without first asking if you may and if they mind. From their response, which will invariably be positive, you can gather whether they are comfortable with sharing ("Of course, help yourself!"), or whether they would prefer you didn't ("Uh... sure..."), and then behave accordingly. Always ask in such a way that it is easy for the other to say no. Always being prepared for the "Yes" which really means "I'd prefer not."

SUGGEST THAT YOUR COMPANION taste your meal, especially if it is delicious. Many people think asking to try food on another's plate is completely impolite and just won't do it. I prefer to think if one is embarking upon or ensconced in any sort of friendship with anyone, it should always be appropriate to ask sincerely and respectfully for what one sincerely and respectfully wants. But everyone doesn't agree and even those who do are sometimes trapped in rusty restrictions. Be kind and generous and patient, and if you accidentally gobble up your meal without offering a taste, apologize.

IF THERE ARE PEOPLE in the restaurant you know and to whom you want to say hello, do so but briefly. A five minute visit either at your table or at theirs is more than enough. If someone you know has not read this page in this book and is lingering too long table side, excuse yourself to make a phone call or some such thing saying, "It was nice seeing you. See you soon," as you leave your own table. You can explain your odd behavior later to your accommodating companion. If the visitor is still there when you return and you wish to be rid of them, simply excuse yourself and your companion, saying you have some private things to discuss. Be sure your companion

---

10 Behind backs, of course, but that is worse. I mention this in the context of restaurants because things people are willing to forgive in private, they are sometimes mortified by in public. Not that many people would warmly tolerate this offense in private either. At a restaurant they can be further mortified that the public might think they put up with it in private. That is when a lover turns viperous and you can't figure out why and they won't tell you because they are paralyzed by their own inability to deal with the subject. What webs we weave and trap only ourselves. Best to ask a frank and unimpeachable friend whether you are guilty of this before it becomes important. Or you can embark on a little self-observation.

feels the same way or you risk offending them deeply by appearing possessive and controlling. It is hard to know, but they will probably give you some clues, like insisting your conversation can wait or actually inviting the visitor to join your table.

INVITE OTHERS TO JOIN you at your table only if you are sure your companion is happy about it. Unless, of course, you don't care if your companion is happy about it. Or if you think they are wrong to be unhappy about it and you are trying to make a point. But in that case we may not be talking about courtship.

DRESS APPROPRIATELY to the occasion. Do not embarrass or concern your companion by being either vastly over or underdressed. There is an enormous landscape of possibilities which are appropriate for everything from midmorning coffee to formal dinners so there is no good reason to be caught with the wrong pants on. On the same note, be clean and smell clean. People have to eat near you, and in many cases you want at least one person to consider getting even nearer to you after the meal. Bathe with soap.

TAKE THE LEAST GOOD seat at the table. If there is a view, give it to another. If one chair appears more sturdy and comfortable than the rest, offer it to another and by whatever means don't take it. If you are the guest of others in their town and the view is really for your benefit, reverse the above admonition. Also, if another is attempting to court you by taking the seat which is less good, allow that rather than getting into a tussle. Accept and submit to courtship. It is not binding.

REMEMBER HOW YOUR favorites like their coffee or tea or water or wine and if it is served wrong, notice and correct it before they do.[11] The best sorts of people hate complaining on their own account, and anyone at all is enchanted by someone noticing and caring about their comfort.

NEVER NEVER NEVER get up to leave without asking the others if they are ready to go and getting a unanimously positive response.

NEVER ARGUE WITH the waiter about the check at the table. If there is a problem with the check, tell the waiter. If the waiter cannot or does not take care of it, or if there is a dispute, excuse yourself and take care of it at the cash register or at the host stand, or on the sidewalk for all I care. Confrontations are terrible for digestion and the possibility that your handling of it will prove impressive is very very slim. It can destroy what might have been a very nice mood, ruining in turn your hopes for a very nice evening.

---

[11] Yes, I'm completely serious.

DON'T GET DRUNK.

DON'T DO DRUGS in the restroom, or at the table for that matter.

DON'T FLIRT in a suggestive manner with restaurant staff nor with other diners.

IF YOUR FOOD IS BAD or badly cooked or if you did not get what you ordered, address the problem immediately and courteously with your waiter. Do not wait or whine or pout or martyr yourself to the meal. What would be the point? Your companion will feel terrible, neither of you will enjoy the evening, and it would have been effortless to resolve had you done so right away. If you can't bring yourself to do anything and your companion offers to, accept. Throw your ego and your fears out and let them resolve that which is immaterial to them. It is a wonderful playground for practicing diplomacy. It's just a restaurant. It might be entertaining for them or something they are good at, and certainly it is always smart to let someone do you a favor. You get to return it later.

IN REVERSE, IF there is anything bothering your companion, ignore their protestations that they don't mind and take care of it. Things like the sun in their eyes, or air conditioning blowing on them, or a chair which wobbles, or a utensil that is not clean, or food that is not cooked properly are the sorts of things one is apt not to want to make a scene over. Certainly, the sort of people you want to be hanging around with won't want to make a scene over something which only bothers them and not that much. That is why you must leap in softly and make the point that even when they would put themselves second, you put them first. The very essence of courtship, I would venture, each putting the other first in a constant expression of regard and affection. Beautiful to watch. Astounding to find oneself within.

SPEAK, FOR THE MOST PART, in a reasonable tone of voice and at a reasonable volume. Others are trying to eat and have conversations of their own. And it is possible your dining companion is among those people who are phobic about feeling conspicuous in public places. You will not change that, and certainly not by being loud.

LET THE RESTAURANT management know if there was any problem with the service or with anything else. Waiters are not paid to snitch on themselves, and management needs to know how things are going. Imagine it were your establishment. What would you like customers to do if they had a bad experience? You would want them to be gracious about it at the time, and then let you know what happened as soon as possible. Your companion will be impressed by your sense of responsibility combined with restraint and good nature.[12]

DON'T BREAK into song.[13]

TRY NOT TO BE extraordinarily special in your ordering. Or if you are, be just as good-natured and flexible as you are persnickety.

DON'T ASK FOR SEPARATE checks except in the most rare of circumstances.[14]

REFRAIN FROM CRITICIZING your companion's choice of food. Make your recommendations, and be done with it. If they want to order something you know is not particularly good at this spot, tell them in a non-judgmental fashion, including why you didn't like it. It might be exactly the sort of thing they love.

CHECK YOUR TEETH, and mustache as well if you have one, for bits of food. Your knife will work as a mirror for this, according to some. Better I think to make a visit to the restroom after the meal, or if you are on very friendly and intimate terms with your companion, ask for a tooth check.[15]

ORDER SENSIBLY AND with awareness of yourself and what you like and what is good for you. When unsure, I will ask the waiter what they really like and then pick from among those choices. This is not fool proof. They may be trying to unload an awful special of some sort and you might fall for it. Another trick is to notice what is being served at other tables and if something appeals to you, ask for it. Some people order very badly, always ending up with something they don't like. Maybe they don't read the menu carefully. Maybe they aren't honest with themselves about what they like to eat. Maybe they harbor delusions about the world and food within it. I can't figure them out. If you are one of those people, work it out. Find a way to order properly. People hate it when their meal is great and they want to eat

---

12 As opposed to what they might think if you chew out the waiter for some small error, or if you let some horrible mishap slide because you don't want to make a fuss.

13 Unless it is one of those really rowdy establishments which encourages that sort of thing, and you know a really good song. Or if it someone's birthday and they will not expire from embarrassment if you sing to them in public. Personally, I like to sing a quiet Happy Birthday in an archaic form of double talk to the birthday person, just to them and whoever is right next to them at a moment when they seem unoccupied with other birthday worries. In a restaurant, very softly, an odd musical whisper near their ear. A private gift which excuses me from attempting to sing along later. It is the only party trick I know. Six year olds love it.

14 I cannot even imagine what those might be. Sometimes you will be dining with someone who will not be happy in any other circumstance, and then you should ask politely for a separate check for them.

15 A disgusting detail that would be nice to ignore, but the very ugly truth is no one will hear a word you say as long as there is food on your face. A good clue that something is amiss is if your companion seems to be trying to get something non-existent off their own face or teeth. On the other hand, warm, good-natured grooming assistance from your companion might be a strong sign courtship is proceeding apace.

all of it, but they have to share because you ordered stupidly. And that's if they are nice. They might just as likely leave you hungry, but enjoy their meal less for watching you pick around your plate.

Mind you, there are a whole slew of things I am not thinking of right off, but which your mother would be glad to outline for you.

COOKING
WITH ANOTHER

In which we consider what cannot be discussed.

COOKING, WHEN IT involves courtship, often involves cooking with another. I would be the last person to forget or deny the potential of such a scene.

And yet I am reluctant to reveal my thoughts on the matter. Why?[1] Because how one behaves while working with another on a sweet or not-so-sweet task, is more revealing of character than anything else I can think of. And I am loathe to point out tricks on how not

---

[1] And why then do I even bother to mention it? Because too many people have complained this chapter is missing and so I thought I would try to write it. But as you will see, I can't. At least you all won't think I forgot such an important topic.

to be a boor in such situations when your boorishness is exactly what your companion needs to see so they can make an informed choice about spending any more time or effort on or with you.

You see the problem.

Perhaps I can look at it from another angle, focusing on what you might want to notice in another while you cook in their company. Interpret for you the more common occurrences and how they might play out. Then you can draw your own inferences about how you should behave in similar circumstances, roles reversed. I warn you now, though. You will be wrong. Your true colors will be revealed. You will stand naked beneath the gaze of your beloved or whomever it is you have been courting and for whatever reasons. Film directors of great reputations and fame have admitted to inviting potential cast members to their home and having them assist in baking cookies or some such seemingly simple event. How much more they learn about the person and their character than they would in a cold reading. How much you will learn about others.

Oh, but we are trapped again, for their behavior is going to be related directly to your own. Unless I can be utterly sure you are being a most valuable partner, compassionate and patient and cooperative yourself, I can hardly point out anything another does as horrid and worthy of concern or flight. It might be reasonable reaction to your being too fussy or too bossy or otherwise unpleasant or even intolerable to work with.

How can I be sure that you are a good companion in the kitchen?

I cannot. You must figure this out on your own. Write your own chapter as homework. All the clues are in this book. Everything you wish I would just spit out and say right now is on these pages. It is also in most of the books on your bookshelf. I cannot bring myself to tell you how to appear to be a good person in the process of cooking with others. You might do as I say, someone will fall madly in love with you, throw their lot in with yours, and discover too late you are humorless, selfish, impatient, unimaginative and not at all the sort of person one would want to love or live with. And they might discover it was I who gave you the power to deceive and they will come after me with lawyers or some other tool of destruction. But mostly I would just feel awful about helping you perpetrate fraud, want to run to the person you deceived and hold them and kiss them and make them dinner and distract them with conversation and music and art and laughter or some such instruments of healing until they are so tired they fall into sound soft sleep.

PAYING FOR IT

In which some of the mysterious social aspects of money and its exchange are respected.

THAT CLATTER OF CHINA and glass and silver, the chatter of a hundred conversations, none of which you have to follow, light bouncing off walls and faces and brass things and glass things and wood things and bottles of wonderfully poisonous things. Stunning hosts, waiters in black and white with clean faces and neat hair. Dark spots where snuggling is overlooked, bright spots where cynicism is almost appropriate. Big loud places, small loud places, the elusive quiet cafe that is still warm and alive. I love restaurants.

And yet there I am, as seldom as I can arrange, surrounded by this sure magic, choosing not to eat. Does this happen to you?

It's about money much of the time. Worse than sex it sometimes seems. I would feel more comfortable even now discussing the details of safe dallying or the effect of controlled breathing on orgasm than the ins and outs of money between lovers and family and friends. And the very people who are looking at this page saying to themselves, "What is with this girl? Why is she so wound up about money? Clearly she has a bit of a problem and should resolve it rather than projecting onto the rest of the world," are the very people who offend others so deeply on one occasion or over the course of many that they end up with friends who will not go out to eat with them, and if forced to, won't order anything, will pick at what they did order, go home and eat leftover tikka masala from the night before when they shared one of those warm bright, careless and safe evenings with others. Perhaps even in the same restaurant.

The trickiest thing. Or not tricky at all. Or extraordinarily tricky for one person and just another meal to the other. And you have no way of knowing if your companion is in the former category if you are genuinely in the latter. Some people simply refuse to eat with more than three other people at any one time, and then only with those people who they know to have compatible attitudes about money and restaurants. Or they dine out only in such situations as they will be able to simply pick up the check themselves and be done with it. Others go about their lives and never notice that some people dread eating with them and avoid finding themselves at a restaurant table with them except in the narrowest of circumstances.

Yes, well, what do I have to say about all this? Not much. I have seen friendships wither over stinginess. Other entanglements dismissed for the opposite reason. Too generous. Frantically so.

No matter what approach to money and the sharing of food one chooses or finds oneself inconveniently possessed of, it should be acknowledged that others notice and are affected. One way or another. Good, bad or indifferent. Sometimes it will match, sometimes it will be in opposition. In any situation, seek resolution that maintains dignity and good humor. It can require a sort of social and economic self-defense.

ARE THERE ANY rules of thumb? Unfortunately not. The rules of behavior that one group considers written in stone comprise for others heinous and unforgivable comportment. The only safe way out of this dungeon of discrepancy between what might otherwise be very close friends is often very taxing on both your pocketbook and your stores of goodwill. It might involve picking up the check discreetly, demurely and often. It might also include on many occasions a bit of improvisational skill as you explain why you are picking up the check. It won't do in most cases to say frankly you do not care to undergo the humiliating process of dividing up the check,[1] that you simply cannot bear the idea of listening to people you otherwise love try to claim they only drank a half a glass of wine, that their salad was a dollar less than someone else's, and who even cares because they never add a reasonable tip nor the appropriate tax to what they think is their share. You end up paying twice what you would have if you had come to the restaurant on your own, you begin to wish you had, and your evening is severely soured by listening to this gibberish.

Another equally miserable resolution, endured most often by women but any light eater is a potential victim, is to good-naturedly agree to split a check equally when one has barely eaten at all, has shared a pasta with another at the table while some of the other diners had grilled sea bass, salad and dessert. Unwilling to ruin the rhythm of the evening by discussing the check, the light eater is in terrible danger of feeling abused and resentful of their brutish and gluttonous companions. What's worse, there are those who consider this a reasonable way to behave at a table of dutch diners. They will even tell you that when the check is to be split equally, they just order whatever they want, and aim for the most expensive stuff at that. You look at them and wonder if you should tell them they can lose friends that way. People are quirky about money. People notice what you do. The only time they don't notice is when they come out ahead. Then they are mercifully blind to what has transpired.

I SWEAR MONEY is more difficult than sex, although the routes through the various impasses are strangely similar. Unstated generosity to the degree you are willing and able, and then the graceful but complete extraction of your own self from abusive situations when you are no longer willing or no longer able. At some point, in either realm, it might be right to let your companion or companions know you are having trouble with a particular thing, are trying to resolve it, but that if they keep up the same behavior it is possible you will simply slip from view. No threats, no ultimatums. Just honesty, honestly owning your own frailties that contribute to the problem. They in turn can choose to modify their approach to whatever it is, or they can choose not to. Later, when you call up to say hello from your new home in the outskirts of Barcelona, they won't be able to accuse you of having been uncommunicative, of not having warned them, of neglecting to give them an opportunity to make the small or gigantic alteration in their make-up. It is some solace.

Back at the restaurant, it is best in many cases, and if at all possible given your finances, to come up with some plausible reason for buying the others dinner. Don't do this all the time, mind you. You do not want to go broke, nor lose all affection for your penurious

---

[1] Sometimes you can be that frank, though, and to wonderful effect. Very advanced stuff, mind you.

friends, nor make them feel you have some odd agenda.[2] Another often successful strategy is to be assertive and fair in splitting checks.

As it turns out, people end up eating out with others who match them philosophically at the table.

Light eaters congregate, allowing only the extremely polite glutton to join them more than once. They will be most elusive in their movement from place to place, knowing nobody is loathe to dine with them. They split the check amongst themselves, sensitive to small discrepancies. They err on the side of generosity. And why not? The check is always pathetically small. A wild boor could easily join them, order a fabulous meal, split the check with them, utterly blind to the structure of the group, and find they have eaten extremely well for extremely little. For this reason, light eaters leave for dinner early and without announcement, or after everyone else is gone.

People who like discussing the bill and deciding who owes what down to the dime, those people who carry little plastic cards for figuring out the tip exactly; they, too, end up dining together. It is difficult for people not raised with such habits to stand them. It seems ridiculous to them not to figure out the check to the minute, and it is ridiculous to everyone else to be so fanatical about a matter of cents. Especially when it is the waiter who most often suffers. However, if one is going to be a fish out of water, this group is not so bad. You will

2 Another extremely rare possibility is that you might make others feel as though you don't think they can pick up the check. This would only come up if you are fabulously rich and already so generous you pick up the check too often. As faults go, that is not so bad and darned forgivable. But be sensitive to the egos of others nonetheless.

only end up paying a bit more than your share to make up for the small tip. A little medita-tion while they figure out the details of the check, or a trip to the restroom can alleviate the small discomfort of watching people you otherwise admire become briefly monstrous.

Meanwhile, people who are careless about money, who eat all they want and then are happy to split the check, knowing they ate as much as anyone and that they will not be caught with the short end of the deal, they also end up eating together. This is generally because no one else wants to eat with them. No one else can afford it. No one else wants to spend so much money on food they don't eat without the pleasure of actually offering a gift to another. This group is usually quite open with invitations to join them, although they are as unwilling as the first group to include a second time someone who has shown them-selves reluctant to play by their rules.

The worst possible position in terms of courtship is to be dining with people who contribute to a check in a miserly fashion, forcing you to make up for their close-fistedness surreptitiously or suffer a scene of money changing. Rather than having made others feel taken care of and honored, rather than feeling good about having given a small gift to others for no reason, rather than having avoided the check squabble entirely and all that that implies for the magic of the evening, you are instead in great danger of feeling resent-ful. Poison to all courtship, and the antidote is capricious and rare. I've never seen it myself. If the culprits persist in their penny-wise ways, or allow you to pick up the check more than twice before saying Oh no, it is my turn, you have several options and none of them are great:[3]

ONE

Stop discussing the check entirely and let the others figure it out. Pay what they think is your share, and then discreetly leave extra to make up for the invariably meager tip. It is most important that the waiter think highly of you. Otherwise you might get hideous service at a later date when you are with less scurvy friends or colleagues.

TWO

Grab the check and say, "I used to wait tables. Let me figure this out," and then do, including a generous tip. Inform each person of exactly what they owe, rounded up to the nearest dollar. One method is to divide the check equally and then add a couple dollars or subtract according to each person's meal. A girlfriend who was a waitress

---

[3] I am making the broad assumption that you do not want to cut off all contact with these peoples, or cannot for business or family reasons. Also, money is a strange thing and does strange things to most people. Surrender. Unless you are tied closely to someone, money quirks usually can be side-stepped. You shouldn't dissolve friendships over it unless it seems to speak of other things.

in Manhattan and is good at this sort of thing recommends this, but adds that you have to do it in a very forceful and authoritative manner. If anyone criticizes your math or claims they owe less, you can chastise them good humoredly about being cheap.[4] The rest of the table should rush to your side in support since to reduce that person's share by even a dollar would increase their own share, and they surely won't want that.

THREE

Stop eating with those people. If you are forced into going to a restaurant with them, and you know you will be made unhappy by the resolution of the meal, refuse to eat for one reason or another. You already ate. You have a date later where you will be expected to eat. You aren't feeling well. Or get whatever you want, but come up with a reason to leave before the rest of them are done, paying for your own meal and tip on your way out. Don't ask for separate checks. It makes the waiters nuts and they still don't get a good tip.[5]

FOUR

Unless you are tormented by such colleagues on the road, you can step lightly around the whole thing by suggesting dinner at your house instead and then tell everyone what to bring. Don't wait for them to ask. "You bring two bottles of wine." "You bring a green salad." "You bring dessert." Contribute something yourself. The end. Or offer the meal to them as a gift and forget about it. It will not be returned. Don't ever mention why you do this. Only agree to go to a restaurant with these monkeys when you feel as though you can withstand the assault on your good graces and your bank account, cheerfully and without remark. Ever. You're an adult. Do what you want to do and don't do what you can't do happily.

FIVE

If it is just a single person who drives you nuts, try to invoke a pattern of alternating who picks up the check, trying as well to be the person who gets the check on the more extravagant occasions so they do not feel, as they are apt to do, that they are getting a raw deal. One day, pick up the check and announce. "I've given up arithmetic for

---

[4] Assuming they are not financially strapped so that a dollar does matter. Be flexible and compassionate.

[5] "What is with this author and tipping?" you are thinking to yourself. It is the first rule of romantic and probably all other courtship. Never undertip. It exhibits stinginess which is a very undesirable trait in a lover or friend or colleague. And if the other ever worked for tips themselves, which many people, especially women, have done, they may, unbeknownst even to themselves, take it as a personal affront and your chances for a successful courtship are scuttled.

good. Let me get this. You get it next time." On the next occasion as you enter the restaurant announce, "Oh boy, you're paying this time. I think I'll have the escargot and chocolate soufflé for dessert!" Wait until they turn white, laugh, and then order your usual sandwich on rye, no pickle.

ENOUGH ALREADY WITH how to negotiate the herds of wild boars roaming the planet. There are plenty of people who are aware and flexible and generous and fair, and as willing and able as you are to pick up the check with a brilliantly fabricated excuse or honest expression of spontaneous generosity if need be. Plenty of people accept a broad spectrum of possible attitudes and behaviors without judgment. Find them and hang around with them.

Those you eat with are those you are closest to. Best to be forgiving and come up with solutions which entertain you rather than throwing out perfectly good people just because their parents missed a couple beats.

PAYING FOR ALL OF IT

There are also plenty of people whom you really and truly do want to take to dinner, who are precious and delightful and who will fight you for the check. Or people whom you must take to dinner for one reason or another. Whatever the case may be. Buying someone or a bunch of someones a meal can be a lovely thing to do, but just as a resentfully prepared meal can be worse than no meal at all, you can easily pay a check in a way that makes others wish you hadn't. Think of all the ways others have made you uncomfortable and don't do any of those things.

Now, how to go about paying for a check so that the gift you are giving is received in that glow of good humor so conducive to any kind of courtship, be it professional, political or personal.[6] Before we start, let me remind you that your underlying motives for picking up the check must be genuine and irreproachable, or you will have to be a better performer than I am. If you are acting from a point of sincere generosity, either from spontaneous or

---

[6] And while the professional and the political are certainly interesting arenas for courtship, it is the personal which has the fiercest reputation. It might seem that you are simply sharing an evening together or a lunch or coffee, and it has become normal to simply divide the check and think nothing further. Yet sometimes, I would venture to say often enough, it is the desire of one or the other or both to feed the other. And splitting a check does not translate into each feeding the other. The impression is that each has fed themselves. Love does not work that way, ever. Each must always be willing to give entirely, carry the whole burden in any situation, and sometimes insist on doing so. Proof? No, not really. But it is not enough to claim you would caress your lover. Not enough to insist and insist upon being believed that you love deeply and unto the ends of the universe. Either you do it or you don't.

premeditated good-will, you are on your way to doing it well. There are still a number of traps. Everyone's parents should have taught them these skills, but unfortunately everyone's parents do not possess them themselves. Fortunately, they are not so difficult to pick up.

At some point the check comes. Do what you want to do, naturally. But if you want to feed someone, try some of the following approaches:

Invite another to dinner. "I want to take you out to dinner tonight," you say to them. "Humor me," you can add, if they look at you sideways. Unambiguous, and the evening should go just fine as long as you behave magnanimously and not tyrannically. Do not undertip nor be precise about it. Do not be rude to your server. Do not chew with your mouth open nor talk with your mouth full. If there is a problem with the bill, address it discreetly and professionally. Do not embarrass your companion. Do not make a big deal out of buying them dinner. It is not a big deal, unless you do it in such a way that they feel very very cared for and complimented and you do not make a big deal of it. Your gift is for naught if they have even the barest suspicion of owing you something. They should feel instead that they have done you a great honor by allowing you to take them to dinner. That they have made you extremely happy by agreeing to spend the evening with you. Of course, that should actually and obviously be the case and you shouldn't have to make any effort to convince them of it.[7]

In the event that there is no reason for you to be taking them to dinner, and you fear they might hesitate to agree to such a thing, you can deploy one of a number of techniques improvisationally at the restaurant.

One possibility is to get it over quickly with the very casual comment as you open the door to the restaurant for them: "By the way, my treat." Or later on, if it is just the two of you, be the one who asks for the check. Do not do it so early so your companion thinks you are trying to cut the evening short. If they appear to be trying to capture the waiter's attention to get the check, outstrip them. Say something like, "Are you ready to go? I'll get the check." When the waiter appears, and without being silly, ask for the check yourself. When the check is placed in front of you, pull it toward yourself possessively or discreetly place it even further out of reach of the other. If the check is not put in front of you, for whatever reason, reach for it immediately and gain possession. Do not let it sit on the table unclaimed. Say in a selfish tone of voice inappropriate in any other situation, "That's mine." You don't have to look at it right away—in fact you probably shouldn't, thereby making the dramatic point that it doesn't matter what it is, it is yours. You certainly don't have to destroy the rhythm of conversation to accomplish this. But you do have to take possession

---

7 By the way, all this is true for the oldest lovers as well as for the earliest moments of courtship.

of it immediately. The longer it sits there, the less convincing you will be when you try to claim you really do want to pay for dinner. "Right," thinks your companion. "Whatever."

Meanwhile, if you are planning to take someone to dinner but you suspect they are not ordering freely from the menu,[8] make it clear it is your treat tonight. Encourage them to order what they want by recommending items on the menu which you have noticed are particularly extravagant. Say, "You should try the abalone! It is delicious here." Remind them it is your treat and encourage them to take merciless advantage. Few will bleed you at the opportunity, and you will set an excellent tone of generosity regardless.

Another trick is to ask for the check, get it and pay it while your companion is away from the table. When it is time to leave and they ask about the bill, you say, "I already took care of it." When they protest, smile and tell them it had been your despicable secret plan all along and now they are your plaything, ha ha ha!

Of course, it is possible that someone does not want to be taken to dinner, is unable to accept a gift freely offered and will insist upon paying their share. If they really do insist and it seems there is some quirk behind it,[9] let it go. Underestimate slightly what they owe and insist that you are right. That gesture should be a gift which they can accept and which they will silently appreciate. Or suggest you were hoping to linger late in a cafe down the road and that if they will let you buy them dinner you would be honored to accept a drink from them later in the evening.

There are so many lovely ways to be generous. All you have to do is think to yourself, "If I were sitting across from myself, what would make me comfortable?" Say and do whatever would make you think, "This is the sort of person I would like very much to be around."

AND NOW WE COME to the most fun part about buying dinner for others. Buying dinner for lots of others. Here's what you do if you have any reason to think others at the table will try to thwart your generosity: At some point during the meal, surreptitiously let the waiter know the check is to come to you. One good trick is to drop by the wait station on your way to the washroom, give them some plastic money and ask them to write up the whole thing before bringing it to the table. Then if there is any dispute, you can claim possession is nine-tenths of the law.

---

8 Women, who tend to be frugal for a variety of reasons, many of which make me so mad I could spit, do this all the time. Keep an eye out for it whether you are a woman or a man.

9 Honestly, why else would someone refuse such a lovely thing as to be taken to dinner? They couldn't possibly be worried about your intentions, could they?

If a meal is leisurely enough and the waiter is not prompt with the bill, you will have plenty of time to excuse yourself for any of a number of reasons, make your way to the host station where you can wait for the bill to be added up, check it, figure the tip, pay for it and return to the table. When it seems to be time to go, or when someone mentions it is time to get the bill, you reveal that it has been taken care of. Nothing anyone can say will change that, and in the end they will be forced into accepting your gesture. However they may insist and seem to refuse, everyone is always delighted to not have paid for dinner.[10] The more nonchalant you are about the whole thing, the more content you seem at having outwitted them in the who's-going-to-pay-for-dinner competition, the more they believe you are truly happy and that they owe you nothing, the warmer they will be toward you and the world at large.

Of course, if it was always understood that you are to pick up the check, you should do away with all such devices and simply be sure to ask for the check and take possession, underscoring your generous intention with graceful action.

---

[10] With the notable exception of some business or political sorts who have very strict and convoluted rules about whom they can accept food from. In the company of such people, it is sometimes entertaining to surreptitiously buy them a meal and then watch them squirm. Mind you, it might be devastating to your greater agenda.

THE END

In which you suffer closing arguments and frail conclusion.

DID CLEOPATRA COOK?

Perhaps not. She was just the sort of person who, by report, wouldn't depend upon cooking skills to attract and keep lovers and other admirers and friends. On the other hand, one might easily imagine she was particularly good at calling for the right bowl of fruit at the right time,[1] and had a cache of chefs waiting to entertain her guests' smallest or most extravagant request at a moment's notice. A version of delivery food. And while we're at it, an excellent opportunity to illustrate for those who thought they didn't need to study this

---

[1] With or without asp, for example, although in hindsight she might have simply waited a moment longer before ordering that last fruit basket.

subject that it is not the quality of the delivery food or restaurants at your disposal, but your discretion in using them. Cleopatra, I'd wager, never frightened off a modest new friend with an overly extravagant curried delicacy that took too long to prepare, nor would she have summoned a gold platter of barbecued eggplant without checking first to see if her guest liked eggplant.[2]

But one might also be willing to place a bet that she had one or two sweets or savories she could make for friends or an intimate without thought, effort or a recipe book. How sweet would that be, seeing the queen of All Egypt, former lover of Julius Caesar himself, patiently and earnestly stirring up some divine snack in the palace kitchen just because your stomach had growled slightly as the two of you languished among silk pillows on the south terrace. How far would watching her whole exquisite self involved in preparing something delectable go toward melting the heart of a reluctant lover?[3] One must believe she had this among her many wiles, even if it only involved knowing where the apricot tree grew in the garden and how to select a ripe one. Someday we might even uncover the hieroglyphic memoirs of a royal insider who will reveal in a titillating, unauthorized fashion that Cleopatra snagged Mark Antony, a most reluctant as well as married and highly principled suitor, one moonless night in just such a manner.

And if you can imagine that cooking might have been in Cleopatra's bag of courtship tricks, why shouldn't it also be among your fewer and less legendary attributes? If even the Queen of the Nile might have found use for a culinary skill or two, if it turns out that even with her collection of charms she did not thoughtlessly feed her guests stale crackers and order inappropriate pizzas, how arrogant would one have to be to refuse knowledge of the kitchen and of food?

TELL ME, WHEN did you realize this is not a book to stretch a repertoire of recipes grown dull? That it is not a book concerned with a more healthy approach to cooking, unless of course you think more friends and less clothing in your life might improve the condition of your heart or somehow encourage your blood to flow more freely. No evidence to the contrary, I should expect it would. Cook as a facet of courtship, even if you court only your own good humor, and see how it goes.

So it is not a real cookbook. So what? There are wonderful recipes all over the place. You could be standing in a bookstore at this very moment or in a kitchen and have a dozen

---

[2] Unless she had some motive in serving them something they didn't like, which is not unthinkable.

[3] The effect of seeing another fully engrossed in whatever they are doing is, in my polling, the most cited reason for falling and staying in love. It need not be cooking. It might be any labor or endeavor at all. Especially if it involves making something. A creative and focused moment. More seductive than any provocative dress or glance. Imagine. Such efficiency. It does make sense though, evolutionarily speaking.

cookbooks within reach. If you had any desire to cook, you have only to find a recipe and keep making it until it works. If there is enough wine flowing and necks for nibbling no one will go hungry, and when you do figure out how to cook, your friends will figure out that they should wait for the main course.

Instead, a book of words to cajole you into considering that cooking may not be a sport reserved for cooks. Neither a chore for the oppressed, nor a pleasure and privilege reserved for the initiated. Only a mystery and forbidden or inaccessible to the degree that you subscribe to fear or other prejudice. Thoughts offered to use as defense against arrogance and its sneers and jeers when someone surprising tucks in dangling necklaces, pulls back unruly hair and says "I'll cook tonight." Encouragement for you to cook well and for no reason beyond that I would like to eat in more often.

PLAYING WITH FOOD

Or, entertaining yourself at home.

HERE YOU WILL FIND what could be taken as recipes by someone who has not read the rest of this book. Really they are only descriptions of how one not very skilled at cooking happens to play with food. As recipes, they are vague and untested. They are rather illustrations. Of course, you might find that some of them sound savory and want to try them. Do as you like, but know there is a stiff undertow. You will be much better off with a real cookbook and only a general recollection of what went on here.

BAKED BRIE

According to the delicious M - - -

WHO CAN EAT IT? A monstrosity of overindulgence lauded by over-dressed host-esses. A blandly rich cheese thing baked in buttery pastry so there is no graceful way of eating it without it dripping oil on your invariably silk clothes which, by the way, you will soon be too voluptuous to wear.

Then the sultry M--- walked into my life bearing gifts of friendship and regard and, one summer's night, baked brie. Oh sure, it is still messy, still frighteningly fat. But now I will be rude to my friends, stiff business contacts, lie to small children and wear cotton for evening if I think it will get me another bite.

Seek out:

> *A brie round — Not too large.*
>
> *Sundried tomatoes — Brought back to life with a minute in boiling water,[1] bathed languidly for minutes or hours or days in olive oil and garlic. Or from the jar in which they were packed in oil. Chopped up, or pureed slightly in the cuisinart. M--- uses tomatoes from her own garden, dried in the sun or the oven. You probably won't.*
>
> *Pastry sheets — The sort you might use for brioche. Or that other, flakier kind used for baklava.[2]*

Slice the brie round sideways so you have two full circles of brie half the original thickness.[3] Spread a thick layer of sundried tomato stuff on the cheese side of one half, and then replace the other half on top. Now wrap this in pastry, however you like. Don't look here for tips. Open a cookbook, or call someone who knows how to cook. Once wrapped, put it in the oven for awhile. Serve without bread or anything except maybe some good wine. Cut into squares and eat with your fingers. Encourage your guests to do the same.

---

[1] You can use the microwave for this. Put the dried tomatoes in a small bowl with a bit of water and microwave for however long . A minute or two or three, depending on how many tomatoes. Remove the tomatoes from the water and bathe in oil and garlic for at least a few minutes before doing anything with them, like putting them on bits of French bread and eating them up.

[2] As if anyone besides M --- would ever make baklava.

[3] Naturally, I've never done this. And I don't really expect you to do it either. But if you did feel bold...

The savory tomato and the spiciness of the garlic cut through the oppression of cheese wrapped in buttery pastry, allowing you to devour much more than you would otherwise find palatable. How fortunate for your tailor.

VARIATIONS

On another occasion, M--- again arrived bearing gifts, but this time the brie was cut with prosciutto. Oh oh. She claims she did everything as above, but using the cured meat instead of the tomatoes. She seems trustworthy. Give it a try.

Another, also beautiful M--- of other, more public fame pats a nice layer of chopped nuts and brown sugar on top of the brie round and bakes it like that. No pastry sheets. No slicing open the round. Easier, richer, sweeter, different. Like herself. Serve with very plain crackers or with very good, also plain bread.

BRUSCHETTA

Italian for savory things on small toast

VISIT ALL THE finest markets until you have obtained:[4]

> *Roma tomatoes*
> *Garlic*
> *Fresh basil*
> *Olive oil*
> *Salt, pepper & sugar*
> *French or sourdough bread — Loaves or baguettes*

Chop up a bunch of roma tomatoes as small as you like them. Use a knife, not a food processor. Chop up several garlic cloves. They should seem like fresh, hard fruit and be sufficiently pungent that people walking into the kitchen should exclaim immediately how good everything smells. Pick the best leaves from a bouquet of basil and chop them up as well. Throw each thing into your favorite bowl as soon as it is chopped. A little salt, a bit more sugar, a grind or two or three of black pepper and several spoonfuls of olive oil. Mix with a wooden spoon and serve on French, Italian or better yet sourdough toast which has been cut into strips. If you use baguettes, slice slightly on the diagonal so the pieces are

---

[4] You might have divined this list from the description on the menu at your favorite trattoria.

elongated. If you have nothing else to do with your hands, rub a peeled garlic clove on the toast before you spoon on the tomato stuff. Brush the bread with olive oil before toasting if you like and if you will be toasting horizontally.

Too easy.

Perhaps, but you might be surprised at how impressed your guests will be by this minor display of Italian flair. Hot jazz or romantic opera is perfect with this sort of thing, though Led Zeppelin may do as well. Check your lighting. If it is very bright, even still daylight, which is fine for lively conversation and summery food that tends to spill and fall all over the place, be sure light is not shining directly on anyone's face or the top of their head. Napkins out and available. Survey the drink situation and correct any empty glass problems. Do all this without anyone noticing and you are on your way to being an extraordinary host; fresh, sultry and spontaneous with a dash of Italy. You might even consider keeping that chopping knife handy to ward off unwelcome amorous adventurers.

VARIATIONS

If you don't like bread, or don't have any that is appropriate, or someone can't eat bread, make up some white rice,[5] let it cool and then toss some of it into the tomato mixture, and then some more and some more until it looks like something you want to eat. Add the rice slowly so you don't add too much. The point of adding the rice to the tomato rather than vice versa is to assure that you won't find you have less tomato than you would like mixed irretrievably with more rice than anyone wants.

Or, add a bunch of torn up brie cheese and more olive oil to the tomato stuff, let it sit around for a half hour or so and then toss with freshly cooked and very hot pasta.[6]

Or instead of the traditional tomato bruschetta, you might experiment with other things on toast, preferably rubbed with garlic. Italian cookbooks will sometimes offer suggestions. I can suggest very good pesto, preferably some that you made yourself with fresh basil, but there are very nice basil pestos to be had in the grocery stores of the larger cities and the smaller, gourmet towns. A strip of sundried tomato on top of the pesto, or instead of. Avocado and very sharp, very thinly sliced cheddar or parmesan cheese.[7] Roasted red

---

[5] Not the minute rice stuff. Who could be in such a hurry as that? Put as much real, washed, preferably basmati rice as you want in a pan, add as much water to cover it plus almost an inch more. Some small amount of salt. Bring to a boil and then simmer covered for about fifteen or twenty minutes. Or measure one part rice to something shy of two parts water. Salt. Ask your mom. Or your former spouse. They'll tell you all about it.

[6] That would pretty much be a recipe gleaned vaguely from the first Silver Palate cookbook, a book you might want to acquire. Those authors in turn gleaned the recipe from a luncheon in the Tuscan countryside. I'd guess someone in that Italian family spent a little time in France. A sublime dish almost any way you make it.

[7] In an even greater variation for the usual wheat-intolerant friend, the bread was replaced by slices of boiled and cooled yellow potatoes. Perfect little canapés, or bizarre bruschetta. They were so good. It reminded me, because I do forget, that restrictions are nothing of the sort. They free you instantly from your own habits.

peppers marinated in olive oil and garlic and cut into strips. Roasted garlic puréed with a little stock and some herbs to make a spread perfect for bruschetta. Some incarnation of those white cannellini beans; cooked, mushed and toyed with.

Mostly, use your imagination and whatever is available at the farmer's market or hanging around from last night.

Caesar Salad

DO NOT PUT whole anchovies on the top unless you know someone loves them. But do use anchovy paste in the dressing. Oh yes. Mom is amazed her daughters keep it on hand as assuredly as they keep dish soap. My lord, she thinks to herself. What else do they have in their cupboards?

Complaining as she will, I mix up things she hates in a bowl. Garlic. Anchovy paste. Lemon is all right with her, I suppose. Not too much parmesan. So much oil? Would I feel better under her attack if I knew what I was doing? I cringe as I choose again to use an egg. When will I stop this madness? Soon, I promise again. And where is the thyme I bought today? That is the secret thing. The thing I would never have thought of but some chef in some forgotten restaurant did. Fresh thyme or dried if need be. It hardly matters. Magnificent or more magnificent. With the olive oil, lemon from a lemon, an egg, parmesan cheese, anchovy paste, pepper from the grinder, the best croutons you can find, which is to say bread pieces toasted with oil and garlic. By Lewis, if you have any luck at all. The most beautiful romaine lettuce the organic farmers from several states have to offer or from a neighbor's garden. Washed and made dry. All tossed together. First everything except the croutons and the lettuce. Then the lettuce, now torn up with hands that might as easily tear another's mind from their flesh, their heart from their soul, in some wooden bowl, old and worn and wide and now full of ripped up green to be tossed with a mixed-up sauce of some thickness. Croutons finally, and then the gesture of completion, freshly grated parmesan and ground pepper.

You might put it on a plate. I suppose you could eat it with a fork. Fingers work as well. Mom tells all her friends that of all the salads in the world she prefers this one. Forgetting how much she hates everything about it.

DON'T FORGET TO serve very good bread and something to drink. The croutons tease rather than sustain, and there is salt in the salad by way of the anchovy and the parmesan. With lots of garlic bread and plenty of wine and conversation you have a party.[8]

Feel free to figure out how make this without the egg.[9]

CAFE AU LAIT

A coffee drink for morning courtship of anyone at all

TRY TO REMEMBER if you have in the house:

> *Good coffee and a means to brew it*
> *Whole milk*
> *A stove-top steamer, or a blender or something equivalent*
> *Sugar or honey, according to taste*

Make a delicious pot of strong coffee somehow, some way. With the melitta or the coffee maker or the melior.

Steam milk with a stove-top steamer.

Or heat two cups of whole milk somehow, some way. On the stove or in the microwave. Then make the hot milk frothy either by putting it in the blender for a minute or by using a minipimer handheld mini blender.

Or come up with your own technique.

Pour the frothy milk and the hot coffee into tall, sturdy glasses or into porcelain bowls which you can drink from. The final color of the mixture is about that of a paper bag. Spoon a layer of white foam on the top if it did not form of its own accord.

Of course you can also do this with a home espresso maker.

---

[8] This was the menu at that wild book party a few years back. I mention it because I don't think anyone noticed. It worked extremely well for an active party. I think there were brownies or some such hand-eaten dessert brought by one of the guests to finish off the evening. Food enough to sustain, but not so much as to sedate. Evocative enough of a meal—being comprised of a first part and a last part—that no one seemed to miss nor long for a traditional middle part.

[9] Feel free to use a recipe, for that matter. Once in a while there will be good one in a cookbook. The amounts as determined by a real chef will be better than anything you or I can do impromptu. Still, you might want to add more garlic, a little thyme. Anchovy paste, if it was left out.

SERVE TO ANYONE who is still in bed, remembering to include a linen napkin, or the best the situation has to offer. Linger nearby, sitting in a chair or lounging on the floor, and offer conversation as accompaniment. Leave if you are not needed, if another courtship is progressing nicely without you.

Serve with fresh bread or muffins or croissants or toast or melon or grapefruit or bagels[10] to anyone who wanders into the living areas.

CHOCOLATE PIE

With apologies to Will Jones and the Lincoln Delicatessen

THIS CHOCOLATE PIE is the best thing ever. Your friends will be so happy you learned how to make it. They will coax and cajole, and you will deign or decline. The inside is too easy, but requires your attention for about thirty minutes. Not that you can't continue your conversation while the electric beaters are beating, but you will not be able to do much else with your hands. The key is fresh eggs. If the eggs are not fresh, the chocolate stuff will curdle or simply not stiffen. And there isn't a thing you can do except throw it out and start over with fresh eggs.

You will find yourself needing:

> *A baked pie crust* [11]
>
> *Unsweetened chocolate — Four squares (i.e. 3 oz.) of very good chocolate, or just three, if you like your chocolate light*
>
> *3/4 cup butter — It must be butter, and the better the butter the better*
>
> *1 cup of powdered sugar — You cannot substitute any other kind of sugar*
>
> *Real vanilla extract*
>
> *Four or five fresh, large eggs — They must be fresh, or this won't work*
>
> *Whipping cream — Heavy cream eventually whipped to soft stiffness*

---

[10] Or leftover pizza or Indian food or garlic bread or leftover carrot cake or cheesecake or fruit pie or whatever anyone might enjoy.

[11] For this pie, try not to buy a pie crust. Better to serve it without a crust at all. Just call the whole thing "chocolate mousse" and serve it in bowls with dollops of whipped cream. Maybe with a crispy cookie for luck.

But people are bowled over by a hand-made pie crust, no matter how bad it might be. It can be tough, uneven, patchwork and partially burnt, and you will still get pie-crust credit. Any recipe for pie-crust will work. Just be sure to do the whole thing really fast. If you have a food processor, you are a fool not to try. What's the worst that could happen? You get covered in flour and someone takes pity on you. The recipe I use is: 1 1/2 cups of flour and 1/2 cup of butter mixed together, and something less than a quarter cup of cold water or orange juice

In this pursuit, tools and appliances are required:

A double-boiler, or a very low setting on your stove, or a microwave oven

An electric mixer

A rubber spatula

A wire whisk

Two bowls — One smallish and one largish

A pie dish (if you do indeed make a pie and not just a bowl of chocolate)

To the heart of the matter:

Slowly heat the butter and the chocolate in a pan, a double boiler if possible. Stir gently with a wooden spoon while they melt into one another. You can melt them in the microwave if you want. Saves time, and if you use the same bowl you are going to mix in there will be less clean-up. But you will miss the high-quality flirting time always associated with the slow melting of anything, but especially of butter and chocolate.[12]

When the butter and chocolate have formed their most perfect union, add the powdered sugar and capful of vanilla extract. Stir it up. Pour into a medium big bowl if you are using a hand-held mixer. Pour into the bowl of the stationary mixer if you are using one of those. Use a rubber spatula to get all the chocolate out of the saucepan. Allow to cool slightly, enough so the eggs won't cook when you put them in. Break one egg into the chocolate sauce and turn on the mixer, starting on low and then increasing the speed. These eggs need more beating than you can possibly imagine until you have actually done it. Several minutes for each one. Add the second egg and continue to mix until the consistency changes again. Add the third, fourth and possibly fifth egg and beat until the mixture begins to hold the patterns made by the beaters. It will noticeably change in color, becoming lighter as it stiffens. It should become solid enough to keep its shape when spooned into the cooled pie crust, or into bowls or just one big bowl if you have opted out of making a crust. Before you spoon it into the serving bowl or pie crust, taste it to make sure it is sweet enough for you. You can add more powdered sugar directly to the chocolate stuff and beat

---

or sour cream added slowly until the whole thing just barely sticks together in a ball. Roll out on a smooth surface, using lots of flour to discourage sticking and turning the flattened dough over when it is half rolled out. Put in a pie plate and bake for ten minutes at 400 degrees. Something like that. Make little cuts in the bottom of the crust before baking, maybe even pour a handful of dry beans into the pan to hold the crust down while it cooks. Otherwise it might turn into a big puffy thing with no room for the chocolate stuff. If it does, poke holes in the bubbles right away; while it is cooking is best.

[12] If your beloved is in the kitchen or within hearing distance, please don't use the microwave. If they are so far away they can't hear it, by all means zap the stuff, finish the pie and go be with them.

for a few seconds to mix. When the chocolate stuff is perfect[13] and has been spooned into a pie crust or something else, give the beaters to someone to lick clean while you rinse out your mixing bowl. Dry the bowl well. Lick any stray bits of chocolate off your friend's face. Place the pie, or whatever it is, in the refrigerator for at least an hour or two or until serving.

Now, turn one cup of whipping cream into whipped cream. The whipped cream should be softer than the chocolate mousse. A trick from an athletic pastry chef is to whip the cream with the electric mixer only until it is just starting to thicken, stopping well before it gains any stiffness. Then finish the job by hand with a wire whisk. This way you can easily control how whipped this cream gets. Or you can turn the mixer to low when the cream starts to keep patterns on the surface. Do not add sugar. If you want, add several drops of vanilla. Serve as a side dish with the chocolate pie or mousse or whatever it has turned out to be. If you have a number of people and someone is unable to partake of chocolate, suggest they try the whipped cream with their coffee.[14]

A FIRST ATTEMPT at this delicacy can be a little disheartening because the beating does take an unexpectedly long time. But it is not actually a long time, so relax. Everyone waits for chocolate and besides, if you are in such a hurry you shouldn't be making dinner in the first place. You should have ordered takeout and bought ice cream and cookies.[15]

---

[13] If the chocolate never really stiffens, but also does not curdle, spoon or pour into the pie crust or bowls anyway. It will chill to a sufficiently firm if somewhat dense thing in the refrigerator after an hour or two.

[14] If you knew beforehand that they could not eat chocolate but decided to make this anyway for your own reasons, please have something on hand that they will enjoy for dessert. Fruit. Cookies. Leftover cranberry crumble. Something you can offer them and which they can decline for other than health or dietary reasons. Since it is somewhat common for people to be unable to eat chocolate, it might be a good habit when you do not know all of your guests very well to have an alternate dessert on hand if you plan to serve this pie. I feel foolish even mentioning this. Of course you thought of it yourself.

[15] Or Scotch whiskey. This most humble and effortless recipe stumbles in late from a small but loud party. Vanilla ice cream, or coffee or toffee or chocolate, I suppose. We preferred the vanilla. Several spoonfuls in a bowl. Then encourage guests to pour Scotch from their glasses over the ice cream to form a caramel-colored sea around the icy islands. Scotch Isles, we call it, because it is close to midnight and we are giddy from a successful show at Monika's gallery. Don't be embarrassed. I should think if the booze is of sufficiently excellent quality and age, you could serve this at the finest of events.

CRACKED CRAB

With Caesar Salad and Bread

FOR THIS MEAL it is handy to live on the west coast and to serve it during crab season when it does not seem like a foolish extravagance.[16] You might also remember there are a good number of people who can't eat shellfish, or some shellfish, because of allergies or pregnancy or environmental conscience or religious affiliation, and if you serve it to them they will be unhappy and unable to eat, and then you will be unhappy and I hope unable to eat. Although they will try to be nice about the whole incident, you will feel terrible and both of you will be hungry. There is another group of people who think shellfish itself is evil for one or more of a number of reasons. One is the possibility of being poisoned by the delicate flesh which does seem especially prone to absorbing toxins from its environment. Another might be the ongoing debate as to whether shellfish has 1000 or 10,000 times more cholesterol than any other known food. These people won't be nice about it, and you will feel awful about having been A) so callous as to have even considered serving shellfish to people you love, or B) so foolish as to have such nervous and inflexible people for friends.

The best approach is to ask very casually upon invitation to dinner if your guest likes crab. Do not reveal any commitment on your part to serve the little sea-creatures. Listen to the response. If it is anything besides "Oh yes, I love crab!", or perhaps, "I don't know, I've never had it," change your plans. Crab is too dear to serve to the unwilling.

Once you feel confident you won't offend anyone with your good intentions, or be offended by their response, go to the best fish market you can find. Ask someone who knows where one can get the best crab.[17] If you don't know anybody or anybody who knows anybody who knows this sort of thing, try calling a couple of very good restaurants that serve fish, ask to speak to someone in the kitchen, and tell them you are trying to find a source for fresh, cooked crab. Most sources supply both restaurants and the public. Buy almost as many pounds of crab as you have people to feed. Ask the people at the fish store to crack and clean the crab for you. They will charge you for this favor. Pay for it, and do not imagine you can do it as well at home.

---

[16] On the other hand, always try to get the far more glamorous Alaskan King Crab, which has a similar season but is extravagant no matter when you buy it. It is more delectable, more dramatic and less likely to be poisoned by the waters near San Francisco. If you purchase the exotic crustacean during the local season, perhaps no one will notice and wonder what you want from them that you should be serving Alaskan crab.

[17] Be careful whom you ask. Knowing whom to ask is a most important skill.

NOW FIND THE BEST bread in town. If you are on the west coast, get the sourest, crustiest sourdough bread possible. Anywhere else, you must find something that will stand up to the crab without stomping on its delicate nature. Nothing whole grain or coarse in any way. Nothing so light and airy that it will go unnoticed. Sweet baguettes are not a fabulous choice unless the bread is very very good,[18] but they are better than anything whole grain and very much better than anything sliced. Italian bakeries are popular in some places and they often have heavier, tastier white breads than you will find in a regular bakery. Something with herbs, maybe. No olives nor mushrooms nor meat nor cheese.

Hop over to the vegetable store and buy a gorgeous head of romaine lettuce. Pick up as well a creamy-looking Caesar salad dressing in a bottle.[19] Check the label and don't buy anything with MSG listed an ingredient. Be a responsible consumer. The ingredients should be all natural[20] as much as they can be. Most importantly, the dressing should be wonderful. It is going on the salad and will also serve as a dipping sauce for the crab. Pick up some garlic or herb croutons, following the same purchasing guidelines as for the dressing. No cooking in the kitchen tonight.

On your way home, stop by a good wine store and get some very light white wine. Many of the Italian whites are excellent with crab. Orvieto, something like that. Ask the merchant for a suggestion.

GO HOME. PUT the wine on ice or in the fridge.

---

[18] This is as good a moment as any to ask that you look at the ingredient list on your bread. It should contain only things you could get yourself at the grocery store. Flour, water, yeast, starter, grains, condiments. Certainly nothing you cannot pronounce or would have to visit a chemist to purchase. Purchasing only such bread as you would make yourself is your only means to encourage bakers to stop putting preservatives and false flavor in breads.

[19] I honestly don't know how to make a Caesar dressing as right for dipping crab as can be found in bottles. Perhaps you can find or develop your own recipe and so enjoy making one part of this supper. I have, out of necessity, taken the point of view that the otherwise embarrassing bottle of dressing is integral to the ease of preparation for this elegant meal, that to chop or stir or whir or otherwise toil would spoil the motion and rhythm of the event. I limit the humiliation of the thing by being careful, as mentioned, in my purchase of the bottle of prepared dressing, convinced that the whole meal would be spoiled by replacing a dressing of choice with a general brand concocted of emulsifiers, fillers and chemically created flavors and colors.

[20] Did you know that the preservatives we eat act as tanning agents and that our bodies don't decompose as quickly as they used to? This is also discussed in the graveyard scene in *Hamlet* when our hero asks the gravedigger how long it takes a body to rot, and the gravedigger replies "Faith, if 'a be not rotten before 'a die (as we have many pocky corses now-a-days, that will scarce hold the laying in) 'a will last you some eight or nine year. A tanner will last you nine year ... his hide is so tanned with his trade that 'a will keep the out the water a great while, and your water is a sore decayer of your whoreson dead body." Nowadays, bodies never rot. Once they're dead, that is. Say, is this appropriate discussion for a cookbook?

Pull from cupboards and shelves:

Two big bowls — One for the crab and one for the salad
One very small bowl — For extra Caesar sauce for dipping the crab and bread
A basket or cutting board for the bread
An extra plate or bowl — For discarding crab shells
Big plates and big cloth napkins for everyone

Let the cracked crab fall from its package into one of the two bowls. Put a large cloth napkin over the top of the crab, or a layer of paper towels, and then cover with ice. Make the salad most casually, washing the lettuce, drying it and tearing it into big pieces. Toss with dressing and croutons just before serving. Put the bread, perhaps partially cut so it can be ripped easily, into the basket lined with an enormous cloth napkin, or leave it on the cutting board, or put it on the table as is.

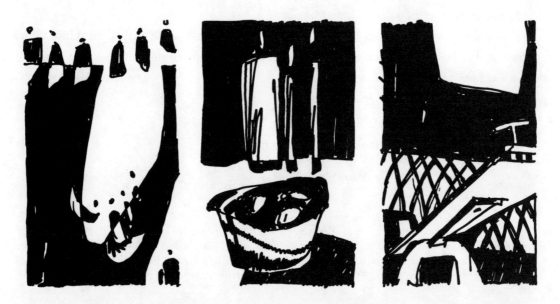

Offer your guests martinis if they like them, or beer or wine or water or juice while you are doing all this.[21]

---

[21] Another nice touch, which I swear I discovered quite accidentally, is to allow your guest or guests to arrive while you are still in the shower. Put on a discreet robe. Preferably a cotton kimono, or some other indifferent, after-bath attire that will not speak loudly of your seductive purpose. Being clean, wet and naked under an unwrappable wrap of plain fabric is enough. Make your excuses for having arrived home late and having been very grimy while you pour drinks for everyone, or at least open a bottle of wine or pull out the gin or vodka, pointing to the cupboard where the glasses are hidden. Then you can decide whether or not you wish to get any further dressed. Often the party will be sufficiently advanced at this point that no one will care if you ever put on any clothes again for the rest of your life. Very dangerous to execute with any but the most pure intentions.

Serve the crab, the salad and the bread, perhaps at the coffee table, seating your guests on couches and chairs, or possibly on the floor if you have a very nice floor and cushions and things to lounge about on. Make sure everyone is comfortable and not too nervous about not being at a table if you are not at the table. Serve the salad with big utensils and have forks out in case someone wants them. You might need some tools to crack the crab a bit more. Nutcrackers work. A wise host will eat everything with their fingers, including the salad, thus giving guests the go-ahead to go ahead and enjoy themselves. Don't speak of it. In fact, don't speak of anything concerning the dinner. Make sure the music is complementary—hot jazz or slow salsa goes well with cool food.

DON'T LET DESSERT ruin the atmosphere. Excellent cookies that someone else made, either a friend, a bakery, a manufacturer or you in a former incarnation from yesterday or the day before. Ice cream, though tonight keep your choice of flavors traditional and uncomplicated.[22] Coffee, cognac, whatever seems right. Don't put yourself out now.

CRANBERRY SAUCE
Remarkably without mention of the berry's medicinal benefits

THE TWO TRICKS to making cranberry sauce that come to mind are: Have the cranberries in the first place, and ignore everyone's suggestions about how to make cranberry sauce.

Fresh cranberries are only in the stores in the late fall and winter. Around the holidays they are on sale and you can stock up. Throw a few packages in the freezer and enjoy them all year.[23]

On the second note, be forewarned that people hanging around the kitchen will invariably tell you to put orange rind or lemon or some kind of liqueur or fruit juice or nuts or spices or whatever in the cranberry sauce. "I have the best recipe for cranberry sauce," they will joyously exclaim, and then list a bunch of delicacies you would have to ask Hercules himself to find for you. How can it be the best recipe when it has so many ingredients in it? Let them make their own sauce. Don't fight or argue with them because they might start helping you make it their way. Just nod your head, murmur something unintelligible and

---

[22] Ice cream should follow the same guidelines as bread: It should contain only ingredients you can, and would, purchase yourself in a food store. And by the way, see footnote 15.

[23] The frozen bags of cranberries are also excellent, as are frozen peas, for throwing on sprains and bruises. Of course, they become useless as food, so if you have a choice, use the peas.

go on about your business. Hum a little or talk to yourself so they think you are nuts and keep their distance. You can even throw out a decoy comment like, "Hmmm, maybe I'll try that." All will be made right at the table if you stand your ground at the stove.

Other than that, you really have only to follow the instructions on the back of the cranberry package. One bag of whole fresh cranberries (about two cups), one cup of granulated sugar and one cup of water. Put all this and nothing else into a sauce pan and cook at medium heat until it is done to the texture of cranberry sauce you like. I cannot give times because it all depends on how hot the stove is and how nubbly you like the sauce. I once hurried them through at a high heat in about seven minutes, stirring furiously to keep it from burning on the bottom, and later cleaning up a horrible mess of splattered cranberry.[24] Better to allow the cranberries to cook for about fifteen to twenty minutes on medium heat, partly covered when you are not stirring them. You'll see why. Time them so the sauce is ready at the very moment you are ready to eat. Or keep them warm. Or heat them up again just before serving. The sauce should be warm or even almost hot when it is eaten. Serve cranberry sauce whenever you or someone you adore feels like it. You don't need a turkey.

A THIRD TRICK for cranberry sauce is to spoon it warm over vanilla ice cream.

GARLIC BREAD

"A jug of wine, a loaf of garlic bread and thou."

EARLIER THAT SAME day, find and purchase:

> *Long loaves of sourdough French bread, or very good, plain French bread*
> *Sweet butter, 1/2 cup per large loaf*
> *Garlic, and lots of it*
> *Aged Parmesan, Romano, or Asiago cheese, grated*

Melt the butter slowly on the stove or in the microwave without cooking or burning it. Add about half as much garlic as you have butter and stir it up. Fresh crushed garlic in a jar is

---

[24] My own fault one holiday. Chatting with some surgeon about the cultural effects of the cruel misuse of interns in the US hospital system, I forgot my one responsibility until people were actually serving themselves plates of food and there was only some canned cranberry concoction with candied fruit and mini-marshmallows in it. I will never forget the disappointment in my sister's eyes and her effort to feign indifference. I persuaded her to take a late spot in the buffet line and had the sauce ready before she sat down to dinner. A narrow save.

excellent for this. Chopping up cloves of garlic is always a good idea, but garlic bread needs an awful lot of garlic and you must choose your battles.

Meanwhile, slice the loaves of bread lengthwise along the side so they butterfly open, just like they do in French films. Pour, spoon and spread the butter and garlic sauce onto the opened bread. This can be a trick as the melted butter sometimes soaks in before you can spread it around. Actually, that is the point. Otherwise you might be tempted to put on less butter and garlic than is necessary for this garlic bread. If you have put enough garlic into the butter, there won't be much of a problem. When all areas of the bread are decorated with butter and garlic, sprinkle both sides of the loaf generously but discreetly with grated cheese.

Now you have a choice. You can close up the bread, wrap it well in foil and throw it in the freezer. Or leave the loaves open and put them, maybe one at a time, into an oven at about 350°F for 7-8 minutes.[25]

I suggest putting a loaf or two into the freezer in any case. It is as wonderful as you might think to pop the neat packet into a hot oven and have fresh fabulous garlic bread like mom never made in just a few minutes. Especially nice if you find yourself cooking dinner for two or three or six or seven or eight when you had had no such intention at all. Keeps your guests from fainting dead away while you figure out what you can possibly make out of the meager ingredients in your refrigerator or while someone goes to and gets back from the store. Garlic bread in the freezer is also very useful for a spontaneous evening. "Say, I just remembered. I have garlic bread in my freezer. I made it last week from some extra loaves of bread. Why don't we make a salad, open a bottle of wine and eat dinner on the porch?" I haven't met the would-be lover who would not say Yes. When you cook the frozen garlic bread, leave it in the foil and cook it at 350°F for about 15-20 minutes,[26] opening it and allowing it to toast for a few minutes at the end.

VARIATION FOR RESPONSIBLE READERS

Still use the best bread you can find. But instead of succumbing to the siren call of butter, use olive oil. Still an astounding amount of garlic. Heat the oil and garlic together with some amount of rosemary, dry or fresh, in a saucepan on the stove. Spoon onto the cut open bread. Bake open in the oven at 350°F for about eight minutes. It's not the same, but it is delicious.

More variations will wander past your eye. Everyone, it seems, has a way to make garlic bread. Notice what you like and copy without remorse.

---

[25] The length of a quick shower, including getting undressed and later putting on a robe; no hair washing unless the hair is very short. If you need more time, say 10-12 minutes, put the oven at 300°.

[26] Handily enough, the time it takes to shower thoroughly, including washing your hair, but still not getting very dressed.

GARLIC, LEMON, PARSLEY & GARLIC PASTA

A ONE-BOWL pasta. Its features being quick and effortless to make in any amount, requiring only one bowl, one pot, one spoon and five minutes.[27] Distilled from several recipes, none of which I could conveniently make in three square feet of kitchen in a fourth floor walk-up in the Left Bank. A platform for unlimited amounts of garlic and it nearly always tastes good no matter what the mood. It also turns nicely into pasta salad for a picnic tomorrow or the next day simply with the addition of some vinegar. As so many others do, this dish depends on a generous hand.

Check to see that you have most of the following things in or near your kitchen:

Pasta rotelle — Nice, but one of the long sorts like spaghetti is fine, too

Garlic — Chopped or crushed, and lots of it

Parsley — Dry or fresh and in copious amounts

Lemon juice — Preferably from a lemon heavy with juice,
but if necessary from a bottle

Olive oil — The best on hand

Black pepper & salt

Crushed red pepper — If you are that kind of cook

Start your water and put the pasta in as soon as it is boiling. Mix up the oil, lemon juice, garlic and parsley in a big ceramic bowl. Use lots of garlic: A big spoonful, or at least two cloves per person to be served (don't mention this to your guests), lots of lemon juice (at least one, really juicy lemon), and a tree of parsley. The pasta won't be as green as pesto, but the parsley should be a presence.[28]

The oil, lemon, parsley and garlic mixture should be about an inch deep on the bottom of the bowl. You can add more of everything if it turns out not to be enough sauce for the pasta you make.

---

[27] Plus whatever time it takes to boil water and cook pasta. But that time doesn't really count because you can be doing all sorts of things, many of which do not involve food, while you wait for physics and chemistry to run their course.

[28] If you made this sauce in a food processor, or with a mortar and pestle if you still live in Tuscany, it is a pesto. Just missing the nuts and an imperative to use Parmesan. You might want to try pushing this recipe in that direction sometime.

As soon as the pasta is ready, and it is as important to not overcook the pasta today as always, strain and throw directly into the bowl. Toss and add black pepper and salt as you like, maybe some crushed red pepper. Don't use cayenne. Serve with grated parmesan if you or your guest would like. The end.

GUACAMOLE
In a manner of speaking

THERE IS SOMETHING vaguely indecent about avocados. Soft and heavy, with an unmistakable, barely perceptible flavor. And the color looks particularly nice being nibbled off fingers.

'Guacamole' only in that it is mainly comprised of squashed up avocados. The sole other ingredients garlic and cream cheese. A friend calls her version, which inspired this and which is finer and paler, Avocado Cream. Hers is a pale green cloud of nothing that will kill you. This one is not so bad.

Amounts? Oh, I don't know. Avocados and garlic cloves are so hard to quantify. The last time I made it—some few moments after a fit friend scorned me for making it at all and so these amounts are probably wrong—I used three medium-large avocados, four ounces of cream cheese and filled the garlic press three times with very sharp garlic. I don't recommend so much garlic. I don't even recommend a garlic press. I was angry. I got crazy. To be sane, try one smallish clove for each avocado. Let set for a while because you can't taste the garlic right off, then add more if you like. Salt and pepper. Jurgen once added a spoonful of apple cider for smoothness.

If you are already tired of this earthly prison, go ahead and scoop it up with nacho cheese doritos. Regular tortilla chips are also good. For something a bit more continental and a bit less embarrassing try French bread or slices of cucumber. Make a sandwich on a crusty roll with long, razor thin slices of cucumber, maybe alfalfa sprouts if you are that kind of girl or boy, and generously spread this avocado stuff instead of mayonnaise or mustard or anything. Very nice. There once was a delicatessen in Cambridge that made sandwiches like this but with a Boursin-like spread. It makes you wonder where you've been cloistered and what else you might have missed. A wonderful afternoon snack while you page through cookbooks considering what to have for dinner.

GUACAMOLE TOO

Another approach to guacamole, more traditional and less disgusting to anyone with a notion of health, comes from some friends who keep kosher and who eat very well. Avocados, naturally. Garlic, as usual. Lemon and cayenne. Seeded and diced cucumber and sweet red pepper. What's so special about that, you ask. Oh, nothing. Try it anyway. So quiet, the coolness of the cucumber and the sweetness of the pepper sneak up on you and make you imagine other things that might be sweet and cool and at the same time soft and rich and spicy hot. Barely even reminiscent of those scoops of green served in self-declared Mexican restaurants from coast to coast.

NOT GUACAMOLE

Perhaps you cut open an avocado planning to smash it into some kind of common dip, but it is so perfect and beautiful the idea of mushing it up makes you cringe. Don't. Change plans. Remove the seed. Place each avocado half on a plate which has perhaps nothing, perhaps something else on it. Pour some sort of delicious vinaigrette dressing into the bowl of the fruit where the seed used to be. Serve it just like that, before dinner and with a spoon. They do it in France all the time. In Italy it would seem they squeeze lime juice onto the avocado and then dribble with some honey. Eat it with a spoon so you won't hurt yourself.

If you intended to do something like this, but the avocado turns out not to be so gorgeous once you open it up, cut it into pieces and toss it with the salad. Or make guacamole of some sort. Or slice or mush it up and put it on sandwiches. Or feed it to the dog. It's very good for fur.

LASAGNA

IN MANY CIRCLES a sort of ambrosia. A peace pipe of pasta. It improves after spending some quiet time in the frigidaire. Narrow slices of layered flavors you can eat with your fingers. On the other hand, it does take some time to make. Not a whole day, mind you, but you should certainly expect to spend a couple of hours putzing around the kitchen. Time and labor intensive, but not so demanding of your culinary skills.

In case you don't know, lasagna is a baked pasta dish comprised of alternating layers of a wide, flat, frilled pasta, tomato sauce, mozzarella cheese, maybe some kind of meat or vegetable, maybe ricotta cheese, maybe some kind of béchamel (white, cream) sauce, and Parmesan cheese.[29]

---

[29] One of the very best lasagnas in the world can be had in Paris, in the shade of Montmartre, at the Scorpio Pizzeria. God knows why. Normally it's not the sort of thing one can successfully order in restaurants.

There might be a lively debate going on somewhere about the proper order of stacking the layers. Not here. You put on what you think it is time for, making sure you get all of them in several times. I usually put some sauce on the bottom of the pan to start, and finish with some sauce under the last layer of Parmesan, but hardly anybody looks to me for cooking advice. Try the back of the lasagna box. The only trick I know is to be in a good mood when you make it. Lasagna, like everything, does not benefit from grumpiness nor stinginess. Serve it with a very Green Salad in a Caesar or vinaigrette dressing, and Garlic Garlic Bread with Garlic. Corn off the cob cooked with butter and salt and pepper is also nice alongside.

Rustle up:

> *Pasta — A box of lasagna noodles*
>
> *Tomato sauce — Some excellent, or better than decent sort.*
>
> *Mozzarella — A ball of it sliced up*
>
> *Ricotta — A pint mixed up with spinach if you like.*
>
> > *Or choose to use a white sauce.* 30
>
> *Grated Parmesan or Asiago or Romano*

For equipment, you might want to have nearby:

> *Pasta Pot*
>
> *Colander*
>
> *Sauce pan*
>
> *A bowl or two*
>
> *Cheese slicer*
>
> *Baking dish of some sort*

Boil your lasagna pasta in a pot, remembering to add a few drops of oil, some salt, and maybe a crushed clove of garlic. It shouldn't be even al dente because it will cook again in the oven. Actually, as long as it's flexible it is probably cooked enough. Strain in a colander and toss with a spoonful of olive oil to keep it from sticking together while you layer it with

---

30 I think white sauce has something to do with cooking together flour and butter until it is light brown (Cooks in the know call this a Roux and pronounce it "roo".) Add milk or cream at a leisurely pace to eventually form a very thick gravy. Actually, this is sort of how you go about making gravy. In any case, I have never really gotten a handle on this particular skill. Ask someone who is a better cook than you are to show you how to make a white sauce some rainy day. There is nothing quite so charming as the sincere request to be shown how to do something. Try not to make the sauce better than they do at some later date when you are cooking for them.

the other stuff. Don't worry if it gets cold during assembly of the casserole. The whole thing gets cooked again.

Slice your mozzarella. This is a good time to have one of those slicers with a roller and a wire or a planar slicer. The cheese should be cold in any case or it will scrunch up when you slice it and make your life momentarily hell. Grate your Parmesan, Asiago, or Romano cheese if it is not already grated. Stir up your ricotta, adding chopped spinach if you like, frozen or fresh. Don't forget to wash it well and drain it in either case. Stir it up.

Where is your tomato sauce? On the stove simmering since Tuesday? Still on the shelf in the supermarket? It really doesn't matter what sauce you use, as long as it is thick enough and very tasty.[31] If you are using something off the shelf, put it in a sauce pan, on low heat, and add some garlic, some red wine, some crushed red pepper, some oregano. I would prefer you do not use mushrooms. If you want to turn this into a pink lasagna, now's the time. Add some cream, sour cream or white sauce.[32] Stir it up.

Arrange the various cheeses, sauces, colander of lasagna and the pan you will be filling up with these sublime strata so the layering process will be convenient for you. Be prepared to make several lasagnas in various cooking vessels, as it is difficult to gauge the amount of stuff you have to work with. Don't worry if all of the sauce gets used up on the first lasagna and the second ends up being primarily cheese. Or vice versa. Everyone likes their lasagna different. Someone is bound to like yours.

Start layering. The pan should weigh about ten pounds per square inch when it is filled. Finish with a light layer of parmesan. If the pan is very full you might want to consider putting a sheet of aluminum foil on the oven rack to catch bubbling cheese and tomato sauce. It is not imperative, not dangerous, clean-up is easier and you can recycle the aluminum. Ask some well-muscled morsel to lift the pan into the oven. Seal up any extra little lasagnas for sojourns in the subzero. They are so nice to heat up on a moment's notice when good people suddenly appear or if you are one night hungry and alone, and worlds better than anything you could buy.

Typically the lasagna will need to bake for about an hour at about 350°F. It needs to bake at a medium heat until it is hot and bubbling. Some people like to bake it covered with

---

[31] This footnote is the only place in the world you will find instructions for Onion Lasagna. Thickly slice as many yellow onions as you can stand. Do not chop them up. Sauté the big, thick, half circle slices with plenty of olive oil and/or butter slowly so that they do not brown but become translucent and start to turn golden. You might consider adding some oregano to them while they cook. Create your tomato sauce around these onions. Make it simple, maybe even using plain tomato sauce with oregano, basil, parsley, red wine, sugar, red pepper, garlic, Italian sausage, whatever, including some cream at the last moment if you want a pink sauce. Use this onion thing as "tomato sauce" in layering the lasagna. That's it. On another day, you might consider trying the recipe for Pesto Lasagna in the first Moosewood Cookbook. Friends swear that it is not difficult to make, and I swear on occasion I have fallen in love with the cook.

[32] Oh, sure.

aluminum foil until the last ten or fifteen minutes, when they remove the foil and let the top brown. I don't like to use foil. Suit yourself. You can accomplish the same effect by making your lasagna in a casserole dish that has a cover.[33]

When you do take it out of the oven, do not try to cut into it right away. You should let it sit for at least ten minutes to let it set. Use this time to make sure everyone is happy and every wine glass is full of Chianti or Valpolicella. Serve generous rectangles on big white plates with lots of green salad and maybe some garlic bread.

Leftover Steak

TAKE HOME THE remains of that too generous steak. From restaurants or barbecues, just ask for it to be wrapped up. It is the one thing people will believe is for your dog. Wrap it up well, put it in the refrigerator and try not to forget about it. A day or two later, find yourself and a friend at home in the most languid sort of way. Without turning on the kitchen lights too brightly (in fact, maybe just a low lamp or bring in a lighted candle), slice up the bit of steak into strips with a chef's knife. Watch the fingers. Sauté them (the strips of steak, not the fingers) slowly for a few minutes in the tiniest bit of butter or oil—or nothing at all if you have the right sort of non-stick pan—until they are hot through. Place them (again, the steak strips) on a nice dinner plate,[34] add a good sized dollop of Dijon mustard, or mustard mixed with some mayonnaise, or maybe some herbed aioli[35] or leftover béarnaise sauce if someone is very, very lucky.[36] Ketchup or yellow mustard would be poor choices.[37] Take the plate and some large napkins back to the floor in front of the fire, or to the bedroom, or the bathtub, or wherever you left this evening's companion ten minutes ago. Yes, ten minutes, that is all it should take. This is for evenings when hunger means something else entirely.

---

[33] Of course, you'd have to actually have a casserole dish with a cover. This might also be a good time to make sure you have a oven that works, and if there is a pilot light, it is lit.

[34] See the Dishes portion of "Setting Tables".

[35] Mayonnaise with garlic, naturally. Also very good with French fries, on burgers, with cracked crab, or salmon. Indeed, there are any number of things you can do with aioli.

[36] And they would be very, very lucky if you happened to know how to make béarnaise sauce. I don't even think I can spell it right without help. It is a tarragon sauce which requires a double boiler and constant vigilance to prepare, but then lasts for a good long time in the refrigerator. A gnarled uncle of mine makes it as though he were trained in Paris to the purpose. It is the only thing he can make that does not involve charcoal and a big sky. It is enough.

[37] I don't care how fond you are of them. They reek of fast food and the associations are all wrong.

NOTE: Don't insist on feeding your companion if it does not occur spontaneously, organically.[38] As always, but in this case especially. Meat is not a particularly playful or romantic thing. Just eating this barbaric and dangerous snack is enough for most people. Especially if they are naked.

NOTE 2: Don't you dare use utensils.

CORA'S MASHED POTATOES

THESE POTATOES ARE served from coast to coast. Sometimes they are served to me, and when I admire them and ask where my host learned the recipe, it always traces back to Cora. They are sublime with roast anything, sautéed anything, grilled anything or by themselves. These potatoes could be the key to world peace.[39] Wonderful as well with some kind of delicious gravy. Always at our Thanksgiving table, always something we are very thankful for.

Get:

> *Idaho potatoes — Two or three times as many as you have people to feed*
> *Butter — A half-cup at least*
> *Sour cream — A pint, really*
> *Black pepper and salt*

You can peel the potatoes or not, as you wish. If you do not peel them, wash them very well, scrubbing with a stiff brush. Cora always peels them. Cut up the potatoes into large hunks about the size of new potatoes. Throw them into a big pot of boiling water with several spoonfuls of salt. Cook for about twenty minutes, or until the potatoes fall apart when poked with a fork. Pour out the water, leaving the potatoes in the pot. Add the cube of butter, or most of it, or more, and mix it up with the potatoes, allowing the potatoes to crumble and the butter to melt. Add the pint of sour cream, or most of it, or more.[40] At this

---

[38] Which is to say they eat a morsel out of your fingers, right under your nose, surprising you terribly. Or perhaps soaking wet or just unwilling to move their hands from wherever they are, they ask you to feed them.

[39] On a diplomatic level, not a universal scale. The ingredients, the industries that supply them and the politics and ethics that support them probably and unfortunately won't hold up in a world scheme.

[40] It is extremely difficult to convince people how generous one should be in making this dish. The amounts are wild and extravagant and utterly immeasurable. You can only achieve the sublime point where Cora has staked her claim by transcending all preconceptions you might possess about amounts and propriety. Best of luck to you. Fear not for all steps along the path are quite satisfying in themselves.

point you might want to be using one of those squiggly potato masher tools or an electric mixer. Cora uses the mixer and the mashed potatoes are like velvet. Sometimes I just use a fork and the potatoes are wonderful though a bit, shall we say, rustic. In any case, smoosh the potatoes, butter and sour cream together until it is a texture you like. Black pepper, taste, add some salt if you like and then taste again. Add whatever you think it needs more of.

VARIATIONS

One of Cora's daughters doesn't like to boil potatoes. She thinks all the nutrition is boiled away and, having small children, she worries about that sort of thing, and besides, she is right. So instead of boiling the potatoes, she bakes or microwaves the whole potato, and then does the butter/sour cream/salt-and-pepper thing on each child's plate, smooshing it all together quite haphazardly with a fork while she talks on the phone, probably to Cora. It is different, less of a knockout, and only slightly less wonderful to eat. How does this vary from a regular old baked potato? Not much, except you may not feel comfortable doing this in this particular manner in a fine restaurant.

Other variations include the use of seasoned salt or other herbs, or garlic. The use of different sorts of potatoes or yams or sweet potatoes. New potatoes are terrific, mashed only coarsely.

IN THEORY, THIS is not unlike how one goes about making puréed anything. The French do this with almost every vegetable. Carrots, beets, turnips, parsnips, celery root, whatever comes up. Cook it and then mash it up, more typically with just a bit of milk or water, salt and pepper.

AN OMELET

Or not, for morning or evening or afternoon

I WOULD LOVE to not have an omelet in this book at all for all the usual reasons. What is worse, although I suppose it hardly matters, is Boursin[41] is the only other ingredient. I am sorry. But if I don't tell you about this omelet and a morning full of sunlight and romance passes into the hands of some horrible ham and cheese thing, I will never be able to forgive myself.

---

[41] Boursin is a soft cheese riddled with garlic and herbs, and which is made in France.

There is not much to say. Make a delicate omelet, adding a small amount of water and maybe some white pepper to the scrambled eggs before pouring them into the sauté pan.[42] Turn the omelet if you like, or mess with it a few times with a rubber spatula or wooden spoon before it sets so the top part is not too terribly liquid.[43] Place small pieces of Boursin all over the omelet, fold up, let set for a minute and serve with a baguette or fresh croissants, delicious coffee and some kind of citrus juice. Flowers should be on the table and music in the air. No one should have on street clothes. Except maybe the person who went out for fresh bread, juice and flowers. When the omelet is gone, go back to bed.

Of course, you can serve this to friends who have come over to your house in their real clothes, if they have brought bread and flowers and fresh juice and fruit.

SCRAMBLED EGG VARIATION

Often you won't be able to find, afford, or otherwise procure Boursin. It can be made, but not without the gelatin-free cream cheese that is almost as difficult to find as the Boursin itself. Plus, sometimes you misplace your omelet making skills.

So, scrambled eggs. As many eggs as you like. Three per person seems right. Depends on the persons and on the size of the eggs. Beaten up in a bowl with a little milk or water

---

[42] Right after a small amount of oil or butter, if you still haven't managed to procure a non-stick pan. Mind you, a non-stick pan is invaluable, both while making the omelet and when it is time to clean up.

[43] Everyone has to figure this out for themselves. Watch someone who does it well and then experiment. Or get someone to teach you. Or open up Escoffier or Julia Child and follow their instructions to the letter until you think you know how to make a delicate omelet. I once possessed this skill but have since let it fall to the wayside. So I can offer no advice, except maybe that you don't have to be very talented to have this be a very effective omelet.

and a spoonful of Dijon mustard. Salt, pepper. Dry, sharp cheese, grated. Cheddar, Emmenthaler, Asiago, Parmesan. There is a dry, aged Jack that is good. Not a great deal of cheese, but some. Try more, try less, if you are not content. And thyme. Fresh, dried fresh, leaves or ground. A little bit or quite a bit. It is very hard to go wrong.

Start cooking the eggs slowly, again in a non-stick pan if possible. Stir lazily with a wooden spoon or a heat-resistant rubber spatula while listening to conversations around you or just to a little Dave Brubeck. Add salt and pepper, thyme and cheese as the eggs begin to cook. Take them off the flame moments before they are as cooked as you want them to be. It is hard to believe, but eggs keep cooking in their own heat. A bare moment before they are perfect, put the eggs on plates with toast and sliced up vegetables or fruit. If you have many hands and much ambition, some thinly sliced zucchini or summer squash sautéed just to softness in butter, thyme, salt and pepper are perfect alongside. They kind of go with the eggs. Or broiled slices of rich red tomato.

If you have much foresight, you can sauté onions slowly to translucence in butter before you begin cooking the eggs. Use the same pan, but put the onions to the side until the eggs are cooking. Add the onions just after you add the cheese. Also very nice, but those damn onions can take fifteen minutes to soften up and if you got a late start on breakfast, which is not an uncommon scenario, they are not worth the wait.

ONION STROGANOFF

Being at once wholly traditional and wholly invented

THIS RECIPE WAS stumbled hard upon late one night in the shadow of Montmartre when there was nothing in the refrigerator. Not even the things that are always there. Bleak house, as it were. And in France there are no twenty-four hour supermarkets. Few late-night dining spots. Fewer still in that part of town. Onion Stroganoff would be worth mentioning as an example of how even the meanest, emptiest refrigerator can be tamed. But as it happens, even when the ingredient situation is not so bleak, when the finest produce and most exotic groceries are available, it is still chosen. Warm with flavors that are strong and savory without depending on garlic or meat. Comforting. Provocative. Neither ethnic nor reminiscent of anything your mother ever made. And it doesn't have any mushrooms.

Careful, though. Some people do not mix well with onions.

Somehow assemble:

> *Onions*
>
> *Butter or olive oil*
>
> *Thyme — Dry and lots of it. Or fresh and lots of it.*
>
> *Worcestershire sauce*
>
> *Black pepper*
>
> *A glass of wine*
>
> *Tomato something — Sauce, paste, juice; not ketchup*
>
> *Sour cream, or creme fraiche if you actually are in Paris*[44]
>
> *Pasta*

Slice as many yellow onions as you can get into your skillet. Three or four works for two hungry people. The more onions the better. Leftovers will be coveted. Slice the onions into generous half circles. Don't chop them up nor slice them thinly or you will have nothing to bite into. Don't use red onions as they dissolve to nothing when exposed to heat.

Cook the onions slowly, very slowly in a good amount of butter—or oil if you choose[45]—and lots of thyme. More than that. The onions should not brown, but rather turn translucent and keep their shape. To that end be sure the heat is low but still cooking.[46] This takes some time which makes some people think it is not a particularly good late night dish. They have a point, but it tastes so warm and sweet and savory in the middle of the night, you might forget momentarily their objections. Besides, you will think of something to entertain yourself while the smell of onions and thyme start to fill up the kitchen. Conversation of some sort can be good. Climb up on the counter next to the stove so you can jostle the onions in their buttery grave with some frequency. When the onions are cooked, add a few ounces of whatever tomato thing is at hand, some appropriate but generous amount of Worcestershire sauce and black pepper. Stir it up slowly while it all continues to cook. Pour in wine whenever you like, a bit at a time starting right before the tomato is added, allowing it always to simmer off right away. When you are just about ready to

---

[44] Luck alone that this was in the apartment that evening. By the way, you can make creme fraiche by mixing together equal parts of sour cream and heavy whipping cream and leaving it out for maybe 24 hours. Mix thoroughly before covering and leaving on the counter. Mix again the next day, and then put it in the refrigerator. No reason to pay the exorbitant prices it sells for in the states. Don't try to do this with anything but all natural sour cream that lists only cream and culture or enzymes as ingredients. on the container. Don't buy anything but this sort of sour cream ever. Have I already mentioned this? Most sour creams are thickened with gums and other things which behave poorly in recipes. Don't buy them and don't use them if possible.

[45] But why? You have to use sour cream later, and so have no chance at all of avoiding dairy, which is the only reason I can think of to not use butter here. Throw in the towel now, or make something else. Or perhaps you could make some kind of roux and add it later to thicken and lighten the sauce. If you can make a roux.

[46] Medium heat, I think they call it.

serve, when the pasta is just about perfect, when your guests are starting to malinger near the stove, add one or two or three large spoonfuls of sour cream, stir, and then add more until you like the color and consistency. If it is too thin, simmer for a minute. Too thick, add very little water. Taste, and make sure everything is well represented in the dish. It could need salt, but probably not. Serve over some kind of fat pasta like linguine or fettuccini. Spaghetti works fine. So does toast. Or rice.

Green salad with nothing except dark lettuce and oil & vinegar & pepper is good right after, or before to distract your guests if it is late and they are fidgety.

DON'T SERVE THIS, or any kind of stroganoff, on warm, starry nights.

PEANUT BUTTER COOKIES

MY RECIPE SHOULDN'T be shared because it comes directly from a cookbook. Meta Given's kitchen treatise. A *Joy of Cooking* for a generation that couldn't possibly conceive of cooking as a joy. Cora was given this book as a wedding present from her grandmother. Now out of print, I find copies in junk shops in small towns famous for rodeos. Everything you want to know about cooking, canning, skinning, roasting, toasting, whatever.

Somehow, some way, find a really good recipe for Peanut Butter Cookies and get very good at making them.[47] They are extraordinarily simple to make and don't require refrigeration or rolling out. A plate of these fat, glittering disks heaped to tottering on a plate makes people sigh with delight. When all else fails, and even when it hasn't, there is no shame in resorting to peanut butter cookies.[48]

Be careful not to encourage the tendency of people to revert to pre-pre-pre-pubescence at the sight of a peanut butter cookie. Serve them with very good champagne and candle light, or some really good, maybe even spiked coffee. Stay away from milk or hot chocolate. That will put your audience into a juvenile mood and then to sleep. As their eyes haze over, you might even be mistaken for someone's mother.

Later, of course, you can sneak down to the kitchen and help yourself to all the nostalgia you like.

---

[47] Or if you like, don't. Refuse to bake, refuse to learn how to make cookies, and leave this particular arena to me.

[48] Beware those few that cannot stand them. They will not be won over, and may even be put in a bad humor by being reminded of what they cannot enjoy.

STILL, I THINK I will tell you. I guess I've changed enough things. Doubling the recipe for all time for starters.

Arrange together on the counter:

> *Flour — 2 1/2 - 3 cups unbleached white* ·
>
> *Baking soda — 1 teaspoon; optional, it turns out*
>
> *Salt — 1/2 teaspoon*
>
> *Butter — 1 cup of unsalted if available, and at room temperature*
>
> *Peanut butter — 1 to 1 1/3 cups of all natural, all peanut peanut butter,*
> *   also at room temperature*
>
> *Sugar — 2/3 cup of the white, granulated sort*
>
> *Dark brown sugar — 1 1/3 cup, well packed*
>
> *Eggs — 2 that are large, but not freakishly so*
>
> *Vanilla extract — A capful or two of the real stuff*

As usual, mix up the butters, plain and peanut, and the sugars, brown and white, altogether in a bowl till it is smooth and tempts your fingers to dip in for a taste.[49] Sift, or mix together with a fork, the flour, soda and salt. Mesh strainers sift well, if you feel you must sift but don't possess a real sifter.[50] Add the eggs to the butter/sugar mixture and mix it up well. Add the vanilla. Then add the flour mixture, slowly, a bit at a time,[51] until it is all mixed in and you have cookie dough.[52]

With your hands make balls of dough more or less the size of ping-pong balls. Maybe bigger. Place them on a cookie sheet. Pour granulated sugar into a small flat dish. Press the prongs of a dinner fork flatly onto some cookie dough to make the prongs sticky and then into the sugar. Then squish down the balls of dough twice, in two different directions, cross hatching the top of the cookie. Press the fork into the sugar each time before you press the

---

[49] Think twice before succumbing to this pleasure if there is someone else in the kitchen. Some people are extraordinarily sensitive to fingers being dipped into food. No arguing with them. They find it disgusting.

[50] Isabel, whose advice concerning cooking is well-heeded, thinks having a good sifter is very important. You are going to have to look into your own soul on this one. I live nicely without one. Not as well as Isabel lives, it must be noted.

[51] If you put too much in at once, you will find it as challenging as synchronized swimming, and about as much fun, to stir without getting flour all over yourself and the kitchen. Which might be entertaining. But if you want to keep this exercise contained, add just as much flour as you can stir into the wet stuff easily, then add more, stir, add more, stir, and soon you have cookie dough.

[52] This whole process will be much easier if the butters are room temperature and therefore soft and pliable at the outset.

cookies. The sugar keeps the fork from sticking to the dough, and later the sugar glitters faintly on the cooked cookie. However much you press the cookies down is more or less how they will stay, so suit yourself.[53] I think I let them hover around a half inch, or just a bit more. Try to keep the depth of each cookie even[54] so they cook evenly.

Bake at 375°F for 10 to 15 minutes. Please don't overcook them. Watch that they set, but do not brown at all. When they come out of the oven, put them on wax paper or parchment to cool, or on a wire rack if you happen to have one. Serve them stacked up in casual opulence on a dinner plate.[55]

PEANUT PASTA

FIND YOURSELF SERENE or mischievous in a kitchen and within grasp of:

Peanut butter — Natural, chunky or smooth, as you like

Vinegar — Rice wine or balsamic or white wine or even white

Soy sauce

Garlic

Ginger root

Sesame oil — Or tahini, or don't worry about it

Hot pepper oil — Or crushed red pepper, or Tabasco, or something spicy hot

Sugar — White or brown, or honey, if there is any left

Broth or fruit juice, or hot water lemon grass has simmered in

Green onions

Chopped cabbage or bean sprouts

Pasta — Spaghetti or some other long sort

Place a big bowl before you. Put in a few very large spoonfuls of peanut butter. Maybe about a cup. Pour in some vinegar, about a fourth of a cup, and about the same amount of

---

[53] As it happens, whether or not they keep their shape is really determined by how much moisture is in the dough, and I have yet to perfect this science. Sometimes they spread out a bit and become a uniform thickness; sometimes they keep what ever shape I pressed into them. If you want them to be more shapely, add a bit more flour to the cookie dough which has not yet been baked.

[54] That is to say, not squished paper thin on one side and left fat on the other the way Oscar, who is six, likes to do.

[55] For heaven's sake, don't ruin the voluptuous effect of these cookies by placing them daintily on a platter, You will make people nervous about disturbing the arrangement when they should be helping themselves with abandon.

soy sauce. A little more vinegar than soy. Pour in a small amount of sesame oil. (If you only have tahini, use a bit of it instead.) Add a bunch of garlic.[56] More than you think is reasonable. Add the ginger.[57] More than you think is wise. Stimulated senses are stimulated senses. Speaking of which, add the hot pepper stuff.[58] Stir until the peanut butter has dissolved, adding a bit of warm broth or some juice to help it along if you like. Add a spoonful of sugar or two or three, or a long squeeze from the honey bear. Stir it up. Ask someone delicious to taste it and see what it needs. Add whatever they suggest if their suggestion is not foolhardy. Taste it yourself and decide what it really needs. It probably needs more of everything except peanut butter. You should be able to just distinguish all of the different ingredients, but no one should overwhelm the others. If you can't tell what it needs, but it surely needs something, it needs sugar or honey. It is best to go easy on the soy sauce at the beginning and add more later.

Wash the sprouts or cabbage and the green onions. Chop up the onions with your chef's knife, way up into the green part.

If you have never made the sauce before, do not start the pasta until you are happy with the sauce. If you are comfortable with the recipe, you can start the pasta water before you pull out the bowl. The water should be ready at about the same time you are stirring up the sauce. Rush back into the kitchen! Throw the pasta in the pot. Just this once, you can use the same utensil you are using for the sauce to stir up the pasta. Finish up the sauce,[59] adding broth or juice or water until the sauce is the consistency of very heavy cream that is starting to turn sour.[60] Maybe a little thicker. When the pasta is al dente—that is when you

---

[56] Garlic, maybe as many as ten cloves, pressed or chopped. Squash the cloves with the side of a chef's knife and then chop them up finely. Or spoon fresh garlic from a jar, as I do now and then. Fresh cloves of garlic are different and better.

[57] Try to use fresh ginger. Several inches of a root, peeled and chopped. It is so much more everything. Sometimes having fallen into the habit of laziness and using the powdered stuff for long months, I have forgotten what this pasta is like with fresh ginger. Then I am surprised and marvel all over again. People will be happy regardless of what you do, but how hard is it to pick up a piece of ginger root when you are at the store?

To prepare the ginger, use a potato peeler to get the rough skin off, or don't. Cut thin, round slices of ginger, then chop it all up. If you don't know how to chop gracefully and effectively with a chef's knife, ask a chef to show you. It involves holding the pointy end lightly against the cutting surface and then rocking the blade of the knife against whatever you want to chop.

[58] Hot pepper oil you buy in the store is definitely oil, but rarely very hot. To make your own sufficiently spicy oil, take an empty jar and fill it with about a cup of light sesame oil, or peanut oil if you are in a pinch. Then pour in most of a bottle of crushed red peppers—the kind pizzerias serve—cover and leave for a few weeks. Now you have the best hot pepper oil in the world right in your own home. Careful though, as it keeps getting hotter as long as there is any red left in the pepper flakes.

[59] By the way, if you do all this right, and god knows how you would do that since I have been singularly unhelpful on the subject, you will end up with about three times more sauce than you or your friends can possibly imagine putting on the amount of pasta you are cooking. Forge ahead. Overabundance can be perceived as a charm in some few circumstances and this is among them.

[60] This is also, more or less, the consistency of motor oil before it has spent any time in an engine.

bite it you can feel it between your teeth but it doesn't crunch—strain it in a colander, rinse quickly with fresh, cool water, and put it back into its pot. Pour a few tablespoons of sesame oil on the pasta and toss. Or don't. Add some sauce, and toss. Add more. Throw in most of the sprouts or cabbage and some of the onions. Add still more sauce if needed. Use your hands, washing them first. Put the whole mess back into the bowl, rinsing the bowl first if it is very messy. Or maybe you put the pasta and vegetables into the bowl of sauce, if you made the sauce in a nice big bowl, and toss right there. (If there really is too much sauce, put it into a jar or other container and save it for later. It lasts forever in the refrigerator.) Throw the last of the cabbage or sprouts and onions on top of the pasta. Give someone a kiss on the nape of the neck as you place a plate in front of them and invite them to help themselves.[61]

VARIATIONS

Replace the beans sprouts or cabbage with julienned carrots or broccoli or nothing at all. Some people do not like or cannot eat sprouts or cabbage. Refuse to make it if the green onions come under attack.[62]

Add fresh basil leaves, cut into strips. Or cilantro.

Include cucumbers. Or serve with cucumbers in an Asian-influenced, vinaigrette dressing.[63]

Cook some rice and let it cool. Chop up cucumbers, red or green onions and maybe some cabbage. Toss with sauce which has been watered down to the consistency of a whole milk.

Sauté breasts of chicken in oil, ginger, and garlic, quickly braising each side, then add water to the pan, cover and let cook for about ten or fifteen minutes. Whatever it takes. Let the chicken cool before tearing it into bigger than bite-sized pieces. You might have to share the last one. Toss in some of the peanut sauce while the pieces are still warm and then either include the chicken on the top of the platter of pasta, or serve in an entirely separate dish so vegan eaters will not be intimidated and refuse to have any pasta at all.

---

[61] I have a confession. This recipe has never worked. I have been making it for about seven years, it is extremely popular and widely requested, devoured and complimented by everyone except my sister who doesn't like it at all, but I have never quite managed to keep it from becoming somewhat dry within about ten minutes of having tossed the sauce in the pasta. I think if the pasta is rinsed, which direction I did include in the recipe, this problem is solved. Who knows. You are most cordially invited to figure it out for yourself. No one cares, but it has always bothered me.

[62] Again, hyperbole. Never refuse anything. Ponder and decline. Choose otherwise. Reconsider and retreat. Surprise with unexpected surrender. But don't refuse just like that simply because I told you to.

[63] I'm not suggesting you make something else. Dilute the peanut sauce with vinegar and oil and a little water. Or combine anew some oil, rice vinegar and a little soy sauce. How hard is that? Cut up the cucumbers into random chunks rather than neat slices for fun and because they are easier to eat with forks and fingers that way.

PESTO

ONE AT A TIME, into the cuisinart, and in the following order:

> *Basil leaves, from several bunches of basil*
>
> Whrr whrrrr whrrr whrrrr whrr.
>
> *Olive oil, about 1/4 cup*
>
> Whrr whrrrrrrr.
>
> *Garlic cloves, as many as you think is appropriate*
>
> Whrrrrr whrrr whrrrr...
>
> *Pine nuts, or walnuts, maybe 1/4 cup as well*
>
> Whrr whrrr whrr!
>
> *Lemon juice or white wine, several tablespoons*
>
> Whrrrrrrrrrr.
>
> *(Melted butter or a bit of cream, if you are completely irresponsible, 1/4 cup of either, and not the cream if you used lemon juice. Lemon doesn't mingle well with milk or cream.)*
>
> (Whrrrrr!)
>
> *Parmesan Cheese*
>
> Whirrrrrrrrrrrr!

Boil water, cook pasta, toss in a bowl with more of this green sauce than you probably think is right. Serve with salad and garlic bread and wine and water which bubbled out of the Italian Alps. The end.

Broadly drawn and tough to destroy. Experiment with extraordinary amounts of garlic. See how bright the green can get with the addition of lemon juice. Serves many. Serves two.

Pesto sauce might also be bought at the grocery store (depending on where you live), can be safely stored in the freezer, and is generally fine. Nothing like making if fresh, but many people have never had fresh pesto and will never know what they're missing.[64] Add sliced sundried tomatoes or sautéed mushrooms[65] for diversion when you toss the pasta.

---

[64] He proclaimed politely that he did not like pesto, believing it to be true, until greater politeness and perhaps curiosity required that he taste freshly made pesto one day at a picnic on the beach. Turns out his disdain sprung from disliking a version found on a pizza made somewhere in the middle of Kansas. Probably in winter. Turns out he likes it just fine when it is well made from fresh basil in late summer. Moral: While you cannot force others to try things they think they don't like, you yourself might make an effort to be aware of the circumstances surrounding moments of judgment, and reconsider with some frequency your tastes.

[65] I've never actually done this because I cannot stand even the scent of cooking mushrooms. But from what I can tell, you just slice them up from top to bottom, and then sauté them somewhat slowly in a bit of butter or oil. In any case, that's what I would do if I had to do something with them.

With the addition of vinegar, it becomes pesto pasta salad. Add some sliced up vegetables, like carrots and zucchini and green onions and peas,[66] and you will be very popular indeed on the picnic circuit.

FROM ELAINE

Slice a sourdough baguette into elongated ovals. Brush with olive oil and toast under the broiler for a few moments.[67] Spread lightly or not with pesto sauce as made above. Decorate with sliced strips of oiled and garlicked sundried tomato. Or several fresh peas, blanched[68] if you think of it.

FOR RUSSELL

As above, but instead of toast, slices of boiled or roasted potato.

PIZZA

ALWAYS HAVE THE number of a very good pizzeria on hand, no matter where you are. By "good" I do not mean you should compete with your friends as to who has the best pizzeria, arguing senselessly about what qualities of pizza are most important, risking foolishly their devotion when you turn your nose up at their pizza of choice.[69] In this forest of flavor and texture and politics, I will trust there is a pizza of which you are enormously fond,[70] and this is the pizza you will share with your friends because you know

---

66 Or again, mushrooms.

67 You have just made crostini, the toasts that form the foundation for bruschetta.

68 I don't understand why it is called "blanching", since my main experience is one of green vegetables becoming more intensely green. Get some amount of water boiling and then put whatever you want to cook into the boiling water for a few moments. For green vegetables like peas, green beans, asparagus, etc., you watch carefully, gently moving them about in the water with a wooden spoon, and the moment they change to a bright green, take them out. Proper blanching also involves rinsing the vegetables in cool water. I don't generally do that.

69 Be gentle in leading them towards a better pizza, especially if they have lost their way so badly that they might even consider ordering Domino's. Don't let them. Not just because the pizza is barely edible, but because the politics that will be supported by your pizza dollar are nauseating. Ask around. I am not familiar with the interior of the country, but on the coasts it is very hard to get romantic with anyone who thinks you support in any manner restrictions on the rights of women to choose what to do with their bodies. How did pizza get so complicated? In any case, since it is always a good idea to support local merchants, unless you live in Detroit it shouldn't come up.

70 Really fond, not just impressed by the sophisticated toppings you could have but never do because who really wants an arugula pizza?

they will like it too. Not because it is such an interesting pizza, but because it will speak to them and to you as a beloved to a lover when you open the box. Only rarely[71] is pizza a good place for culinary adventure.

I recommend garlic, but I think I am almost alone in this. As one who hates mushrooms, I warn you to find out beforehand if your pizza partner or partners like mushrooms. If they don't, leave them off. Putting them on half is a solution, but a bad one. The way you shares pizza is very indicative of how you are. When someone says they don't like something, it is not very nice to say, "OK, I'll just put it on my half". Think of what that might lead to. What if one day you express a dislike for whips and chains, and your partner takes the same approach as you did with the mushrooms? On the other hand, if the person who doesn't want or like mushrooms orders the pizza with mushrooms on your half anyway, accept their gesture graciously and try to get a commitment out of them that night.

The same approach should be taken toward meat, which to some people is very akin to being asked if they like whips and chains. Or anchovies. Or olives.

I find that a pizza cluttered with peppers and onions in addition to the garlic, goes over well with a great number of people. Sausage added to that, if you have a crowd of carnivores, is a bliss not easily described.

Always share pizza. Always have too much. Be loved. Be happy.

YOU WANT TO make your own pizza? Seems like a bit of work to me, though others insist nothing could be easier. A recipe for a crust can be found in many cookbooks, and then just about anything can be arranged on the surface. Some sort of tomato or herb sauce, vegetables and savory meats, sliced garlic and other condiments, various cheeses. A pizza stone is nice and helps the crust cook evenly, but I have had lovely pies made for me on plain cookie sheets.

Suit yourself. I order pizza, and shower friends who choose to make the pie themselves with praise and compliments and the most sincere tribute of eating up every bite.

---

[71] Although famously as well in the case of Mr. Puck.

POTATO LEEK SOUP

with thanks to Mrs. Oswald

COLLECT QUIETLY from a variety of sources:

Leeks — Washed well and sliced up
Potatoes — Washed well if you do not peel them
Butter
Broth — Full of flavor, from vegetables or a chicken
Fresh dill
Black pepper
Salt

Sauté in butter and at the bottom of a nice big soup pot two or three or four well-washed and sliced up leeks. They should get soft and fall to pieces. Kind of like you do. Meanwhile, somewhere nearby, cut up several pounds of well-washed or peeled potatoes into large pieces, way too big to eat in one bite. Throw the potatoes into the pot and cook them for a moment with the leeks. I don't know why. Add broth or water to cover the vegetables plus two inches or so.

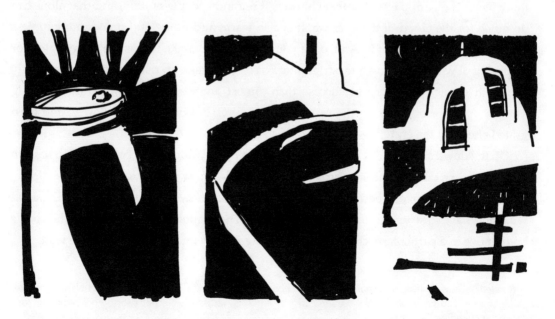

Let simmer for awhile on the stove. Thirty minutes maybe. Until the potatoes get soft and fall apart when poked gently. Kind of like I do. Portion by portion, put the soup in the blender for a brief turn. Return the puréed soup to the pot. Add a handful of fresh dill, or several tablespoons of dried. Pepper and salt.

IF YOU SERVE THIS soup to people who do not much like you, they will reconsider their opinions. If you serve it to people who already like you a bit, you will find it to be the sauce of friendship. If you serve it to people who already love you, be prepared to rise mightily in their estimations and please remember to behave humbly in your newly exalted position.

RISOTTO

Which is to say round rice, slowly and gorgeously cooked

YOU SHOULD GET a real recipe for risotto. There are several excellent cookbooks full of nothing but risotto recipes.[72] A friend even made excellent risotto from a recipe on the back of the risotto bag. It had amounts like ".6 gallon", which were a little hard to decipher, but it still worked.

Risotto has several charms, one of which is that it does not involve wheat, and so for those people who have wheat allergies, and there are many, it is a great alternative to the more usual choice of pasta. Another charm is it reminds people of Italy, and that alone can do much for the mood of the evening. It is also warm and filling and unassuming, unless you make a big deal about it. And, once you learn how to make it, it is the perfect ploy for disposing of whatever is in your refrigerator.[73] You can make up risotto recipes more easily and with greater assurance of success than almost anything else. Just do the Five Big Things: Butter or oil, cooking the rice, adding alcohol, hot broth added slowly, and hard grated cheese at the end.

On the down side, the rice takes about fifteen to twenty minutes to cook and you have to stand there the whole time stirring it. On the up side, most people look adorable stirring something on the stove, especially if it smells really good and your audience is drinking good wine and have ideas and humor to sustain them. The motion of stirring makes the cook's body move in a particularly charming, undulating fashion and few will mind the wait.

---

[72] *Risotto: A Taste of Milan*, an exquisite jewel of a book by Rosario and Constance Arkin Del Nero has everything you need to know, and looks beautiful in your kitchen, unlike that other risotto cookbook everyone including myself seems to have.

[73] Once I made risotto with apples, onions, raisins, thyme, and German beer, just because that was what was in my teeny tiny refrigerator and I didn't feel like walking down five flights of stairs to get some real food. Not very Italian, but no one complained.

Risotto makes a splendid non-meat meal which is not too disturbing to non-vegetarians. It is also good with sausage, or seafood, or poultry, or served next to a roasted something.

A RECIPE? WELL I suppose I could give you the general outline, just to assuage your fears about the whole thing. Don't take this as gospel, though.

Gather:

> *Arborio rice — 2 cups*
> *An onion — White or yellow*
> *Butter or oil — About a third of a cup*
> *Broth — About 6 cups, simmering on the stove*
> *A glass of dry wine*
> *Grated parmesan — A fat handful or two*
> *Other stuff you want to put in the risotto*

Start with some kind of well-flavored broth simmering in a saucepan on the stove. Could be anything, depending on what kind of risotto you are making. If you are making risotto for the first time, which is likely if you are actually using this recipe, it doesn't matter as long as it is good. Low salt vegetable broth cubes or packets from the grocery store, for example, are fine. Not great, but fine. Because it is so easy, I usually cut up leftover vegetables, including an onion and some garlic and herbs, and simmer for a half hour while I prepare the other ingredients. Some recipes are even fine with water. Hot, of course.

Melt about 1/4 cup of butter, or some combination of butter and oil[74] in the bottom of a large sauce pan. If you like onions, chop one up and sauté it in the butter for several minutes, until the onion softens. Or do just that but with several shallots instead. Pour in about two cups of arborio rice.[75] On medium heat stir the rice in the butter and onion until the rice starts to snap and pop. Don't let it burn. Pour in almost a cup of dry white wine and watch it fizzle and steam away.[76] Just as the rice is starting to stick to the bottom of the pan, pour in a ladleful of simmering broth. It must be hot in order for the rice to absorb it properly, which is to say, quickly. Stir the rice until the liquid is absorbed. Pour in another

---

[74] The del Neros insist that you not use oil. In Spain they use oil and it is just fine. As it happens, I have used olive oil and it was very fine. In any case, don't use margarine, no matter how much you think it is a good idea, if for no other reason than the dye in it makes the risotto a funny color.

[75] Arborio rice is a short fat Italian rice perfect for this dish. It is widely available, but not always in your neighborhood grocery store. Try a specialty market, or a cookware store. Or use regular rice if you cannot find it. Do not use instant rice. Ever, for any reason.

[76] Risotto requires alcohol at this point for chemistry reasons. But it can be anything. Red or white wine, beer, champagne, depending on the rest of the ingredients you are using. As long as it is dry and flavorful. So don't use Budweiser. Or Night Train. Or Asti Spumante. Or Southern Comfort.

ladleful. You will add about six or seven cups of liquid in this manner. When the rice is cooked to your liking—or al dente, which is to everyone's liking—turn off the heat, add a couple handfuls of grated cheese, Parmesan or something like it, stir briefly and deeply, and then cover the pot and let it sit there for a few minutes while you check to be sure the table is set and everyone has a glass of wine or whatever. As you do have a moment before the risotto is ready, you might toss a salad and put it on the table with the risotto.

There you are. Something resembling a recipe for risotto. The recipe on the rice package suggested the Parmesan cheese be mixed with about an eighth of a cup of cream before being added to the risotto. It was a delicious spin, and a very rich one. It also proved to be more prudent to leave the cover off at the end to allow a little of that extra liquid from the cream to evaporate.

MAY I ADD that risotto is under appreciated as a leftover, either cold, straight from the fridge, or padded into little paddies, or rolled into balls around a piece of cheese, and then sautéed slowly till warmed through in a little butter or oil,[77] or reheated howsoever you choose. If you have extra risotto, and it was any good to begin with, don't throw it out. Keep it and fight over it tomorrow.

MIDNIGHT ROAST TURKEY

Along with suggestions for stuffing and instructions for gravy

THERE ARE DAYS of the year when a turkey roasting in the oven is a lovely and expected thing. Expected to be lovelier than it often is due to a certain amount of nostalgia and aptitude for delusion on our parts. But delicious and perfect even when it is far from both.

Holidays we put aside. The secret time when a roast turkey in the oven will create happinesses never dreamed of is at night, long after dark, any time of year.

Here's what you do:

Buy a turkey, a large but not very large turkey. It can't be too small nor just the breast because it has to require several hours of cooking and has to have a place for stuffing. Maybe 11-13 pounds. At least ten.

---

[77] Or nothing at all, if you have a good non-stick pan like I told you to buy.

Next, figure out how you want to make stuffing. The stuffing you can buy in a box in the store, adding an onion and butter or whatever the instructions say, is not so bad. There is a recipe for apple and onion stuffing in the *Joy of Cooking* which historically has been a good choice. James Beard offers an excruciatingly simple stuffing with tarragon and pine nuts. My mother's stuffing recipe which exists only in her head involves celery, onions, dry bread, sage, and a few other things, but nothing at all exotic or even unlikely. It would be the best thing, and exactly what one wants when they smell the turkey roasting late at night and are too serene to find pleasure in anything clever or sophisticated.

On an evening when you have plans to go out and to come back eventually, make your stuffing, stuff it into the turkey, and stuff the turkey into the oven. It is an excellent idea to place the turkey on a baking dish which is larger in circumference than the largest part of the turkey. Breast down. It is also an excellent idea to figure out how to twist the legs of the turkey so they might be fastened together near the opening where the stuffing was stuffed. Use string, or fabric scraps or dental floss or whatever will not melt, burst into flames, or poison the turkey as it cooks. But don't worry too much about it.[78] Figure out how much time the turkey should roast in the oven at 350°F by multiplying the weight of the turkey by 18-20 minutes. 12 pound turkey; 240 minutes. Four hours or a little less. Just enough time to go to a movie and do some leisurely people-watching afterward. Call up some good friends who live nearby, or rustle up any house guests and go out. Bring them all back to your kitchen around midnight and take the turkey out of the oven. Hang around for about fifteen minutes, about the time it will take for everyone or just yourselves to settle around the kitchen table or start up a game of cards or caps or some conversation. Carve up some of the turkey onto a plate, scoop out some generous amount of stuffing and add that to the plate and let them at it. Beers, wine, fizzing water with lemon, tea. Very nice.

And now you have turkey leftovers in your refrigerator without having become sick with overeating the day before. You might even want to try making gravy the next evening with all the turkey drippings you were too tired and happy to deal with the night before when you just threw the whole thing in the refrigerator. Great time to practice making gravy, away from the maddening crowd.

You don't know how to make gravy either?

All right. Awful as it might sound, take all the fat drippings from the pan in which you cooked the turkey and put them into a large skillet or sauté pan. A sauce pan will work if you have nothing else. You might want to heat up the whole roasting pan on the stove for

---

[78] There is no way to describe how to do this. Fortunately, no matter what you do it will be fine. You don't even want to hear the stories about turkeys roasted unfastened and upside down so that they were too suggestive to carve at the table, nor turkeys roasted in ovens smaller than the turkey itself on pans smaller still, nor of the smoke which ruined a week's work in the dark room. All the birds were perfect and were gobbled right up.

a few minutes to melt the turkey drippings so you can pour or spoon or siphon them out of the pan. Make sure you get everything stuck to the bottom of the pan. Those bits are where a great deal of the flavor lives. Or, if you have removed the turkey from the pan for carving purposes, and the roasting pan seems sturdy enough to withstand the direct heat of the stove and a lot of stirring, go ahead and make the gravy directly in it.

In any case, heat up the drippings so they are very hot, nearly sizzling. Into this pot of not quite boiling oil, pour a mixture of flour and water which you have previously stirred up with a fork such that all the flour has dissolved without a lump into the water. Something less than a quarter cup of flour, and enough water to turn it into a thickness you can pour. With the stove on medium heat, pour the mixture into the center of the pan, the hottest part, right over the heating element of the stove.

Use a wire whisk[79] to stir the flour mixture into the drippings, keeping it right in the middle if you can. Keep stirring it and letting it cook on medium heat until the flour mixture itself starts to bubble and cook. It is very important that this stuff cook before you start adding liquid to make gravy.[80] If it doesn't cook sufficiently, you will have pasty, tasteless gravy. Unfortunately, this is the time when most of your guests will become skeptical and start offering suggestions. Unless they have worked as professional chefs in fine restaurants or you have other reason to heed their advice, don't listen to them. Just keep going, following your instincts and these vague instructions. Gravy is a deeply personal thing, a path you must find and break for yourself.

Is the mixture bubbling? Does it seem there is cooking going on? Suddenly pour in half of a glass of wine, preferably dry red wine, but whatever it is you are drinking will be fine,[81] stir and allow the alcohol to sizzle off for a moment. This step, loud, surprising and somewhat dramatic, usually shuts everyone up for awhile.

All you have left to do is add milk a bit at a time and keep stirring until the gravy looks like the sort of thing you want. This just takes time. Pour in some milk and allow the sauce to thicken again as you stir. Do not be afraid of lumps. Keep stirring. The sauce will alternate between being too thick and too thin and then too thick again, but paler in color than

---

[79] I should have mentioned right at the beginning: You are going to be very glad to have a wire whisk for this chore.

[80] This whole process is the same as described for a white sauce or a roux in the recipe for lasagna. Again the same advice holds: Ask someone who knows how to cook to show you how to do it, and then experiment and perfect from there according to your own good sense and imagination. Or just leap in untutored and keep trying until you get it right. That's what I did. To shy to ask for help. Or too lazy to try something new when a better cook is in the kitchen and willing to do it themselves.

[81] If you are drinking Scotch or Cognac or some other distilled and aged thing, that is fine too, but pour in somewhat less than you would wine. If you are drinking vodka tonic or just tonic or a soft drink or juice or light beer, keep drinking and look around to see if anyone else is drinking something a little more savory and appropriate and use that. Thank whomever it is whose drink you just used and suggest they go find themselves another.

the last time it was too thick. Stop when it is done to your perfection, whatever that might be. Salt and a generous amount of black pepper might be added at some point. Taste before adding salt, as some roasted meats have a great deal of salt packed around them. Obviously you will know if this is the case if you made the meal yourself, but you might be making gravy at the meal of another.

Serve with the turkey, stuffing and mashed potatoes. Cranberry sauce. Steamed green beans or a green salad with lots of vegetables in it. Pumpkin pie is an excellent dessert, or the chocolate pie. Another day, gravy on toast or sandwiches or salads.

TOAST

OUR CULTURAL BIAS, our weakness. Remarks that we cannot live by bread alone do not imply a need for other food, but rather that in addition to bread we require other things less measurable by weights and scales. Bread alone will do for physical sustenance. And if it is toasted to perfection, it may also embody and express that other thing which we cannot live without. Whatever you choose to call it.

Toast. Bread made warm again. It is the food of comfort for most of our culture and many of those cultures which have influenced our own. It is eminently sharable. It requires no utensil to eat. Bread and toast are the only things on the table which have absolutely resisted knives and forks and spoons.[82] Bread and toast are always eaten with bare hands, torn apart even in the finest restaurants, eaten with fingers, piece by piece, dipped in olive oil and balsamic vinegar and garlic, dabbed with butter, made heavy with preserves or soggy with gravy and brought to the mouth by fingers which can be most properly licked clean as long as no slurping is audible.

The perfect food. Unassuming, uncomplicated, effortless to prepare, and by its very nature meant to be shared. Bread comes in a form too large to be eaten only by one person. Toast cools too quickly to be hoarded.

Anything said here reflects the prejudice of one who has lived primarily in the cosmopolitan centers of the northern and western hemispheres in the very last decades of the twentieth century. Which may still not explain why I cannot imagine sliced white bread, even when perfectly executed into toast, ever furthering a romantic campaign. Even for those people who were raised on it. It reeks too much of lunch boxes and single servings of barbecue flavor potato chips and twinkies. Takes the mind right back into the

---

[82] Of course you can and should on occasion eat a salad with your fingers, but there will be people who will never think that you are right to do so.

school yard. Not where you would have it. Kind of like serving someone milk with their peanut butter cookies.

We can live on bread alone, but make it real bread made from real stuff. Not the watered down version we feed, lamentably, to children.[83]

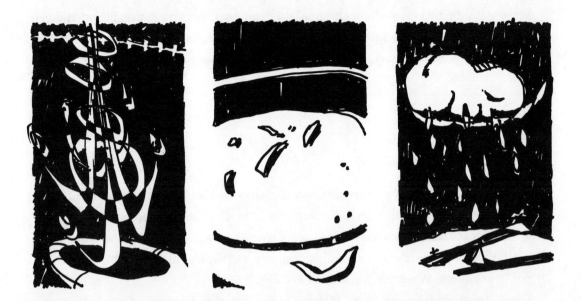

Which is not to say all white bread is bad. Some of the most celebrated breads on earth are made from nothing but white flour, water and salt.[84] Sourdough bread, for example. Or the French baguette. It is very little short of miraculous what transcendent substance can be created from those ingredients which in other circumstances would produce a disgusting glue. It is the bacteria, of course, which changes everything. The yeast or starter. That extremely unsanitary and barely controllable phenomenon which is not unlike love itself— it works or it doesn't and if it doesn't there is nothing to do but throw the whole thing out and start again. Add the grace and gifts of the bakers themselves. Magicians.

And then there was bread. But it might not have been a white bread. It might have been rye, or darkened with molasses, or herbed or whatever. Sprouted grains, many or just one or two. Variety. Even the very same stuff made in the same place by a different baker, or by the same baker in a different place, can be very different. The air itself, the timing, the amount of kneading, all combine to make bread different all the time, or nearly the same each time if you frequent the same bakery.

---

[83] Rabble rousers will point out that plenty of people were raised on seven-grain bread. Yes, they were. But adult teeth can also bite into seven-grain bread. There is enough flavor to continue entertaining and challenging a jaded and disintegrating sense of taste well into old age.

[84] Which, by the way, is not the ingredient list for most loaves of white sandwich bread.

Fine just so, but sublime when toasted. To be honest, I can't say why. Maybe because it is made hot again. Challenging and interesting on the surface, warm and soft inside. Again, like love. When bread is still warm from the oven it can be hard not to just eat it straight off, even if you had bought it to make toast. Conversely, bread which is no longer very fresh is made edible again when toasted and dribbled or spread with something full of fat or flavor. Bruschetta and the like might even benefit from slightly stale bread, toasted, which does not get soggy so quickly as fresh.

Regardless. You toast the bread, in the toaster, in the toaster oven or even in the real oven if you have nothing else. Prepare it as you will. Butter or oil or nothing. Jam or some kind of preserve. Marmite, if your love is British and you have a taste for it. Perhaps on the side. Or rub with a clove of garlic as they do in Spain. Serve on a small plate. Serve on a linen napkin or something more coarse. Serve with coffee or wine or with a beer very very late at night. Offer juice. Add a salad and call it lunch.

Here's the trick, though, the thing which will draw that attracting other into your web of intrigue; embedded so far into this section few will read it, giving the advantage to you:

Slice the toast not just in half, but in quarters. Long slices, rather than the square or triangular quarters popular among the under ten set.[85] Put the whole bunch of them on a plate and place that plate in a spot convenient to all present. You will be surprised how many people who insisted moments before that they were not hungry and did not care for any toast, who were obstinately maintaining their distance from you and from that compromising position of accepting food from another, let alone sharing food from the same plate, how many of those people will help themselves to the crisp fingers of bread toasted. Small enough that it is not too much of a commitment. Already cut so they do not have to break off a small enough piece to suit their intention, tricking them into participating in this plain ritual. Offering them food not as a substitute for love and affection but rather as an expression of just that. Feeding them the way they need to be fed so they might be fed even if it is not the way you would have them fed. You would not be loathe to strategically place enticing morsels of food for a nervous and wary cat who has been hanging around, unsure of how to be fed but clearly hungry. Neither should you feel manipulative nor deceptive for coaxing another to participate in such a way. You know it is not always easy to jump right into a situation. One is not always sure which foot goes first. Help that could never be asked for, given.

If they withstand all of your imperceptibly gracious gestures to make it easy for them to join in a social intimacy, then perhaps they aren't hungry. Or perhaps they cannot eat bread for one reason or another. They will generally be quite willing to admit that, if it is

---

[85] Anytime you can distinguish yourself from the under-ten set—except in the realms of spontaneity and imagination and sincerity—you should.

the case.[86] Or maybe they are the sort of person who cannot bear sharing food. Hates eating anything that is not complete and presented on a plate just for them. Some people are like that, and in some it is just a quirk and not in fact a sign they are going to be selfish in other arenas as well. People raised as smaller members of large families often suffer from the phobia of sharing. They believe they are unlikely to get much if they have to fend for themselves from a communal dish. So they demure and wait until something is just for them.

Of course it is always possible that someone genuinely does not wish to share toast or anything else with you. Not much you can do about that. At least you didn't slave over a hot stove for hours to find it out.

TROUT[87]

For the cuisine impaired

BUY OR CATCH and clean as many trout as you have people to feed. Slip into their slit-open bellies some bits of butter or dribbles of olive oil, slices of lemon and sprigs of parsley.[88] Wrap first in parchment paper, then in aluminum foil, making sure the little fish packets are sealed up well. When your guests begin to arrive, ask one of them to start the barbecue.

You can skip the foil if you plan to cook the trout in the oven rather than on the barbecue. Or you can skip the parchment paper if you do not plan to live long enough to end up senile.

Just before you are ready to serve a first course, be it pasta or salad or soup or some delicacy brought by one of your guests, ask someone handy to put the little trout packets on the barbecue. Maybe ten minutes later, ask them to go turn them over. Don't worry if you or they forget. When everyone is done with their first course, hand someone a plate and some kind of utensil appropriate for picking up foil packets from a hot grill and ask them to go fetch the trout. That same person is ideally positioned to then transfer the packets to each guest's plate. While they are out getting the fish, you might want to give everyone new plates, especially if there is tomato sauce or something equally messy on the old plates.[89]

---

86 Don't forget to offer them something else.

87 Or salmon or any kind of fish, really, or meat or vegetable for that matter.

88 For fish other than trout, never mind the belly part. Just sprinkle or place on or near whatever you are cooking and wrap up as usual.

89 If it seems that the sauce or other remains from the first course would complement the grilled stuff, leave the plates from the first course on the table. Unorthodox, but possibly brilliant.

Everyone is responsible for opening their own packet and for negotiating the fish—and its bones and head and eyes and everything that might come with a fish—for themselves.

A DRAMATIC AND primitive main course that requires no skill on the part of the chef. If you can wrap presents even badly you can do this.

In the event you are doing this for only one other person, be very sure the person likes to barbecue, or at least will enjoy trying. If not, turn on the oven and throw the fish in there. Set the temperature at about 375° or 400° Fahrenheit, and be sure the fish cook for at least ten minutes, fifteen is better. Best to err on the long side, as the fish will not dry out, sealed up as they are.

You might also want to be sure your most important companion likes fish.

MAURIZIO'S VEGETABLE SOUP

MAURIZIO DOESN'T KNOW how to cook even more than you don't know how to cook. He thinks you can microwave bread and get toast. But somehow or another he makes vegetable soup. I myself don't know how to make vegetable soup and only like to eat it if it is made by someone else and served to me in a comfortable bowl, with the perfect spoon and fresh or warm bread within reach.[90] Which is exactly what he did on a few occasions, probably extending our marriage slightly past what should have been its run. Powerful stuff, soup.

And he insists I told him how to make it. One day when I was very sick and wanted my mother and soup to materialize from hundreds of miles away but knew deep in my heart that wasn't going to happen.

Here, I'll tell you what I told him and you can see if it works for you:

"Maurice, take all the vegetables in the refrigerator, chop them up into big pieces and put them in a pot of water on the stove. Medium heat is probably good. If you want to, when they are cooked, use my minipimer to purée it. Just salt and pepper will be fine, I think. I'm going back to bed." Of course, I said it in French, so who knows what passed between us.

---

[90] You think I'm kidding. Really, I won't even ladle it out of a pot myself, much less turn on a stove to heat it up. I won't even order it for myself in restaurants. And yet I love it so when it appears in front of me or in front of someone sitting next to or across from me.

It was delicious that day, and every other time he made it. Go figure. Maybe he has the soup gift.[91]

VEGETABLES

SO YOU THINK it would be lovely, caring and possibly even romantic to serve your guests foods that are actually good for them. Well. I suppose vegetables are nice for that sort of thing. Certainly there is no harm in trying. Go look in any cookbook published after 1970 or in France and find a recipe that appeals to you and takes advantage of whatever vegetables are in season.[92]

What else? Do I have any suggestions? Effortless vegetables that will make eyes gleam and get lips licked? Why, yes, as a matter of fact I do. I rarely eat the things myself so I forget about them. Tomato sauce with garlic is enough vegetables for the day as far as I am concerned. And weren't there some onions in that risotto? But for my treasured guests, I might make one of the following vegetable things:

MARINATED GRILLED VEGETABLES

Make a marinade out of whatever you like, being sure to include an oil and an acid. Garlic, ginger, hot oil, capers, crushed red pepper, sugar or honey and little bit of water added to olive oil and balsamic vinegar, plus small amounts of sesame oil, soy sauce and rice wine vinegar if I am feeling sophisticated and complex and they are in my cupboard, is what I usually do.

Cut up whatever vegetables you found at the store that day. Sliced eggplant, halved tomatoes, onions, squash, zucchini, big pieces of any color pepper, whatever. Put the pieces of vegetables into the bowl of marinade, replacing the ones at the bottom with the new ones until all of them are quite messy and you are too. Wash your hands, wrap up the bowls of marinade and vegetables and put them to the side, or into the refrigerator if you are not planning to barbecue within a few hours. When it is time, say about

---

[91] Some people have it, you know, and the rest of us don't. It is a very good idea if you don't have it to make friends with people who do. It is also a good idea to memorize Potato Leek Soup, which for some reason doesn't require the soup gift to make well.

[92] Tempting as it is to have vegetables and fruit out of season, they are rarely any good. They might look beautiful, the color chemically or genetically manipulated to please your eye, but they will almost always be flavorless. Read MFK Fisher, *With Bold Knife and Fork*, the chapter, "Having Fallen into Place" for more considered opinion on vegetables. She loves them as I don't.

Also, there is a cookbook called *More Vegetables, Please*. Get that one.

forty-five minutes before you want the vegetables to be ready, ask someone to start the barbecue.[93] When the barbecue is just perfect, have someone grill the vegetables. Most of them will take about five minutes all told, some on each side. You will have to figure out how you like them.[94]

Serve them on a big plate. Let people eat with their fingers. Later on, marvel at the night sky and toast marshmallows over the embers.

ASPARAGUS

Buy the slimmest asparagus you can find. If you can't find asparagus as slim as your little finger, don't buy any at all. If you do manage to buy asparagus, trim off the ends to your liking. Trim off the smallest bit of the cut ends even if they are already perfect, as they will have dried out en route to your kitchen.

Choose a pan that is as long as your asparagus in at least one direction. I trim asparagus so short a medium-size sauté pan is just fine. Heat something less than an inch of water to boiling in the pan. Put in your asparagus. With a wooden spoon constantly and gently move the asparagus from the bottom of the pile to the top so they all get equal time at all the various levels. Go into a short trance as you watch them turn from a perfectly fine green to a most beautiful bright, baby-leaf green. It will only take a very few minutes. As the last ones are beginning to change, turn off the heat and start transferring them from the pan onto a plate. One exquisite woman serves them like that with dinner, grating curls of fresh Parmesan cheese[95] onto the spear ends of the asparagus. Or you can place them on the coffee table or counter, wherever your guests are chatting each other up before dinner, and let them at it. Give them a small bowl of dipping sauce made of Dijon mustard and mayonnaise, or a curry sauce, or a thick Caesar dressing, or something smooth and savory. Or nothing. Squeeze a lemon over the plate.

---

[93] I realize that I am a little cavalier about having someone always on hand who is willing to barbecue. It is not that I live surrounded by chivalrous and talented barbecue wizards, but rather that in most cases someone with nothing to do will be happy for a purpose. And if no one volunteers right off, I find that if you start right in with a very low level of professionalism, someone will quickly take over the job. If no one does, the truth is that barbecuing is not very difficult and kind of fun as well. Why else would men leap up to do it?

[94] I burnt a bunch of eggplant black a few parties back, just before a very nice tall friend "rescued" me from the chore of barbecuing. After everyone got done teasing and making hilarious comments about my ability to barbecue, they gobbled down the eggplant like candy and begged for the recipe. I lied to them, if you want to know. Told them my secret marinade ingredient was mace. The point is, it's hard to barbecue badly enough to matter.

[95] With a funny contraption she has for the purpose, but you probably don't. Plain grated is lovely as well.

MUSHROOMS

Every now and again I come across a recipe for mushrooms that makes me ache with desire to like them. Usually the recipe involves butter, a sauté pan, salt and pepper and wine, red or white, or maybe Cognac. You can probably figure it out.

Gently clean the mushrooms, slice thinly, cook slowly. Even the plainest stateside mushrooms sound good prepared like this, although imagine instead a more rich and interesting mushroom. There are magnificent and exotic recipes for mushrooms, many of which are too laborious for me anyway, but which you might try. Look in an old French cookbook and do whatever it recommends.

I will mention that when buying mushrooms, look under their caps. The membrane that forms the underbelly of the mushroom should be mostly or completely intact. They should be firm and fleshy. You should be excited about getting them home and preparing them.[96]

GREEN BEANS OR STRING BEANS

Snap off the ends which were attached to the plant. Then do just exactly what you might have done with the asparagus. Even the color change is similar. Serve with a bit of grated cheese, or, in a fit of bold creativity, with a light Italian tomato sauce. Or toss with butter and lemon and garlic. Or dribble with olive oil and possibly a little balsamic vinegar. Or just olive oil and black pepper. Or nothing.

TOMATOES[97]

Take a bunch of roma tomatoes, very red and vine-ripened if possible, and slice them in half the long way. Place them sliced side up on a plate on which you will be happy to serve them. You don't want to touch them again until you eat them. Spoon onto each one some kind of marinade which includes garlic and some sugar or honey in addition to the oils and acid. I usually also include ginger and a little hot oil as for the other

---

[96] Fantastic, don't you think, that I mention them at all, especially since they are not even a vegetable. They are a fungus. A thing which grows in the dark and under rocks. Vegetarian cultures in India spurn them, mistrusting anything so indiscriminate about where it grows; that does not care for sun. I understand mushrooms have virtually no nutritional value, although I like to think they offer minerals or something. For courtship, however, they are invaluable. They are sensual and earthy; deeply and subtly flavored; oddly, even obscenely textured. People who enjoy them, enjoy them, if you catch my meaning. More than other things. I will love them.

[97] These tomatoes were first made with the intention of barbecuing them with the rest of the marinated vegetables. They never made it to the barbecue, becoming instead a favorite recipe. And yet another which I do not eat myself. I hope you are all enjoying yourselves.

vegetables.[98] If the tomatoes seem a bit hard and unwelcoming toward the marinade, stab them with a fork a couple times to give the sauce somewhere to go. Leave them to set around for awhile, an hour or two at least, overnight even in the fridge, and then serve them before dinner, with dinner or afterwards if you forget about them. If you happen to make too many, or forget to serve them, chop them up, cook them slowly in a sauce pan until it looks like a tomato sauce, and then toss with long pasta. That will make someone happy as well.

ARTICHOKES

I am not sure artichokes count as a vegetable at all. First of all, it is a flower, a thistle at that. And then so little of it is eaten, artichokes mainly being an excuse to scoop up some kind of sauce. But people love them and consider you very darling for having made them. So go get some, one per person if you are feeling bountiful. Don't bother getting any at all if you can only find ones that are bug-bitten and small. Once home, cut off the stems flat so they will sit nicely on the bottom of a big pot. Place them there in about an inch or so of boiling water, cover, and then let them steam-cook at a low boil for forty-five minutes. Take them out, put them on plates, and give them to people. You can place a few in the middle of a noisy hoard, along with that mustard sauce or some kind of herbed aioli,[99] just as you might the asparagus, and let them fight among themselves. Give them a knife or two for the final moments. It is very entertaining to see how people negotiate responsibility for the task of cutting out the heart and the subsequent sharing of it.[100]

---

[98] That's only because it is so extremely unlikely that I would ever have two different marinade recipes in my head at the same time, much less make them both on a single evening. And since I don't actually eat any of this stuff, I am hardly going to get bored and make up a new marinade when this one works just fine. Actually, it works for meats as well, if you happen to cook that sort of thing. Mind you, you could be bold and brave and do much much more.

[99] I know that many people are used to melted butter with their artichokes, and they might very well ask you for some. Even if you have butter on hand and are inclined to pander to small demands, don't. Melted butter is fine for a moment, but most unappealing as it cools. You don't want anything like that on your table or within sight of your guests. Also it is messy in a manner which is not so much sexy and charming as messy. And it doesn't have much flavor. Just fat and for no other reason than one is used to it. The worst of all worlds. Make some excuse, or say "ok" but then forget to fetch any. The artichokes will be gone too quickly for it to matter much, and if your charming refusal provokes bad will or even a fight, what an easy way that was to discover your beloved's true colors. Aioli, once again, is garlic mayonnaise.

[100] I do not care for artichokes particularly, so my enjoyment of the fray is uncolored by desire to leap into it, which would be most inappropriate action for a host hoping to make her guests feel treasured. If you do not think you can serve artichokes without trying to snag the heart and a good portion of the inner leaves for yourself, refrain from serving them unless everyone, including you, has their own.

BROCCOLI AND CAULIFLOWER

Steam them. But not on my account.

BEETS [101]

Boil them, or roast them with an inch of water in the roasting pan, either way for a really long time. Almost an hour. Lazy and luscious, and you don't have to worry if you happen to be distracted for twenty or thirty minutes during the course of preparing dinner.[102] Let them cool enough to handle before you peel them. The skin slips right off with the slightest encouragement. Then you can slice them up and eat them with your fingers. Or you can dribble them with some kind of dressing. Or you can cut them into big chunks, toss with a curry vinaigrette[103] and serve them with dinner in a bowl which sets off the color of the beets.[104]

CARROTS

Figure out how to make a great salad with carrots. There is a carrot salad popular in France which is just exactly like celery remoulade. Both are divine but I don't know how to make either. It can't be too hard though, since French people are willing to make it. Shredded carrots and a slightly garlicky, mustardy, red wine vinaigrette (with no sugar or anything sweet because carrots are so sweet), and maybe raisins, maybe green onions, maybe roasted chopped up nuts.[105] Or the curry dressing mentioned for the beets.

A good man I know who has a talent for vegetables makes a carrot salad with ginger and nuts and raisins, but not too many. There are recipes for this sort of thing. Another

---

[101] I'm kidding, right? No, not at all. They are exquisite to people who like them, and of such a gorgeous color you would be a fool to insist on remembering and despising those beets from a jar your mom made you eat when she did not have time to cook up some yummy Brussels sprouts for you. Get over it. All the most delicious and successful sensualists I have ever met are very fond of beets. Take from that what you will.

[102] You should be so lucky. And you should be ashamed if you have to decline temptation because something fragile and temperamental is on the stove. I don't have to tell you what else is fragile and temperamental.

[103] Let's see . . . garlic and curry powder mooshed up together with a mortar and pestle. Mix in olive oil, red wine vinegar, salt and pepper. Something like that is what I was told.

[104] A white one, for example. Some pale blue porcelain or rich yellow ceramic, maybe.

[105] This I served with an accidentally very spicy black bean chili and rice. It was a perfect foil, both aesthetically and for its cool, sweet, acidic flavor. Actually the salad itself was an accident as well, my having grated way too many carrots for the cakes I was making on that particular birthday. I'm thinking it would complement many bland or spicy things. I am also thinking this is as good a place as any to admit my prejudice against overly sweet dishes for the main meal. Partly personal taste, and partly a rejection of mid-century habits. It seems to me to recreate the cloying foods of our mothers and grandmothers, while delicious to some palates, would simply remind guests of their mother's or grandmother's table, of celebratory meals and the carrot salad an aunt always brought to pot luck. Nostalgia is nice, but you don't want to be mistaken for anyone's mom in a blur of flavor-induced emotion. In courtship you want to distinguish yourself from everyone's grandmother, unless of course you are their grandmother.

friend used to julienne carrots (make them somehow into slim strips), stir fry them with morsels of chicken and serve with rice. Mom and many other moms know how to roast carrots with roasting meat, a skill you might acquire if you don't have any moms handy.

The only thing I know how to do with carrots, besides eat them raw, is to cut them up into pieces which are too big for a single bite and cook them slowly for what seems like forever in a sauté pan with a bit of oil or butter and a million small amounts of white wine and black pepper, letting it cook away and into the carrots. Eventually you have marvelous carrots worthy of offering anyone.[106]

SALADS

Learn how to make a very good salad without putting yourself to too much trouble. Or resign yourself to making a perfectly fine one out of green lettuce, oil and vinegar, red or green onions, salt and black pepper. Bits of avocado, shredded carrots, chopped nuts, or pieces of papaya are all nice additions to the simple salad if you happen to have them lying around the house.

If your greens are very good, you can toss them with only a bit balsamic or red wine or other favorite vinegar and maybe a bit of olive or nut oil and have a lovely light salad. Richard tosses red or green leaf or butter lettuce with mostly just olive oil and salt and just the smallest amount of red wine vinegar, finishing with ground pepper. In a

---

[106] Oh yes, and I can make carrots into a cake, but I don't know that that counts as a vegetable dish.

wooden bowl it can be very perfect. Notice what interesting salads, with and without lettuce, are served up in imaginative restaurants, and then try to mimic them. Or get into the habit of always asking someone to bring a salad. Most people are delighted to do that and you don't have to think about salad or vegetables again for the rest of the week.

UNCOOKED VEGETABLES

Something short of a salad. Cut up fresh vegetables and put them on the plate with other food. Slices of very red tomato from a garden.[107] Long slices of green or red pepper is a favorite in my family. Others like other things. Apples and other fruit can also be used in this way.

INDIRECT VEGETABLES

Use vegetables when you are cooking other things. Asparagus and tomatoes in the risotto. Peppers and onions or carrots and bean sprouts or cabbage in the pasta. Peas and who knows what all in the rice. Vegetables in the soup. It's not so hard.

YOU SEE, I AM not unfamiliar with vegetables. And you may also see that not liking vegetables is not a good reason not to make them for others. First off, others like them. Secondly, they are economical in comparison to almost anything else you might make. Third, they are a handy means of introducing color to sometimes visually bland plates of food. And they are good for you. And if you get good at preparing them, you may find yourself liking them more and more. You may find one and then another, slowly over time, suddenly to your taste when before you grimaced at the thought. Your skin, your humor and your health will improve, and that might lead to many things.

---

107 I'm pretty serious about the garden. It needn't be yours. No point in using tomatoes from the store, unless they are vine-ripened and exorbitantly priced, or it is the height of summer and there are nothing but deep red tomatoes, cheap for the asking. Otherwise tomatoes are flavorless and even their color is disappointing. Barely ok as an ingredient, and worthless in this context. Sticks of celery would be better.

COOKBOOKS

Variously recommended books to cook from.

FANNIE FARMER COOKBOOK

Fannie Farmer

The basic book, much like the *Joy of Cooking*. But for some reason it seems a little easier to use. You be the judge.

JOY OF COOKING

Marion Cunningham

This is the book everyone thinks they must have. But indeed it is interchangeable with the *Fannie Farmer Cookbook* mentioned previously. Much of the same stuff, although the latter was updated by Marion Cunningham somewhat recently. Look at both, or just accept the one you are given.

SILVER PALATE

Julee Rosso & Sheila Lukins

The first of their books, comprehensive and full of invariably wonderful recipes. Like all their books, the indexing is odd and difficult. But the book is organized into meaningful chapters. Their other books are very good, though not so transcendent as this one and are still more difficult to navigate.

THE FRUGAL GOURMET

Jeff Smith

Dimitris recommends this as the best $6.50 he spent on his kitchen. "He explains about knives and what pots and pans to have in your kitchen, and about mushrooms. And after you have made three or four recipes, you have everything you need for the rest. He doesn't go weird or anything like that." Sounds like a book I should probably read. Although that bit about the mushrooms probably explains why I haven't. Dimitris also recommends Jeff Smith's other books, but not so highly as this first one.

GREENS

Deborah Madison

Cuisine as offered at Greens at Fort Mason in San Francisco—a most elegant and delicious restaurant sitting on a dock of the bay and serving no meat of any sort. Winner of the Most Borrowed Book award three years running. Sometimes I have to borrow my neighbor's because mine is too far away.

THE VEGETARIAN EPICURE

Anna Thomas

An excellent cookbook, even for non-vegetarians. There's got to be something on the
plate besides meat, you know.

WORLD OF THE EAST VEGETARIAN
COOKING *Madhur Jaffery*

Often the messiest book in a kitchen.
Pages stuck together, bits of food crum-
bling off when you browse through.

LOUISIANA KITCHEN *Paul Prudhomme*

Just exactly what you think it is: Recipes
and comments from New Orleans' most
famous and perhaps favorite chef. Don't
know. Don't live there. If Cajun and
Creole speak to your soul, this is the book
to have.

THE FOOD OF SOUTHERN ITALY

Carlo Middione

Sharon recommends it first among her
books on cooking in the Italian fashion.

ITALIAN COOKING IN THE GRAND
TRADITION

Jo Bettoja and Anna Maria Cornetto

Classic, traditional, home cooking the way
Italians do it: Grandly.

LA TECHNIQUE *Jacques Pepin*

No recipes, just how to cook in the French
fashion.

THE HOWS AND WHYS OF FRENCH
COOKING *Alma Lynch*

Understand French cooking. Impress
friends and frighten enemies.

MASTERING THE ART OF FRENCH
COOKING *Julia Child, Simone Beck, and
Louise Bertholle*

Perhaps more difficult to follow than *The
Hows and Whys*, but it probably depends
who's doing the following.

THE ESCOFFIER COOKBOOK

Escoffier

It is unlikely that you will ever follow one
of these recipes. They are even more
vague than the ones in this book. Much
better, of course. But read around and
learn lots. Especially note his instructions
for scrambling eggs.

CHEZ PANISSE VEGETABLES

Alice Waters

Just because it is so beautiful and because
you should eat more vegetables. It is too
recently published to know what kind of
cookbook it is. However, if I had to eat
vegetables, I would like to eat them at
Chez Panisse. Alice Waters has almost
single-handedly brought organic farming
back to life. Your life, if you have any
sense. And what she does with plants once
she gets them into the kitchen is enough to
make you blush at not liking them.

BREAD *Beth Hensberger*

Or any of her books about breadmaking
that appeal to you. There are new ones all
the time, and can be found in every cook-
wares store.

THE SIMPLE ART OF PERFECT
BAKING *Flo Braker*

Good explanations of baking chemistry so
you are less likely to have great accidents
when you are toying with recipes from
other sources.

THE ALICE B. TOKLAS COOKBOOK

Alice B. Toklas

Americans in Paris. While Gertrude Stein
did what she did best, Alice Toklas took
care of the home—the main responsibility
apparently being to keep cooks in the
kitchen and food on the table. Understand
the German occupation of France as culinary crisis.

SHOPPING LISTS

Ingredients you may need for various styles of cooking:
French/Continental, Asian, Mexican, Italian and American.

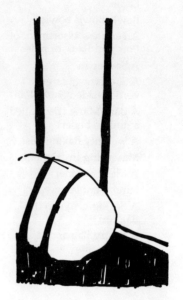

FRENCH/CONTINENTAL

(See Alma Lynch, Jacques Pepin, Julia Child or Alice B. Toklas)

FOR STARTERS
- Access to Good Bread, freshest possible
- Access to Good Cheeses

STAPLES
- Butter
- Eggs
- Cream
- Sugar
- Flour
- Salt
- Pepper

PLUS:
- Wine for cooking with
- Some sort of fruit jam or preserve
- Coffee, and the means to prepare it
- Potatoes
- Rice, long grain
- Bacon
- Lentils, lovely little green ones if you can find them
- Access to or know how to make, Veal, Chicken, and Fish Stock
- Parmesan Cheese

AS YOU GO SOUTH...
- Access to Good Fish
- Garlic
- Basil
- Tomatoes
- Lemon

MEATS
- Access to Good Meat, Chicken, Fish, Beef

VEGETABLES
- Leeks
- Carrots
- Celery
- Petits Pois, which is to say small peas (in your freezer)
- Onions
- Access to Good, Seasonal Fruits and Vegetables

HERBS, SPICES
and other Tools for flavor
- Shallots
- Capers
- Parsley
- Thyme
- Tarragon
- Chervil
- Marjoram
- Fines Herbs (Parsley, Thyme & Tarragon all mixed together)

CONDIMENTS
- Olive Oil, Walnut Oil, Vegetable Oil
- Vinegars; Red and white wine, Balsamic
- Good French Mustard

FOR DESSERTS
- Butter
- Flour
- Sugar
- Cream
- Vanilla Extract
- Creme Fraiche
- Almonds
- Really Good Chocolate, Bittersweet
- Allspice

TOOLS
- Knives
- Wire whisk
- Wooden Spoons

Ladle
Bowls bowls bowls
An endless assortment of Pots and Pans, or at least:
A Saucepan
A Sauterne (a large, vertical-sided Sauce Pan)
A Bain-Marie (also called a double-boiler)
A weighty Baking Dish
Measuring Instruments
A Mesh Strainer
Parchment Paper
A Springform Pan (for Baking)
A Pastry Bag and attachments

A Cuisinart, probably
A Tart Pan(round, with a bottom that comes out.)
A silly Hat and an Apron

YOU NEED TO:

Know how to use a Knife.
Love food and want to spend time enjoying it.
Be able to make a sauce.
Be willing to use butter.
Have an understanding of Cooking with Wine.
Know how to use a Wire Wisk.
Have Discretion.

Be able to be doing two or three or four things at once and not get upset.
Know how to buy and serve wine.
Understand Cheese as an ingredient and as a Course.
Recognize and respect the intrinsic value of the individual ingredients.

(Would all the novice cooks please skip directly to the section on Italian cooking.)

ASIAN
(See Barbara Tropp, *Modern Art of Chinese Cooking or China Moon Cookbook*)

STAPLES

Sesame Oil
Soy Sauce (Chinese and Japanese Tamari)
Rice Wine Vinegar
Balsamic Vinegar
Rice
Several kinds of Noodles
Fish Sauce
Hoisin Sauce
Fermented Black Beans
Chili Paste
Sugar
Corn Starch
Ginger
Garlic
Crushed Red Pepper
Peanut oil
Access to an Asian market
Cilantro (also called Coriander or Chinese Parsley)
Decent Seafood
Eggroll Wrappers (keep in your freezer)

FOR SOUTHEAST ASIAN CUISINE:

Peanut Butter
Tamarind Paste
Dried Salted Shrimp
Coconut Milk

FOR JAPANESE CUISINE:

Dashi Flakes
Kombu
Mirin (Japanese rice wine vinegar)
Sake
Miso

TOOLS

A Wok
Sharp, solid Knives
Wire Strainer
Wooden Spoons, both large and small

YOU NEED TO:

Know how to use a knife.
Have unlimited patience for chopping.
Be able to cook rice.
Be willing to use pork (for Chinese Cuisine).
Be unafraid of boiling oil.
Acquire a feel for the brisk frenzy of stir-frying.
Never whine about spicy food.
Have no problem with sodium.

MEXICAN/SOUTH AMERICAN
(See Diana Kennedy)

STAPLES
Access to Good Tortillas, both corn and flour

Beans, several kinds, dry and canned

Rice, long grain or basmati

Tomato Sauce

Chiles, canned and fresh

Cheese: Cheddar, Jack, Queso Fresco, maybe

Sour Cream

Cilantro

Oregano, the Mexican variety if you can find it

Chili Powder

Cumin

A light Oil

Corn Meal (Masa Harina)

Good Beer for drinking

PRODUCE:
Tomatoes of all sorts, fresh and in cans

Bell Peppers

Chili Peppers: Jalapeno, Serrano

Green Onions

Sweet corn (or in your freezer)

Potatoes (for South American meals)

Limes and Lemons

Avocados

Onions

Garlic

TOOLS
A Pot

A Frying Pan

A good Spoon for scooping

Wooden Spoons for stirring

A long Fork

A reliable Cheese Grater

Maybe a Casserole Dish of some sort

YOU NEED TO:
Have respect for good tortillas.

Be able to enjoy cilantro (many people think it tastes like soap.)

Know how to cook beans.

Have a sense of humor about beans.

Be able to cook rice.

ITALIAN
(See Carlo Middione or Marcella Hazan)

STAPLES
Olive Oil

A nice amount of good brand of Dried Pasta, on hand at all times

Polenta

Arborio Rice

Garlic

Basil

Oregano

Rosemary

Onions: red, white and yellow

PLUS:
Porcini Mushrooms

White Beans

Nutmeg

Spinach

Parmesano Reggiano Cheese (the imported stuff)

Tomatoes, fresh and various sorts in cans

Pine Nuts

Wine, red and white for cooking and drinking

Ricotta Cheese

Mozzarella Cheese (in the freezer)

Lemons

Mushrooms

Anchovy Paste

Olives, a good green sort and a good black sort

Milk or Cream

Access to really good Vegetables

Access to good Fish

Access to good Proscciuto

A recording of La Traviata

Ice Cream in your freezer

Bittersweet Chocolate

TOOLS
Knives

A Big Pot, at least 8-quarts, for cooking pasta

A big Sauté Pan

Knives for chopping

Spoons for stirring

Forks for poking and turning

A Colander

A Baking Dish or Casserole of some sort

A Grater

A Food Processor, maybe

YOU NEED TO:
Have had sex, really good sex, this year.

Love your mother.

Have lots of time and be willing to spend it eating.

Be a good natured person.

TRADITIONAL AMERICAN
(See your mother, or someone else's mother.)

STAPLES

Butter
Milk
Eggs
Yellow Cheese of some sort: Cheddar, American, something
Whole Wheat Bread (in your freezer, at the very least)
Cornmeal
Potatoes, Onions, Carrots, Celery
Salt & Pepper
Bacon
Sugar
Flour
Rice
Noodles of various sorts
BBQ Sauce
A wide selection of Campbell Soups
Onion Soup Mix
Chicken
Ground Beef, and other beef
Pork or Ham
Bread Crumbs

Frozen Peas and Corn
Tomato Sauce
Tomato Paste
Ketchup
Mustard
Mayonnaise

PLUS:

Worcestershire Sauce
Tabasco Sauce
Dill Pickles
Beer, for cooking and drinking while cooking, especially barbecuing
Cream Cheese
A Good Butcher
Access to Wild Game
Baking Powder
Baking Soda
Jell-O, or at least know what to do with it
Strawberries
Chocolate
Bananas
Brown Sugar
Cinnamon
Nutmeg
Vanilla

Pecans
Walnuts
Peanut Butter
Honey

TOOLS

Knives
Pots and Pans
A Baking Dish or two
A Roasting Dish with a Cover
A Barbecue Grill and Utensils
A Colander
A Damn Good Gin Martini, or someone who knows how to make one
A Blender
A Can Opener
Bottle Opener
An Electric Stove

YOU NEED TO:

Have no regard for the fat intake of anyone around you.

NOUVEAU AMERICAN
(See some cookbook published this year.)

STAPLES

Extra Virgin Olive Oil
At least Five Variously Flavored Vinegars
Fresh Herbs Grown in a Window Box
Tri-colored Fusilli
Sundried Tomatoes
Portobello Mushrooms
Snow Peas
Wine from France and California

TOOLS

Good Knives
A Trust Fund

A Cork Screw
A Garlic Press
A Cuisinart
A Juicer
A Lemon Zester
Orchids, on your window sill (they love the steam)
A very tall Pepper Mill
And a Salt Mill
A collection of Vases and a Cutting Garden
Pate Knives
Cheese Board
A Laptop
A Gas Stove

YOU NEED TO:

Have nothing better to do.

PLAYING WITH FOOD

A belated index.